Leonard Howard L Irby

The Ornithology of the Straits of Gibraltar

Leonard Howard L Irby

The Ornithology of the Straits of Gibraltar

ISBN/EAN: 9783743325531

Manufactured in Europe, USA, Canada, Australia, Japa

Cover: Foto ©Andreas Hilbeck / pixelio.de

Manufactured and distributed by brebook publishing software (www.brebook.com)

Leonard Howard L Irby

The Ornithology of the Straits of Gibraltar

THE ORNITHOLOGY
OF THE
STRAITS OF GIBRALTAR.

BY

Lieut.-Colonel L. HOWARD L. IRBY, F.L.S.,

LATE SEVENTY-FOURTH HIGHLANDERS.

SECOND EDITION.
REVISED AND ENLARGED.

WITH AN APPENDIX

CONTAINING A LIST OF THE LEPIDOPTERA OF THE NEIGHBOURHOOD.

FLUMINA AMO SYLVASQUE INGLORIUS.

LONDON:

R. H. PORTER,

18 PRINCES STREET, CAVENDISH SQUARE.

1895.

CONTENTS.

	Page
LIST OF ILLUSTRATIONS . .	v
INTRODUCTION . .	1
APPENDIX .	311
INDEX TO BIRDS	317

LIST OF ILLUSTRATIONS.

FULL-PAGE PLATES.

		Page
Bearded Vulture. *Thorburn*	*Frontispiece*	
Blue-winged Magpie. *Thorburn*	To face	83
Black or Cinereous * Vulture. *Thorburn*	,,	145
Golden Eagle. *Thorburn*	,,	171
White-shouldered Eagle. *Thorburn*	,,	173
Descent to Nest of Bonelli's Eagle. *Smit, after Verner*	,,	175
Interior of Cavern with Nest of Bonelli's Eagle. *Smit, after Verner*	,,	177
Booted Eagle. *Thorburn*	,,	181
Mediterranean Peregrine. *Thorburn*	,,	191
The First Rise of the Grey-lags, Laguna de la Janda. *Smit, after Verner*	,,	217
European Bush-Quail. *Thorburn*	,,	241
Bustard-Driving. *Smit,* after *Verner*	,,	255
A Deep Place in the Malabrigo Soto. *Smit, after W. F.*	,,	279
Whiskered Terns at Home. *Smit, after Verner*	,,	293

ILLUSTRATIONS PRINTED IN THE TEXT.

NOTE.

THE Illustrations printed in the text (excepting the two diagrams of Bird) are from photographs taken by Major Willoughby Verner, Rifle Brigade, of places visited by the Author in 1894.

Map of Morocco ... { at the end of volume.

* Misspelt "Cinereous" on Plate.

LIST OF ILLUSTRATIONS.

FULL-PAGE PLATES.

		Page
Bearded Vulture. *Thorburn*	*Frontispiece*	
Blue-winged Magpie. *Thorburn*	To face	83
Black or Cinereous * Vulture. *Thorburn*	,,	145
Golden Eagle. *Thorburn*	,,	171
White-shouldered Eagle. *Thorburn*	,,	173
Descent to Nest of Bonelli's Eagle. *Smit, after Verner*	,,	175
Interior of Cavern with Nest of Bonelli's Eagle. *Smit, after Verner*	,,	177
Booted Eagle. *Thorburn*	,,	181
Mediterranean Peregrine. *Thorburn*	,,	191
The First Rise of the Grey-lags, Laguna de la Janda. *Smit, after Verner*	,,	217
European Bush-Quail. *Thorburn*	,,	241
Bustard-Driving. *Smit, after Verner*	,,	255
A Deep Place in the Malabrigo Soto. *Smit, after W. F.*	,,	279
Whiskered Terns at Home. *Smit, after Verner*	,,	293

ILLUSTRATIONS PRINTED IN THE TEXT.

	Page
Diagram of Bird	vi
Diagram of Inner side of Wing	vii
Terrace on the north side of San Bartolomé	26
El Organo, near Tarifa	30
Peasantry, Tapatanilla	32
Laja del Ciscar	33
Nest of the Black Wheatear	42
Nest and Egg of Griffon	148
Cave with Griffons' Nests	150
Young Griffon in Cavern	150
Nest of Neophron, showing Crag	153
,, ,, nearer View	153
Nesting-place of Neophron	155
Nest of Bearded Vulture	157
,, ,, ,,	160
,, ,, ,, ,, near View	160
Nest of White-shouldered Eagle	172
Laja de la Zarga, Nesting-place of Bonelli's Eagle and Griffons	176
Nest of Snake-Eagle in Cork-tree	183
Another Nest of Snake-Eagle in Cork-tree	183
Laja del Ciscar	310

Map of South-western Andalucia } at the end of Volume.
Map of Morocco

* Misspelt "Cinerous" on Plate.

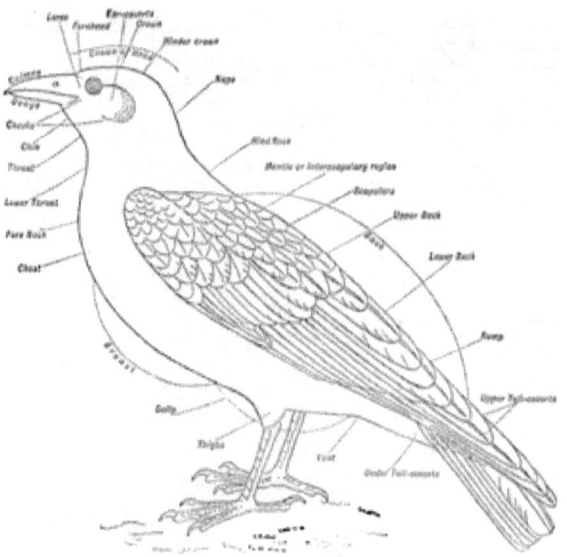

Diagram of a Bird,
TO ILLUSTRATE THE TERMINOLOGY OF THE PLUMAGE.

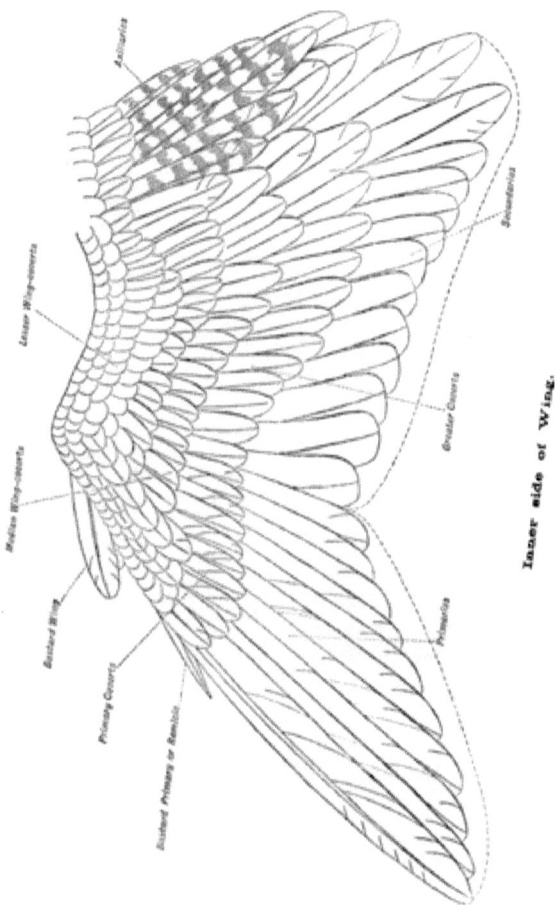

ORNITHOLOGY

OF THE

STRAITS OF GIBRALTAR.

INTRODUCTION.

The list of birds and ornithological notes contained in this book are compiled from observations made on both sides of the Straits of Gibraltar—on the African side within a region extending from Tangier southwards to the lakes of Ras el Doura, beyond Larache, and eastward from Tangier to Tetuan and Ceuta, not reaching inland more than ten or twelve miles; on the European side is included that part of Andalucia which would be bounded by an imaginary line drawn from Gibraltar to Málaga, thence to Granada, Cordova, and Seville, along the delta of the Guadalquivir to Cadiz.

Nearly all the information relating to the birds of the Spanish side of the Straits is collected from personal observations made during a more or less prolonged stay at the Rock, between February 1868 and May 1872, and again from February to May 1874, but including during this time only one summer period, viz. July, August, and the first half of September. For the first three years of my residence at Gibraltar I was quartered with my regiment, the remaining time being passed there chiefly with a view to ornithological pursuits, from time to time making excursions, generally of about a fortnight's duration, to some part or other within the districts above mentioned, but chiefly confining my attentions to the country within a day's journey of Gibraltar.

The observations on the Moorish birds are in a great measure culled from the MS. of the late M. F. Favier, a French collector well known to the ornithological world, who, after a residence of about thirty-one years at Tangier, died there in 1867. I was informed that he had left a MS. written in French, containing his notes on birds; but was not permitted by the owner to do more than glance at it, although he offered it for sale at what seemed to me a very exorbitant price. Fearing to lose a book which might prove of considerable utility in the pursuit of my favourite science, I yielded to his demands and secured the coveted prize, but found upon perusal, amidst a mass of bad grammar, bad spelling, and worse writing, which cost many hours to decipher, that it did not contain so much information as there was reason to anticipate, a good deal of the matter having been copied from other authors.

However, there was some grain among all this chaff; and such facts and details as are considered worth recording are given below with Favier's name attached, and supplemented by my own observations in Morocco. These notes are kept separate from those referring to the Spanish side of the Straits.

This little work is, it may be distinctly understood, not intended to give any special information to scientific ornithologists, but is published with the view of assisting with trustworthy information any amateur collectors who visit Southwestern Europe; and it is hoped especially that it may be useful to officers who, like the writer, may find themselves quartered at Gibraltar. For it admits of little doubt that the study of Natural History will always help to pass away with pleasure many hours that would otherwise be weary and tedious during the time military men may have to "put in" at dear, scorching old "Gib."

There is ample room, for any one with energy, to work out a great deal more information on the birds of the Straits; but it must be remembered that little can be done in hasty visits of two or three months, or by comparing skins secured by assistants, called "collectors," who know nothing of the habits of the birds they send to those who employ them, and upon whose veracity even as to locality the employer cannot implicitly depend.

It may be as well to notice such papers &c. as have been published hitherto relating to the ornithology of the district of the Straits. Dismissing the Spanish lists as meagre and full of errors, we commence with the papers written by Lord Lilford in 'The Ibis' for 1865 (p. 166) and 1866 (pp. 173 & 377). In addition to the interesting facts they contain, these essays are the first which give any reliable information on the subject, and lay, as it were, the foundation of all the work that has since been done with regard to Spanish ornithology.

Since then Mr. Howard Saunders has written, also in 'The Ibis' (1871, pp. 54, 205, & 384), a "List of the Birds of Southern Spain," extending as far eastward as Minorca and as far to the north as the fortieth degree of latitude, thus comprising a very large area. He has also contributed some other papers to 'The Ibis' (1869, pp. 170 & 391), which, altered and considerably enlarged, have appeared in 'The Field' under the head of "Ornithological Rambles in Southern Spain."

On the African side, Mr. G. W. H. Drummond Hay (Proceedings Zool. Society, 1840, p. 133) gave a list of birds noticed by him at Tangier, but only fifty-five in number, while Mr. Tyrwhitt-Drake wrote a list of the birds observed by him in Tangier and Eastern Morocco (Ibis, 1867, p. 421); and a "List of Birds seen near Tangier" appeared in 'Naumannia, but only a list, and not a very accurate one.

ns of birds, generally speaking, have very few dates appended; the exact localities where a species may be found are seldom indicated; the period of migration is also not often stated. "Breeds plentifully," "appears in winter," "a regular visitant," "abundant in spring,"—such are usually the vague remarks given with each species.

Many of the ornithological papers in periodicals and journals are written up from one or two passing visits, often very short ones; and some of the writers possess a power of vision truly astonishing. They see a bird in the distance, imagine it to belong to a certain species, at last believe it to be such, and end by placing the name in their note-book, to appear in due time in print.

The only way to avoid such errors is never to include any bird in a list except when actually obtained and identified. It often happens, also, that the bird *seen* and included is one which it would be quite impossible to distinguish from another closely allied species without handling them both.

These remarks may, no doubt, appear very invidious; but it is want of accuracy in such matters which renders utterly futile any attempt to make out the distribution of birds.

Local names, often trivial and unimportant, must generally be accepted *cum grano salis*; for, unless long resident and conversant with the language of the country, the compiler is apt to fall into the same class of errors as those of the celebrated Count Smorltork, who would probably have written the English name of the Curlew according to the story told of a gunner in the Eastern Counties, who, when asked by a portly old citizen, "What do you call those birds?" replied, "Bless you, Curlews we generally calls 'em; but when we're vexed with 'em, we calls 'em beggars." These vernacular names are most useful, of course, in the case of the more common species, and in Andalucia are, in many instances, of Arabic derivation, relics of the Moorish occupation and of days when under their rule Spain was flourishing, when all that is worth seeing was built, all that is artificially good being remnants of the work of the then industrious Moors. Where are the latter now as a nation?

As a proof of the inaccuracy of local nomenclature, a single name is often applied to several species, sometimes not even belonging to the same genus. Thus *Aguila*, *Aguilucho*, according to the ideas of the individual, may be any of the Diurnal Accipitres, from a Lammergeyer to a Lesser Kestrel; and they are even occasionally used to designate the Raven!!

So *Bujo* applies to *all* Owls, *Culiblanco* to *all* Wheatears; *Chorlito*, the real name of the Golden Plover, is used for various Waders; while *Pitillo*, *Frailecillo*, *Andarios*, *Correrios* are indefinite names applicable to any small Waders and some larger ones. *Pito real* near Gibraltar is *Picus major*, our Great Spotted Woodpecker; near Seville it is *Gecinus Sharpii*, the representative of our English Green Woodpecker (*G. viridis*). *Carpintero* in Central Spain, according to Lord Lilford, is *Picus major*; near Gibraltar it is the Great Titmouse (*Parus major*). *Lavandera*, or "washerwoman," according to localities is either a Wagtail or a Green Sandpiper. *Quebrantahuesos*, "bone-breaker," properly applies to the Lammergeyer; but where that species is absent it is usurped by the *Neophron*.

These, among other instances, prove local names to be only an assistance, and not always to be taken to signify the bird to which they are affixed.

On the other hand, some names are distinctive, as *Abejaruco*, Bee-eater; *Abubilla*, Hoopoe; *Abujeta*, Godwit; *Alcaravan*, Stone-Curlew, &c.

The Moorish Arabic names are for the most part copied from Favier's MS.; but none are quoted unless corroborated by reference to natives of the localities in which the birds were shot. It may be further added that, as it is a matter of considerable difficulty to express Arabic words by English letters, in this work a mere approximation to the sound is attempted to be given.

In the interest of the sportsman and the amateur collector of specimens, it has been endeavoured to give a few hints as to the localities where each may best gratify his tastes; but it would be foreign to the purpose and inapplicable to the limits of this work to reproduce any of the varied information which is to be found in the pages of Ford and other guide-books. In the country districts of Spain, and especially throughout Andalucia, nothing ever changes except the Government. The country is still the Spain of Ford, we might almost say of Don Quixote, and will probably remain so for centuries, except as regards the power of the priesthood, which is gradually waning and will doubtless soon cease to exist.

In a general sense, travelling in Morocco is attended with more expense and less comfort than in Spain. The total absence of inns in the former country (except one or two at Tangier and a few coast-towns) renders it necessary for the European traveller to carry about not only a tent but a good deal of extra baggage, cooking-appliances, &c., which would otherwise be superfluous. The *impedimenta* are transported on the backs of mules, which may be hired at the rate of one dollar *per diem*. One or two Moors must also be taken to pitch tents, load and unload the pack-animals, and so make themselves generally useful, which they always do. They were usually paid one and sixpence a day each. The only provisions which can be procured at the country villages consist of fowls, eggs, butter, milk, and kuskoo-soo; the latter is a peculiar preparation of flour, and may be considered the national dish of Morocco. It is therefore advisable for a party travelling in the interior to provide themselves with some tins of preserved meat and vegetables, as well as with whatever wine, spirits, &c. they might require. The most satisfactory way of making an expedition through the country, I have found by experience, is to contract with a respectable Moor, who will usually defray the entire expenses, including hire of baggage, animals, servants, cook, and meals, exclusive of wine, at the rate of five dollars a head *per diem*.

As far as I have had opportunities of judging, I have reason to consider travelling in Morocco to be unattended with any danger near the coast, but not east of Tetuan, in the Riff country, or in mountainous districts; and to Englishmen the natives are certainly better inclined than to any other European nation. The late Sultan, however, issued an edict to the effect that he would not hold himself responsible for the life or property of any Christian who at the time of any outrage should be unattended by a Moorish soldier; and a mounted soldier to act as guard can always be procured on application to the Consul of the nation to which the applicant belongs. Any party intending to make an expedition further than ten or fifteen miles from Tangier should provide themselves with this necessary functionary, to whom they must pay one dollar a day. This sum is generally considered to be exorbitant; and it certainly is so in a country where the necessaries of life are far cheaper than in any country in Europe. The real truth, however, is that the Moorish authorities throw as many difficulties as they possibly can in the way of inquisitive European travellers, well knowing that, were the interior thoroughly opened up, the vile system of oppression and misgovernment to which it is and has been for so long a victim would vanish before the opinion of the civilized world.

The vicinity of Tangier is as good a ground for the ornithologist as can be wished anywhere; but it has been a great deal worked up by Olcese, who succeeded Favier as the naturalist of Tangier. About twelve miles to the south are the lakes of Sharf el Akab, well worth visiting for aquatic birds. The country beyond this to Larache is not good until within the neighbourhood of that town, where there is plenty of both marshy and dry ground, the latter, in places, better wooded than usual. Near Larache, on the north bank of the river, are the ruins of the ancient Lixus, at or near the spot where Hercules is supposed to have conquered Antæus, the founder of Tangier, which takes its name from his wife Tinga.

South of Larache are the lakes of Meshree el Haddar (the talkers' ford) and Ras el Doura, the latter running for miles southwards in the direction of Rabat. These lakes swarm with every kind of aquatic bird, according to the season; but in the breeding-time the mosquitoes are enough to drive any European away, besides which the nests are so plundered by the Arabs that it is hardly worth while going there for them. Further south than this I have not been, and refer my readers for any information to Mr. Drake's paper in 'The Ibis' (*l. c.*).

Eastward of Tangier, taking the road to Tetuan, there is little or nothing to be done in the way of birds until the latter place is reached, after a long and tedious day's journey; indeed all that part of Morocco which I have visited is very wearisome to travel over, except near Tetuan and Ceuta, where the mountains break the sameness of the route, and where alone any true beauty of scenery is to be found.

Of these hills only those in the immediate vicinity of Tetuan can be visited, owing to the lawless character of the hill tribes and their Mahometan prejudices, and, last but not least, owing also to the exaggerated stories made up to prevent any European from travelling about. In a stream from one of these mountains, to the south of Tetuan, a species of trout (*Salmo macrostigma*) is found; they are also probably met with in other places, which are forbidden ground to the European.

The country about Tetuan is alike interesting to the ornithologist and favourable to the sportsman; about Martine are some fine marshes, while beyond Cape Negro, towards Ceuta, is a large, irregularly shaped, shallow laguna, called Esmir, with great masses of rush and sedge interspersed with tamarisk bushes, separated from the sea by a wide sandbank covered with brushwood; this laguna and marshes are by far the best ground to be seen on either side of the Straits. Proceeding from Esmir, towards Ceuta, the road lies either on the shore or along the usual scrub-covered country till, turning to the left by some Roman ruins, a pass leading up to the Sierra Bullones is entered, when the scenery becomes very fine, the track ascending by the side of a bright clear stream, through bushes sometimes so thick as to completely shut out the sky overhead, at other times passing through heather, in places twenty feet high. The path becomes gradually worse, till the climax is reached in the ascent of a steep hill where the brushwood tears the load off the mules, and with the stones and rocks nearly renders progress impossible. Once, however, at the top, a fair enough road is found leading to the village of Beut, situated in a sort of plateau at an elevation of about 1000 feet, separated from Jebel Musa by a deep valley, a high range of rocks, and another shallow valley.

About here nothing, ornithologically speaking, is to be seen (excepting a few Choughs) that is not to be met with elsewhere. We found an Eagle nesting on the north face of the range south of Jebel Musa: the nest was in a most difficult position to get at; and not being able to reach any place near enough from which to shoot the Eagle, we left the eggs as worthless, because unable to identify the bird: however there is little doubt that it was the Golden Eagle. We saw some apes about the rocks; they were rather wild, and lost no time in making their way to the top.

The view from this sierra (Apes' Hill of the English, Jebel Musa of the Moors, Sierra Bullones of the Spaniards, Abÿla of the ancients) is magnificent, and baffles description, well repaying all the trouble and difficulties of the ascent.

To the south beyond Tetuan lie, half hidden in blue mist, the snow-streaked mountains of the Atlas, stretching far away out of sight, the summit of one vast snowy pile rather to the south-east appearing to be as high, and looking quite as white, as the Sierra Nevada, near Granada, which is also distinctly visible to the north-east; but this African snowy range seems further off. Below to the east, stretched out as if on a ground-plan close to your feet, is Ceuta, with its ugly white-washed Spanish forts and towers, between which and the Tetuan river looms the gloomy headland of Cape Negro. Westward of this are range after range of comparatively low dark hills, rolling away towards Tangier and Cape Spartel, here and there one or two being topped with a few crags and rocks. Far to the west is the Atlantic, leading to the deep-blue Straits, looking, as they separate Europe and Africa, like some mountain-lake.

Tarifa, to the north-west, is clearly visible, as are the crags of the Sierra de San Bartolomé, the sandy cliffs of Cape Trafalgar, and the long spit of land on which is the light-house; while all the grey, bare, barren-looking Spanish sierras look, with the sun shining on them, as if they lay within a stone's throw.

Gibraltar was shut out from our view, owing to the pleasantry of some Moors, who rolled large stones down the only path leading to the summit of the highest peak, and so prevented us from ascending. However the view we did get was such as can never be forgotten, and it was long before we descended to continue our hunt for birds.

The tops of these mountains, which are 2600 feet high (the highest part of Jebel Musa is about 2800 feet), were covered with thousands of violets then in full bloom. The flowers were light-coloured when growing among the stones and waterworn rocks exposed to the sun, dark when shaded and growing among the stunted bushes which were scattered about here and there: their scent was perfect. Very few other flowers were growing on the tops; but most conspicuous among them was the Gibraltar candytuft; and the everlasting palmetto was met with at the very highest places. The base of all these crags or cliffs is approached by a steep talus of small broken rocks, among which grows a very thick jungle of stunted cork- and olive-trees about 15 feet high.

On the north side of the range next to Beut and at the western end of it, at the base of the cliff, is a wide cave, which, at some distance from the entrance, branches off into two distinct caves, one going up hill, the other down. My companion ascended the upper one till he heard in the darkness the growling of some beast, probably a lynx or some wild cat; so he returned, and we collected together from outside a lot of dead sticks and rubbish, which we dragged up in the darkness as near the animal as we could judge to be well within range: we then set fire to it, and stood ready for a shot; but it was no use; the brute, whatever it was, only retired further in, growling away more than ever.

The light of the fire proved the cave to be some hundred feet high, gradually narrowing to the top from the bottom, which near the entrance is about 12 feet wide, thus showing it to have been formed by two gigantic rocks or cliffs flung against one another at the time these limestone mountains were thrown up from the bottom of the sea, which in remote ages doubtless flowed over them. On both sides of the Straits, *i. e.* at Gibraltar and Abÿla, these fissures or caves are common in the limestone; but this particular one fairly rivals the well-known St. Michael's Cave at Gibraltar, and had, from the marks of fire, been inhabited at some not very distant period. The floor in places was quite a foot deep with the guano of Rock-Doves (*Columba livia*), numbers of which flew out from the nooks and crannies of the rock.

As far as we could understand from the Moors, who, living near Ceuta, spoke a few words of broken Spanish, there was a story of a Moor having ascended this cave till he came out somewhere at the top of the mountain; be this as it may, there was a fine breezy draught of air blowing downwards, which sent the smoke of our fire towards us till we, instead of the beast for whose benefit it was intended, were nearly suffocated.

Having no means of getting torches to further explore the cave, with heavy hearts we left the unknown animal to growl himself to sleep; the Moors insisted, by the way, that what we heard was a "djinn," or evil spirit!

The south-east part of the range of the Sierra Bullones is a different formation, and we could trace signs of lead-ore and antimony in more than one place. Whether any mines will ever be worked in Morocco is doubtful: there is plenty of ground; but at present it is forbidden to look for minerals by the enlightened and despotic Moorish government.

The track or road from Ceuta to Tetuan, after quitting the mountainous district, passes through the interminable scrub usual to the Mediterranean coast; and bad as are mountain tracks in Spain, this one beats them all in roughness; and, owing to the weary sameness of going up and down hill after hill, the journey seems endless.

En route, however, by the shore, nearly opposite Tarifa, lies, shrouded in large thick bushes, the ruins of Alcazar Leguer, a large old castellated Portuguese fort, built about the beginning of the fifteenth century. Some parts of the walls are in fair condition; but the interior is very much dilapidated, and the whole overgrown with wild olive- and fig-trees, brambles and rubbish, desolation beyond description, its only tenants being Owls and (say the Moors) evil spirits. A covered way, formed by two parallel high walls with banquettes on their tops, runs down to the sea-shore, where it is broken down and blocked up with sand; the ruins show signs of unskilful workmanship, and contrast very unfavourably with those of Roman construction, besides which, from being principally built of soft sandstone, they are much weather-worn where exposed to the rain.

Wherever I have wandered about in the coast-districts of Morocco the country is singularly destitute of trees of any size, what few there are being in the santos or graveyards. The consequence of this is, there is no change in the landscape; stunted bushes, rocks, and cultivation constitute the general view. Nevertheless the climate is splendid and healthy, perhaps better than that of Andalucia; and one quits it with the regret that such a fine country should in these days of civilization be, as it were, utterly wasted—a land rich beyond most in soil, minerals, and natural advantages of all sorts, within four days of England, remaining without any real government, without roads, bridges, or any means of communication, owing to political necessities abandoned to barbarians, whose chief object seems to be to keep the country as much as possible secluded from the prying eyes of Europeans.

Migration, Shooting, &c.

The migration of birds, although a most interesting subject, is yet very imperfectly understood, and reliable data from different countries and places are still greatly wanted to elucidate it. Without doubt caused by the absence or abundance of food, which in turn is caused by difference of temperature, the passage of birds in these parts begins with most species almost to a day in the spring, usually lasting for about three weeks, though some, as the Hoopoe and the Swallows, are more irregular in their first appearance; and with these the migration lasts throughout a longer period.

Few, indeed hardly any birds, do not migrate or shift their ground to some extent. I can name very few which do not appear to move, viz. Griffon Vulture, Imperial Eagle, Eagle-Owl, Blue Thrush, all the Woodpeckers, Tree-Creeper, Black-headed Warbler, Dartford Warbler, Crested Lark, Chough, Raven, Magpie, Red-legged and Barbary Partridges, and the

Andalucian Quail. Generally speaking, it seems to me that in the vernal migration the males are the first to arrive, as with the Wheatears, Nightingales, Night-Herons, Bee-eaters; but this is a theory which requires more confirmation. Some species, as the *Neophron* and most of the Raptores, pass in pairs.

Most of the land-birds pass by day, usually crossing the Straits in the morning. The waders are, as a rule, not seen on passage; so it may be concluded they pass by night, although occasionally Peewits, Golden Plover, Terns, and Gulls have been noticed passing by day.

The autumnal or return migration is less conspicuous than the vernal: and whether the passage is performed by night, or whether birds return by some other route, or whether they pass straight on, not lingering by the way as in spring, is an open question; but during the autumn months passed at Gibraltar I failed to notice the passage as in spring, though more than once during the month of August myself and others distinctly heard Bee-eaters passing south at night, and so conclude other birds may do the same.

We have (*vide* Andersson's 'Birds of Damara Land,' pp. 18-21) an account of the swarms of Hawks which appear there at the time they are absent from Europe and North Africa; so it may be reasonably inferred with regard to one species, *Milvus migrans* (the Black Kite), that some of the vast numbers which pass the Straits of Gibraltar retire in autumn through the tropics to South Africa.

The best site for watching the departure of the vernal migration is at Tangier, where just outside the town the well-known plain called the "Mâshan," a high piece of ground that in England would be called a common, seems to be the starting-point of half the small birds that visit Europe.

Both the vernal and autumnal migrations are generally executed during an easterly wind, or Levanter: at one time I thought that this was essential to the passage; but it appears not to be the case, as whether it be an east or west wind, if it be the time for migration, birds will pass, though they linger longer on the African coast before starting should the wind be westerly; and all the very large flights of Raptores (Kites, Neophrons, Honey-Buzzards, &c.) which I have seen passed with a Levanter. After observing the passage for five springs I am unable to come to any decided opinion, the truth being that as an east wind is the prevalent one, the idea has been started that migration always takes place during that wind. Nevertheless it is an undoubted fact that during the autumnal or southern migration of the Quail in September, they collect in vast numbers on the European side, if there be a west wind, and seem not to be able to pass until it changes to the east; this is so much the case that, should the wind keep in that quarter during the migration, hardly any are to be seen.

On some occasions the passage of the larger birds of prey is a most wonderful sight; but of all the remarkable flights of any single species, that of the Common Crane has been the most noteworthy that has come under my own observation.

On the Andalucian side the number of birds seen even by the ordinary traveller appears strikingly large, this being, no doubt, in a great measure caused by the quantity which are, for ten months at least out of the year, more or less on migration; that is to say, with the exception of June and July, there is no month in which the passage of birds is not noticeable, June being the only one in which there may be said to be absolutely no visible migration, as during the month of July Cuckoos and some Bee-eaters return to the south.

Though shooting is hardly a subject within the design of an ornithological brochure like the present, yet it generally happens that an ornithologist is also a sportsman; and therefore a few lines on the subject may be acceptable.

In the coast-districts of Morocco no large game is found

within reach of the European sportsman, excepting wild pigs, which are only to be obtained by the battue system of driving the jungle with beaters and dogs, sitting for hours waiting for the chance of a shot, a class of amusement dignified by the name of a "boar-hunt"; sometimes, where the country is sufficiently open, the real sport of pig-sticking can be had.

No doubt further in the interior there is other large game; but with the exception of shooting an occasional gazelle and a few pigs, there is no opportunity of using the rifle.

The small-game shooting is very good; the abundance of Barbary Partridges in some districts is miraculous; but when killed they are of little value in a culinary point of view, being more dry and tasteless than the Spanish Redleg (*Caccabis rufa*), now so well known in many parts of England.

The number of Snipe in some seasons is very great, especially at Meshree el Haddar, where, and also at Ras el Doura, Larache, Sharf el Akab, Martine near Tetuan, and Esmir near Ceuta, as good snipe- and wildfowl-shooting as may be wished for can be obtained. But it is, as ever in Europe with Snipe, always uncertain sport, as one day swarms are met with, and perhaps on the next day hardly any are to be found. The absence of roads and bridges renders the country in wet weather at times impossible to travel over, the tracks becoming a succession of mudholes, and the rivers impassable torrents. This, added to the unpleasant certainty of living under canvas during rainy weather, is a great drawback to winter shooting.

Another, in my opinion insuperable, objection to shooting in Morocco is, that if any great quantity of game be bagged, it has to be thrown away, as, unless within twenty miles or so of Tangier, it is useless. The Moors, being Mahometans, will not eat any thing killed by a Christian or infidel; and killing for the mere sake of slaughter does not come within the creed of a true sportsman. In Spain all this is very different, as any one and every one is only too glad to accept of the surplus game.

In many parts of Morocco rabbits abound; and hares are in places plentiful. Woodcocks are sometimes tolerably abundant; Quails, of course, are in swarms during migration; and there are a great number of Little Bustard.

Shooting in Andalucia is far more satisfactory and pleasant sport than on the African side. In the first place, accommodation can always be had in a house of some sort, which in warm weather, however, usually swarms with fleas; but by taking your own blankets and a camping-palliasse, which can be refilled at each resting-place with chopped straw, one can generally, by the aid of a liberal use of either flea-powder * or albo-carbon (naphthalin), manage to cheat the vermin of their nocturnal banquet. It is almost absolutely necessary to take this powder with one, as sleep in some of the dens where I have passed the night would have been impossible without using it. Another most useful item is an india-rubber flexible bath, as it is not always that a "*lebrillo*" or large earthenware pan big enough to wash in can be obtained.

In addition to the shelter to be got in Andalucia there are roads; and bad as some may be, they do afford means of communication; and there are bridges, though not always placed in the right situation; for in places you see a bridge built across a gully without any road on either side of it, and others where the stream has quitted its old course for a new one—single instances out of the many thousand strange and wondrous *cosas de España*.

The large game is more varied and plentiful in Andalucia than in Morocco. In most of the wooded valleys of the sierras, near Gibraltar, there were a good many roe-deer (*corzo*) and a few wild pigs; in some of the high sierras near Ronda, Ubrique, and in the Sierra Nevada the Spanish Ibex is sparingly found;

* This vegetable powder is made from a species of Feverfew (*Pyrethrum roseum*), and is quite innocuous except to insects; many other plants of the Chrysanthemum group are equally offensive to parasitic insects.

but it is extremely difficult to get them without organizing a regular drive or *batida*—a very expensive affair, requiring a party of several guns, who must take tents, cooks, &c. up into the mountains; and then, if successful, as far as sport is concerned it is hardly worth while sitting for several hours behind a stone, nine times out of ten without even seeing an ibex. It is very difficult to stalk them, as they lie hidden in the thick stunted fir and other scrub which is scattered in large patches on the mountain-sides, and are so wary that you cannot come suddenly on them like roe-deer. However, in an ibex-shooting expedition, one is amply repaid by the magnificent scenery and the novelty of the affair; but as far as shooting goes it is a failure, and every ibex killed by a Gibraltar party costs more than I should like to state.

Ibex drop their young about the end of April; on one occasion a shooting expedition with which I was present succeeded in getting two, both of which I sent home to the Zoological Gardens; but unfortunately they did not long survive.

I am informed that "Ibex, as late as 1830, frequented the sierras above Algeciraz, but a disease which broke out among the tame goats was communicated to the Ibex, who all perished."

In the Sierra Morena, near Palma, a little to the west of Cordova, are red deer strictly preserved and well pastured; the "heads" of the stags are very fine, which is not the case with those of the Coto Doñana, near San Lucar de Barrameda. All these, however, being wood-frequenting deer, the antlers do not branch out very widely, most of the heads being rather narrow. It is in small-game shooting that Andalucia excels, though it is in no way equal to that of the countries lying east of the Mediterranean. Foremost, both in numbers and sport, is Snipe-shooting; for in some seasons, about November and December, if the weather has been dry, it is equal to any that can be obtained; but all depends upon the weather, which, if wet, causes the birds to disperse over the whole country, while if it be dry they remain in the sotos or marshes, and when flushed return almost immediately. Some of the best sport I have had with them was by waiting in favourite ground while they kept coming in, flying high up overhead, and then swooping down and pitching within a few yards. Fifty couple have been bagged in a day by one gun, and that a muzzle-loader, thirty or twenty-eight couple a gun per day being often obtained. The proportion of Jack-Snipe is about the same as in England, and they keep to the most wet and muddy spots. Snipe, as a rule, in Andalucia are far wilder than in other countries, which is no doubt caused by the nature of the marshes, which, often quite dry at the end of summer, are in winter regular lakes, only at their edges affording any resting-places for the birds, the cover being usually thin and bare.

There are many acres of ground flooded with water, from about six inches to a foot in depth, the whole dotted over with tussocks standing an inch or two above the water, and about a foot apart from each other. This tussocky ground is most difficult both to walk over and shoot on, as the tufts are not broad enough to stand on with both feet, and these slippery lumps of mud and grass standing above the water enable the Snipe to see a long distance, and cause them to rise very wildly; while they also have a most provoking habit of flying up just as you are trying to balance yourself on one of the tussocks. The result, if you fire, is most probably a miss, and down you slip into the water, lucky if on your legs and not on your knees or, as happened to me more than once, on your face. There is, however, one point in favour of all these sotos: they have a firm bottom, the mud is never deep, and there are no quaking bogs or dangerous morasses as in Ireland. A retriever, it is almost needless to add, is perfectly indispensable for this kind of sport, saving (in addition to many birds that would otherwise be lost) much time and the bad temper which results from not being able to find birds that have fallen. Snipe in Andalucia are very seldom seen together in lots or wisps, though occasionally in very wet stormy weather small wisps appear. The best localities which I have visited in Andalucia are the marshes near the edges of the Marisma, or delta of the Guadalquivir, below Seville, especially just beyond Coria del Rio, and near the Coto del Rey and the Coto Doñana; one spot near the Palacio of the former place, las Carnicerias, is excellent. At Casa Vieja, or, more properly speaking, Casas Viejas, some forty miles from Gibraltar, is very good ground, particularly in the first part of the season; there are also good marshes near Vejer. Late in the season, near Taivilla and Tapatanilla, on the road from Tarifa to Vejer, at times Snipe are also to be found very plentifully, but are very wild, and it is impossible to make a large bag as there is no cover.

The wildfowl- or duck-shooting in dry seasons is very fair in the early part of the winter, before the lagoons and rivers are filled up by the rains, there being then very few wet spots, and the birds crowd together in the small pools which remain between the high banks of the river-beds, and can be easily approached; but later on, when these streams are brimful or, rather, overflow their banks, and when the lagunas are sheets of water without rushes or cover of any sort at the edges, it is almost impossible to shoot ducks by day except by making "hides" with sticks and stones, and sending some one round and trying to have them driven over you. At flight sometimes very fair sport is to be had for one or two nights; but after that the fowl know the place, and either come very late or avoid it altogether. For flight-shooting a good retriever is absolutely necessary; for it is, in the dark, impossible to find the spoil; and if left till morning, the Marsh-Harriers are at them by break of day, leaving nothing but bones and feathers. To my mind there is very great charm in flight-shooting, and a naturalist while waiting will see and hear much that is pleasant and perhaps some that is new to him. This sport requires, too, considerable skill in judging the distance, and sharpness of vision in being able to catch a glimpse of the ducks as they pass over. It is a great help if you can place yourself so that you face the west, and thus get the birds in the evening light, when they can be seen coming a very long way off; but if they come from the eastward, and you are obliged to face that way, they never show till close on you; and the croaking frogs make an almost deafening noise, so that you cannot, as in England, hear the sound of the ducks' wings.

Immense numbers of Wild Geese in some years are found in the winter months about the Laguna de la Janda, and below Seville, in the marshes of the Guadalquivir. They are of course very difficult to " get at"; but as they pass the day on the ground at the edge of the water, and always have certain favourite spots to which they resort, they are to be got by digging or making "hides" at the places they most frequent. In the morning, at sunrise, they collect on the water, in some places in hundreds, and swim about feeding for an hour or two on some substance which they pick up from the bottom of the shallow water; after this they disperse and take to the shore, where, if left undisturbed, they pass the day sleeping and pluming themselves. There is one of these goose-haunts near the Palacio of the Coto del Rey, a little to the south-east of it. One morning in January, having the day previously made a hide among some tufts of rushes, I went and laid up before sunrise to await the geese, which arrived by degrees in flight after flight, till there must have been within a mile of me, at the lowest computation, between three and four thousand; I shall never forget the sight, and I lay concealed watching them for at least two hours. I could not distinguish amongst them more than one lot of about a dozen Bean-Geese; the remainder were all Grey-lags. Some hundreds were within about a hundred yards, and it was very amusing to see them feeding, fighting, and playing with one another; but somehow they were evidently suspicious of the patch of spiky rushes in which I was lying flat in the slight hole which had been made between two tufts of rushes and covered over with others dug up by the roots, and arranged so as to look as if growing. Unable to turn on my side or move in the least, I was so cramped that it was all I could do to remain there; but after a time a large lot of geese began to set in towards my position, and in a few minutes more I should have had a good family shot. I had plenty of chances of firing, but could not have got more than a couple; besides which I liked to watch them, so waited on in hopes of a good lot coming close to me, when, alas! cries of alarm were heard from the birds furthest away on my right, and after a minute or two they began to fly up, and I could see against the sky a man riding towards them. The geese in front of me all pricked up their heads and were getting ready to be off; so I was obliged to jump and send both barrels at them as my only chance; and by good luck, or rather thanks to the large shot, two were killed, but not enough to recompense one for lying cramped up for so long; nevertheless I was more than repaid by the sight of so many wild geese and some other fowl close to me, and being able to watch their movements. Any one who would take the trouble to try punt-shooting with a big gun below Seville on tidal waters might make some wonderful bags, as the enormous quantities of Geese, Wigeon, and other ducks can only be approached with the aid of a punt. When near the edge of water you can always approach Ducks with a stalking-horse; and Geese will allow this on their first arrival, but soon become too wary.

Golden Plover are extremely abundant in vast flocks from November to March. On their first arrival they are not so wild as afterwards. They can always be "got at" with a stalking-horse; but as good a plan to shoot them as any is to stand still in some place which they frequent on a windy day, when they will often fly within a few yards. Peewits are numerous, but not worth shooting, as is the case with Curlews; but the latter are, as elsewhere, much too wary to allow themselves to be shot, and during the whole time I was in Andalucia I never but once had the chance of killing one.

Woodcocks in some seasons are numerous; but five or six couple in a day is a very good bag, very different from Albanian shooting. Red-legged Partridges (*Caccabis rufa*) are not worth the trouble of going after, either for sport or for the table; in some places there are a good number, but not near Gibraltar; they are the chief object of sport with the Spaniards, who kill them at all seasons, even shooting them from the nest. Quails are, during the *entrada* or autumnal migration, so extremely abundant that, if there has been a westerly wind for a few days in September, when they are on passage, there is really no limit to the number that may be shot. About Tarifa at that season every gun-possessing man and boy turns out with all the cur dogs in the town, and, regardless of each other, they fire in all directions, so that it is a service of danger to go out near them. If the wind during their passage remains in the east, the Quails pass on, and little or no sport is to be had with them. A west wind appears to detain them and prevent their passing the Straits, though it does not seem to retard their migration by land.

The remaining small game to be noticed in Andalucia are Bustards, hares, and rabbits. The Great Bustard is only to be got with any certainty by driving. The Little Bustard, more wary still, is only to be shot in the end of July and in August during the extreme heat of the day, though rarely they can be driven over a gun by getting under the bank of a river or such like shelter, and sending a man round to put them up; but on rising they usually mount up very high, in this respect differing from the Great Bustard, which seldom flies high enough to be out of shot if you are directly underneath. Hares (*Lepus mediterraneus*) are a much smaller species than in England, about the size of a good average English rabbit, not very abundant anywhere and frequenting open flat and cultivated districts, never being found among woods or high ground. Rabbits, of course, are abundant but very small, rather less in size than the New-Forest rabbit, which is the most diminutive race in England. A shooting-license, easily obtainable through the aid of any British Consul, is requisite in Spain; and though seldom asked for, it is better to have one. The form and cost of one varies according to the Government, and therefore is seldom alike two years in succession. A close time has been established, but, needless to say, in the wild districts is not regarded.

Here follows a partial list of the Mammalia of Andalucia, with their local names, which may be useful to the sportsman. Of course there are other species of small Mammals to be found, especially among the Bats; with the names of the latter I have been kindly assisted by Lord Lilford, who has personally obtained them all in Andalucia. Those marked with an asterisk I have obtained myself or seen " in the flesh."

Greater Horse-shoe Bat	Rhinolophus ferrum-equinum.
*	R. euryale.
Lesser Horse-shoe Bat.	R. bihastatus.
	Dysopes rueppellii.
Barbastelle	Barbastellus communis.
*Noctule	Vespertilio noctula.
*Mouse-coloured Bat ..	V. murinus.
*Schreiber's Bat	V. schreiberi.
Long-eared Bat	V. auritus.

V. schreiberi, *V. murinus*, and *R. euryale* are found in caves near Casas Viejas—the two former species in countless numbers.

MAMMALIA.

the dung at the bottom of the caves being from four to five feet in depth. The Spanish name for all is *Murcielago*.

		Spanish names.
*Hedgehog	Erinaceus europæus.	Erizo.
*Shrew	Sorex araneus.	Musaraña.
*Mole	Talpa europæa.	Topo.
*Badger	Meles taxus.	Tejon.
*Common Marten Cat	Mustela foina.	Foina.
*Polecat	M. putorius.	Turon.
*Weasel	M. vulgaris.	Comadreja.
*Otter	Lutra vulgaris.	Nutra or Nutria.
*Genet	Viverra genetta.	Gineta.
*Ichneumon	Herpestes ichneumon.	Melon, Meloncillo.
*Wild Cat	Felis catus.	Gato montés.
*Spanish or Spotted Lynx	F. pardina.	Gato clavo, Gato cerval.
*Wolf	Canis lupus.	Lobo.
*Fox	C. vulpes, var. melanogaster.	Zorro.
Squirrel	Sciurus vulgaris.	Ardilla.
*Fat Dormouse	Myoxus glis.	Liron campestre.
	M. nitella.	Raton careto.
*Dormouse	M. avellanarius.	Liron de los Avellanos.
*Brown Rat	Mus decumanus.	Rata.
*Mouse	M. musculus.	Raton.
*Black Rat	M. rattus.	Rata negro.
*Long-tailed Field-Mouse	M. sylvaticus.	Raton de campo.
*Water-Rat	Arvicola amphibius.	Rata de agua.
*Field-Mouse	A. agrestis.	Topino.
*Hare	Lepus mediterraneus.	Liebre.
*Rabbit	L. cuniculus.	Conejo.
*Wild Pig	Sus scrofa.	Jabali, Jabalina.
*Red Deer	Cervus elaphus.	Ciervo.
*Fallow Deer	C. dama.	Gamo, Paleto.
*Roe Deer	C. capreolus.	Corzo.
*Ibex	Capra hispanica.	Cabra montés.

In this book I have endeavoured to name with each species of bird some definite locality where they may be found, which is rather necessary, as certainly on the Spanish side of the Straits birds are very locally distributed, perhaps more so than in most countries I have visited. It is difficult to surmise the cause of this, as precisely similar tracts of country within no very great distance of each other are not always frequented by the same birds. On the Spanish side, without doubt, the most common bird as regards numbers is the Goldfinch, and the most universally distributed the Stonechat. The number of birds of prey is very great, chiefly feeding on rabbits, rats, mice, reptiles, and insects; they are very useful, and as the ground-breeding birds suffer much in the nesting-season from snakes and lizards, those birds of prey which feed chiefly on these enemies of the smaller birds render their lesser brethren valuable protection. The number of little birds, especially during the season of migration, is sure to be noticed even by the most unobservant. Immense quantities of Larks, Finches, and even some of the Warblers are brought into the markets; but as a Spaniard seldom shoots at such small fry, they are chiefly netted, caught at night with a lantern and bell, or snared with bird-lime (*liga*).

The best localities for an ornithologist living at Gibraltar to obtain specimens or watch migration is the country west of an imaginary line drawn due north from Gibraltar as far as the latitude of Seville. Within this district, part of which is given in the Map attached to this volume, as much can be done as is possible in three or four months' time; and the district is large enough to require many years to work it out thoroughly.

In the immediate vicinity of Gibraltar (or el Peñon, as the Spaniards call it), the Cork-wood of Almoraima and the level ground, mud-flats, and old salinas "between the rivers" on the way to Algeciraz offer to the collector capital ground for work. In the Cork-wood particularly several birds are found breeding which do not seem to nest elsewhere. The ground north-east of Gibraltar is to a great extent covered with scrub and brushwood; and little is to be done in the bird line in that direction.

The sierras being too far distant, cannot be worked from Gibraltar; it is necessary to go to Algeciraz, Facinas, Pulverilla, or some *cortijo* near the hills you wish to work. Very deceptive in appearance, looking quite low and easy to ascend, it takes three or four hours to reach their tops, which, bare, rugged, and wild beyond description, are alone worth visiting for the view, which, always grand, on a clear day is magnificent, that from the Peñon del Fraile to the west of Algeciraz being one of the finest. From these mountains run down numerous wooded valleys (*gargantas*) clothed with cork and oak trees, many of very large size, though badly mutilated by being lopped by charcoal-burners. The rocky streams which flow down these valleys are fringed with rhododendron, arbutus, holly, hawthorn, laurestinus, oleander, bay, myrtle, giant heather, cistus, and many sorts of ferns, conspicuous amongst them being the *Osmunda* and maidenhair, while here and there is an occasional *Caladium* with its huge leaves reminding one in shape of elephant's ears: the leaves of this plant, called *hojas de llama*, are much used by the country people as a medicine for fevers; many of the rocks and all the trunks of the cork-trees are festooned with hare's-foot fern (*calaguala*), also used medicinally.

In spring these ravines are, from their natural beauty and the colour of these various shrubs and flowers, so picturesque that one cannot help lingering about them merely to admire the charming scenery, becoming apt to forget the birds for which one is in search. These places are seldom visited by an Englishman, only by stray smugglers, goatherds, and charcoal-burners; and every pass, hill, valley, in fact every well-marked situation, has its name, many more familiar to me than the streets of London.

Those valleys most worth visiting near Gibraltar are the Garganta del Capitan, to the north-west of Algeciraz, on the way to Ojen by the mountain-path of la Trocha, which is within easy distance (five or six miles) of Algeciraz. The valley of the Guadalmalcil, halfway on the road between Tarifa and Algeciraz, is also very beautiful; but the Garganta del Helecho (Valley of the Ferns), south-west of Pulverilla, is perhaps the best for shrubs, flowers, and ferns. The "Waterfall" valley, near Algeciraz (la Garganta del Aguila), is tamer than any; but above the cascades or waterfalls it improves on acquaintance. This ravine, however, is well known to every one who has been at Gibraltar as the regular rendezvous for picnics, the very name of which is enough to destroy any merits that the scenery may possess. Towards Tarifa and beyond, on the road to Vejer, the country is not so pretty, opening out near Facinas to the vega

TERRACE ON THE NORTH SIDE OF SAN BARTOLOMÉ.

of the Laguna de la Janda; thence cultivated ground, or *campiña*, stretches away to Medina Sidonia and on to Jerez. On the right and left of this road, however, are three isolated rocky ranges—those of la Sierra de San Bartolomé and la Sierra de la Plata being to the left, that of la Sierra de Enmedio to the right; these ranges are the breeding-places of Griffon Vultures and other rock-breeding birds, and are well worthy of a visit.

I here give the names of a few of the rocky cliffs which should be visited by those who wish to see such places:—la Laja de la Zarga and la Silla del Papa, in the Sierra de Plata; la Laja del Ciscar[*], to the east of and near Taivilla; Piedra de Paz, near Paterna; la Laja de los Pajaros, los Jolluelos, and la Laja de Peñarroyo, near Casas Viejas.

There are also magnificent cliffs in the Sierra de las Cabras, east of Alcala de los Gazules, and hundreds of others which I saw but could not find time to visit. I did not care to send "collectors" to bring eggs without the birds to which they belonged; or, as is often the case with these worthies, they would have brought eggs with birds to which they did not belong, and, with unblushing effrontery, sworn perhaps, as I have known them do, that a Turkey's egg was taken by them in a high cliff, and belonged to an "Aguila de las rocas."

It is to be hoped that this book may not be the cause of the useless or unnecessary destruction of any bird, and especially that dealers may not profit thereby. All mentioned is intended for the benefit of true ornithologists, and not for those who are never satisfied unless killing or having killed as many rare birds as possible.

It will be seen that there is sport to be had in Andalucia; and the shooting has the charm of a varied bag, and the freedom to wander where you like, as a rule; added to which it is necessary to work for your game, which, in my idea, adds much to the pleasure of sport. The climate, too, is all that can be wished, especially in spring, when there is something most exhilarating in the air; but in autumn, until October, it is too warm to go out with pleasure, and the sun-baked, tawny, dusty, thirsty-looking country has lost all the beauty of its flowers and the verdure of spring. To see Andalucia, it should be visited in

[*] This name is from "ciscar," to besmear, the whole face of the laja being so whitened by the Vultures' droppings as to be conspicuous some miles off.

March, April, and May, in order to thoroughly appreciate both the climate and the scenery.

Another hint which I would fain give is to be as civil as possible, and conform to the customs of the country. The Andalucian peasant, courteous and polite, is at heart a *caballero*, and very different from the inhabitants of the towns; at the same time he is proud and independent, and, to humour him, he must be treated on terms of equality. Above all things remember that it is no use attempting to hurry in Spain, where patience is more severely taxed than in any other country, and where *no corre priesa* is the order of the day. Certainly the best cure for impatience is to pass a few months among Spaniards.

Here ends this Introductory Chapter, with apologies for its shortcomings in the fact that it is the concoction of one who detests pen, ink, and paper, and who is more at home with the gun, rifle, or fishing-rod; so, in the manner of the country which to me has so many charms, let me conclude with the farewell and time-honoured salutation, *Vaya Vd. con Dios.*

EL ORGANO, NEAR TARIFA.

Since the preceding was written, alas! more than twenty years ago, the writer has on several occasions in winter and spring visited his old haunts, the last expedition being made in company with Major Willoughby Verner, Rifle Brigade, who was quartered at Gibraltar from 1874 to 1881, and who has since made frequent visits. To him I owe many records of his practical observations, as well as to Mr. Meade-Waldo for some notes made by him during a visit to Tangier in the spring of 1892.

Captain Savile Reid, late Royal Engineers, contributed a paper to 'The Ibis,' 1885, "Winter Notes from Morocco"; while Mr. Abel Chapman wrote in 'The Ibis,' 1884, "Rough Notes on Spanish Ornithology," and in many of his Chapters of his 'Wild Spain' he treats of Andalucian birds.

"Aves de España," by Don José Arévalo y Baca, vol. xi. 'Memorias de la Real Academia de Ciencias' (Madrid, 1887), contains some information on Andalucian birds, and all given on personal observation is no doubt *bonâ fide*, but unfortunately he often quotes one upon whom we cannot rely.

There is now, in 1894, little change in the country near Gibraltar, except in the dress of the peasantry, who have discarded most of their picturesque provincial costume, even the old sombrero is rarely seen, and replaced by the felt hat of the London rough; while the "fair" sex have left off the grace-giving mantilla and even in wild out-of-the-way places adopted caricatures of modern fashions.

There seems, if possible, more poverty, and in the winter of 1893–94 there was *mucha hambre* and actual deaths from want; and had not the early spring of 1894 been exceptionally wet, there would have been a serious famine.

Among changes in the immediate vicinity of the Rock, a serious one for the Garrison is that the right of shooting over all that part "between the rivers" to as far as and including the Cork-wood has been hired and monopolized by some Gibraltar merchants, so the British officer, who used to go where he wished, has no chance of a day's gunning: he must either cross the Straits or make an expedition into Spain—an expensive affair, which takes a day *en route* and another on return.

It is much to be regretted that the Garrison could not have arranged to hire this shooting, so as to enable officers to have a day's sport; but the chance has passed away, probably not to return. In addition to this there are many other places marked *acotado* (preserved), which used not to be so, and many more

PEASANTRY, TAPATANILLA.

guns are carried in the country, which has caused a great decrease in the resident birds of prey during the last twenty years. About Gibraltar the Griffon Vulture is as numerous as then, but the Bearded Vulture is gone. In the provinces of Málaga and Granada many Vultures, Bearded and Griffon, are reported to have been destroyed by poison, laid for wolves &c.

As few genera have been given as possible: the present rage is to give as many as any excuse can be found for, and will soon result in every bird having a separate genus; and in addition some writers now give a bird the same generic and specific name, thus making as much confusion as possible in nomenclature.

The unfortunate part of ornithology, as at present practised, is that it is chiefly confined to the slaughter of birds, whose skins, when compared and examined by table naturalists, are upon the slightest variation in plumage made into new species, without any knowledge of their habits, notes, &c. Much more can be done by observation than by the gun, and when a bird is destroyed all chance of noticing its habits is destroyed likewise. Measurements of length given are only an attempt to show the proportionate size of a species. Measurements, in the writer's opinion, are of little use, especially as hardly any two persons measure a bird in the same manner.

LAJA DEL CISCAR.

Order **PASSERES**. Family **TURDIDÆ**.

Subfamily TURDINÆ. Young spotted.

1. Turdus viscivorus, Linnæus. **The Mistle-Thrush.**

Spanish. Charla (Chatterer).

"Found near Tangier, always singly and very sparingly in company with *T. musicus*, on passage. They arrive in November, but do not stay near here, returning to recross the Straits in February."—*Favier.*

They occasionally nest near Tangier, as in 1869 I saw eggs taken near there.

The Mistle-Thrush cannot be said to be common near Gibraltar, being most so in winter. They are considered to arrive and depart with the Woodcocks; but a few pairs nest in the Cork-wood and other wooded districts.

Axillaries *white*; a white patch on end of inner web of two outer tail-feathers on each side.

Young. Spotted with buff and black on head and back. Length 11 inches.

2. Turdus musicus, Linnæus. **The Song-Thrush.**

Spanish. Zorzal.

Favier's note applies to this bird on both sides of the Straits, and is as follows:—"The Song-Thrush is a winter resident in great numbers, being the most common of the Thrushes, arriving in large flocks in October and November, departing in March."

On the Spanish side they chiefly frequent the wild olive-trees, on the berries of which they feed. The first date of arrival noticed at Gibraltar was the 22nd of October; and the latest day on which I observed them was the 1st of April.

Axillaries *buffish yellow*; eye-stripe scarcely developed.
Young. Spotted; the feathers of upper surface with pale centres. After first moult young resembles adult, but has pale ends to the wing-coverts. Length 9 inches.

3. Turdus iliacus, Linnæus. The Redwing.

Spanish. Malvis.

"This Thrush is very rare near Tangier. I have only met with two, between November and March—one in 1852, the other in 1864."—*Favier.*

Mr. Meade-Waldo observed them on the 17th of February, 1892, near Tangier.

In Andalucia the Redwing is abundant in winter, in company with the Song-Thrush.

Axillaries *chestnut-red*; well-defined *whitish streak* over eye, reaching to nape. Length 8¾ inches.

4. Turdus pilaris, Linnæus. The Fieldfare.

Is not mentioned by Favier, but Mr. Meade-Waldo found Fieldfares in abundance on the Moorish side of the Straits in the spring of 1892. On the Spanish side I never met with any, but they are reported by Arévalo from Granada.

Axillaries *white*; rump *slate-grey*. Length 10 inches.

5. Turdus merula, Linnæus. The Blackbird.

Moorish. Tchau Tchau (*Favier*). *Spanish.* Mirlo.

"Resident near Tangier and very plentiful, nesting three times a year."—*Favier.*

I found a nest in Morocco built in a prickly-pear hedge. The Blackbird nests at Gibraltar, and is resident and very common in Andalucia: in the winter months their numbers are greatly augmented by migrants.

Male. Black; bill orange-yellow.
Female. Brownish black or reddish brown; bill brown.
Young. Like female, but more spotted; the male with blackish bill. Length 10 inches.

6. Turdus torquatus, Linnæus. The Ring-Ouzel.

Spanish. Chirlo.

"Is only met with in small flights on passage near Tangier, crossing to Europe in March and April, and returning in the autumn to pass the winter further south."—*Favier.*

I only observed the Ring-Ouzel near Gibraltar on passage in the spring, the earliest dates in each year being the 8th of April 1868, 20th of March 1870, 9th of April 1871, 12th of March 1872, 28th of March 1874; but they are known to breed in the mountains near Granada, and Mr. Saunders records a nest near Colmenar.

Male. Uniform brownish black, with *white crescent* on chest.
Female. Lighter; crescent narrower, washed with brown.
Young. Spotted. Length 11 inches.

7. Monticola cyanus (Linnæus). The Blue Rock-Thrush.

Moorish. Tchau-tchau zerak. *Spanish.* Solitario.

Favier states that the Blue Rock-Thrush, which is as common in suitable localities in Morocco as in Andalucia, is migratory, passing north from February to May, and passing south from August to September. I never could detect any migration on the Spanish side, and consider it one of the very few birds which are stationary, not even shifting their ground—though, perhaps, in other countries circumstances may cause them to migrate.

Abundantly distributed on all rocky ground, even on sea-cliffs, and often seen on house-tops in those towns which lie in their districts, they are always to be found at Gibraltar in unvarying numbers, frequenting daily the same spots, and attracting considerable notice both from their melodious song and conspicuous habits.

I here repeat a note made about their nesting, which has already appeared in Dresser's account of this species:—"A pair nested in a hole outside the wall of my stable at Gibraltar in June 1869. Five eggs were laid, which were hatched about the 20th. The nest, composed of small dried bits of roots, was very scanty and ill put together. When the young were hatched, I broke through the wall from the inside of the stable to the nest, making the hole large enough to admit a small cage, in which I placed the nest and young; and then hung an old coat over the inside hole, so as to shut out the light from the inside, cutting a small slit in the coat through which to watch the old birds feeding their young within six inches distance. Both birds fed them, at intervals of not more than five minutes. The food consisted almost entirely of centipedes (*Scolopendræ*), with now and then a large spider or bluebottle fly by way of change. Where they could have found so many centipedes it is difficult to imagine, as they are insects which lie hid all day under stones &c. The head was always bitten off, and the insect so mangled as to be quite dead. Two of the five young died in the cage, from the old birds not being able to get at them. Of the other three, only one attained maturity, living till October, when, to my great regret, he went the way of all pets. He was very tame, and of most engaging habits and disposition—in fact, what the Spaniards call '*simpatico*.' In his early days he was fed on bread and bruised snails; later on he had more fruit, which possibly killed him.

"The Blue Rock-Thrush very often perches on trees, and at Gibraltar and Tangier is frequently seen on the house-tops, though generally observed on bare rocky ground. They are sometimes found in wooded places, if there are any high rocks; for instance, a pair nested at the first waterfall near Algeciraz, which is in the midst of a dense forest. They have a habit in the courting-season of flying straight out from a rock, and then suddenly dropping with the wings half shut, like a Wood-Pigeon in the nesting-time. The Blue Rock-Thrush is very fond of ivy-berries and all fruit."

It seems that they nest more than once a year, as on the 25th of April Mr. Stark found a nest with young about a week old, and on the 3rd of May a nest with five eggs hard sat on, the one in my stable being hatched in the end of June. One set of eggs obtained by Mr. Stark were of the usual delicate pale blue colour, but marked with small russet spots at the large end, somewhat like eggs of the Black Wheatear (*Saxicola leucura*).

All the nests built on ledges of rocks and open to view are larger and better-built than those placed in holes.

Verner tells me (1894) that they still occupy the same situations on the Rock as they did twenty years ago; and he knows no bird whose eggs are more difficult to find, as during time of laying and incubation they seem to know if they are watched; and the nests on the Rock are, as a rule, more difficult of access than in the sierras. He found on May 22, 1875, five young able to fly; May 13, 1877, five young fully fledged; March 23, 1878, nest just finished; April 24, 1879, nest just completed, first egg on April 13. They never seem to lay more or less than five eggs: this out of many nests he found.

Male in spring. Uniform slaty blue; head and neck with silvery gloss; in autumn and winter with narrow whitish margins to the body-feathers.
Female. Browner than male. Length $8\frac{1}{2}$ to 9 inches.

8. Monticola saxatilis, Linnæus. The White-backed Rock-Thrush.

"Is found on passage only near Tangier, crossing to Europe in April. Is a scarce species, and very rarely obtained during passage."—*Favier.*

I saw several near Tangier on the 16th of April, 1872, and one on the 30th of March, 1874, also numbers passing at Gibraltar on the 4th of April, 1870; and one was seen there returning on the 26th of September, 1868.

According to Arévalo this bird nests in all the mountain ranges of the Peninsula.

Tail *chestnut*, two centre feathers darker than others; axillaries and lower parts *chestnut*.

Male. Head and neck blue; centre of back nearly *white*.

Female. Brown, mottled. Length 7½ inches.

9. Saxicola œnanthe, Linnæus. The Common Wheatear.

Spanish. Culiblanco, Ruiblanca: but these names apply to all the Wheatears.

"This is the most common of the 'Traquets,' except the Stonechat and Whinchat, but is only seen near Tangier on migration in small flights during March and April, returning in September."—*Favier.*

Wheatears are abundant in Andalucia, but seen only on passage. First noticed on the 4th of March in 1870; a single male bird at Tangier on the 26th of March in 1874; many seen near Alcala del Rio on the 4th of April; again passing in numbers at Gibraltar on the 12th of April. Wheatears were plentiful near Casas Viejas at the end of October and the first part of November, being last seen on the 13th of that month. I have a note also of observing six or seven in the middle of the Bay of Biscay on the 9th of October, when they settled on the steamer, keeping with us till night.

Axillaries white, with dark centres. Rump *white*.

Male. Above pale slate-grey; below white; ear-coverts black.

Female. Above dull brown; below buff; ear-coverts dark brown.

Young. Like the female, but spotted with dark markings on feathers above and below.

Both sexes in autumn are alike, resembling female in spring, but have buff margins to all the feathers. Length 6 inches.

10. Saxicola stapazina, Vieillot. Western Black-throated Wheatear.

"Passes near Tangier during March and April, returning in September. Is the most frequent after the Wheatear, with which bird they travel."—*Favier*.

Is in Andalucia apparently less common than the Black-eared Wheatear, perhaps because they frequent higher ground; at least I have noticed them more about mountain-tops. First seen 17th of March, 1877 (*Verner*), 23rd of March, 1894 (Tapatanilla). They nest about the same time as the Black-eared Wheatear, which they resemble in habits, nest, and eggs.

Axillaries black; two-thirds of two centre tail-feathers black with the basal third white, the others white tipped with black.
Male. Crown, back, rump, breast, and belly white, suffused with buff on back and breast. Chin and upper throat black. Length $5\frac{1}{4}$ inches.

11. Saxicola albicollis, Vieillot. The Black-eared Wheatear.

According to Favier, this bird is less common than *Saxicola stapazina* near Tangier, but is met with in the same way. Near Gibraltar they appeared to me to be the most frequent, and were first seen there on the 3rd of April, 1870, when several were noticed; and on the 15th of March, 1872, one was observed, and a single bird at Tangier on the 14th. Seen at Tangier on the 18th March, 1894, by Mr. Irby, 60th Rifles, and by myself on the 23rd at Sierra Retin. They breed on the "Queen of Spain's Chair," laying about the first week in May, building a loosely constructed nest among stones and rocks, very often in the same situations as the Blue Rock-Thrush. The eggs are light blue, with a zone of brown spots at the large end.

Throat white.
Male. Marked as last, but has head and back more whitish, but generally suffused with buff; lores and patch round eye to side of neck black.
Female. Brownish where black in male. Length $6\frac{1}{4}$ inches.

12. Saxicola leucura (Gmelin). **The Black Wheatear.**

Spanish. Sacristan (the Sexton); Pedrero (the Stone-mason).

This bird is merely named as occurring near Tangier by Favier, but is found in Morocco in suitable localities.

On the Spanish side the Black Wheatear is a common and conspicuous bird at Gibraltar, and to be seen throughout the year; elsewhere some are migratory, arriving in March, and only found on bare rocky ground. The nest is sometimes in clefts of rocks, so deep in as to be inaccessible.

Mr. Stark took a nest on the 25th of April, near Gibraltar, containing four pale blue eggs hard sat on, marked with a zone of light reddish-brown spots. The nest was very large, loosely built with grass and heather-roots, lined inside with finer grass, two or three feathers of the *Neophron*, and one bit of palmetto fibre.

The name of *pedrero* is applied to this bird from their curious habit of placing small stones as a foundation to their nest, and frequently, as when open to view, making a sort of wall or screen of stones in front of the nest.

Verner remarks that they much resemble the Blue Rock-Thrush in habits; and all the many nests found by him had foundations of small stones—the first two had foundations only, but the third had a slight wall in front—and until he heard from me that this bird was known near Málaga as *pedrero* he was much puzzled to account for the stones being so placed. In some instances the foundation appears to be useful in keeping the nest dry.

The most remarkable nest we met with was on the 6th of April, 1894, in a small hole in the roof of a sandstone cave in the Sierra Bartolomé. This nest, which I myself saw *in situ*, was made of grass and fibres lined with finer fibres of the palmetto, without wool or feathers: the cavity was filled by the nest and by the foundation and barrier of stones in front; the latter was 9 inches long, the same in width, and $2\frac{1}{2}$ inches high. Verner removed the stones and found that the wall in front

42 TURDIDÆ.

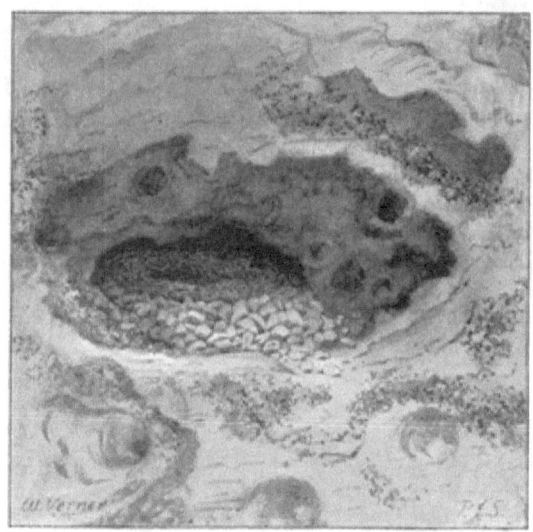

NEST OF THE BLACK WHEATEAR.

consisted of no less than 282 stones, while the foundation was formed of 76 more, a total of 358, the largest being 2 inches long by ¾ inch wide and ½ inch deep, weighing 2 oz., the total weight of all the stones being 4½ lbs. A representation of this nest is given: the cave was about six feet high and nearly circular, with a diameter of about twelve feet.

Verner found the usual number of eggs to be five, occasionally only four; and they appear to be irregular in laying, one nest having fully fledged young on the 10th of April, other birds not laying till the end of that month.

Male. General colour black; rump and under tail-coverts white.
Female. Sooty brown where black in male, and tinged with brown on the white parts. Length 6½ inches.

13. Pratincola rubetra (Linnæus). The Whinchat.

Moorish. Erdan (*Favier*). *Spanish.* Zarzalera.

" Is only a passing migrant near Tangier, crossing to Europe in April and May, returning to winter further south in September and October. Is the most common of the Chats, except the Stonechat."—*Favier.*

The Whinchat is met with as above, on the Spanish side being first noticed on the 7th of April; on the 20th, in 1870, many hundreds passed at Gibraltar, also on the 12th of the same month in 1872, and I noticed them as late as the 3rd of May. They return in September, being never seen in winter, and are not yet known to breed in the south of Spain.

Male. Chest orange-rufous; white line over eye from bill to nape; basal half of tail white, rest black.
Female. Like male, but paler.
Young. Like old female, but more spotted, with white tips to the feathers. Length 5 inches.

14. Pratincola rubicola (Linnæus). The Stonechat.

Moorish. Bou-erdan. *Spanish.* Caganchina, Cagaropa.

" The Stonechat is resident and most abundant about Tangier, being seen in all directions, perched on the tops of plants, bushes, and hedges. They nest from March to July. Some arrive from Europe in September and October, leaving in February and March."—*Favier*.

This bird is also on the Spanish side one of the most common and at the same time conspicuous birds. They increase perhaps in numbers in autumn and spring, but are as common in winter as in summer. I found a nest with five eggs hard sat on the 10th of March, and have no doubt that they breed more than once in the season.

Male. Head, chin, and throat black; breast orange-chestnut; upper tail-coverts whitish, spotted with black. Tail blackish brown; outer web of outside feathers edged with buff.

Female. Upper tail-coverts reddish brown; lower parts rufous.

Young. Spotted. Length 5¾ inches.

15. Ruticilla moussieri, Olph-Galliard. Moussier's Redstart.

Under the synonym of "*Ruticilla erythrogastra*"—a large eastern Redstart—Favier, in his notes, has included Moussier's Redstart; but his description fully identifies it as a male *R. moussieri*. He mentions one killed in 1848. I obtained an adult male at Tangier on the 14th of March, 1872, and saw three others killed in that month in 1874; since then they appear to be of irregular occurrence in spring.

I never obtained one on the Spanish side of the Straits, or saw a Spanish specimen.

Male. Crown, sides of head, back, and wings black; white line over eye from forehead to nape. White patch on wing. Rump, upper tail-coverts, tail (except the two brown centre feathers), and underparts pale chestnut.

Female. Much as female of Common Redstart, but smaller and russet-red below. Length 4½ inches.

16. Ruticilla phœnicurus (Linnæus). The Common Redstart.

Moorish. Houmeira (reddish). *Spanish.* Culirojo.

"This Redstart is only found on passage near Tangier, crossing the Straits in March and April, returning in September and October. It is not so common as *Ruticilla titys*, and is seldom seen settled on rocks."—*Favier*.

The Common Redstart is seen in great numbers near and at Gibraltar on passage. My earliest dates of arrival noticed were the 4th of April 1868, 5th of April 1869, 22nd of March 1870, 28th of March 1874 (Tetuan), 23rd of March 1894. In 1872 they passed in great quantities on the 12th, 13th, 14th, and 15th of April, the last noticed being on the 26th, in the Cork-wood.

They are not known to remain and nest near Gibraltar, but are reported by Arévalo to do so near Granada.

Rump and tail chestnut; axillaries *chestnut*, or rufous.
Male in spring. Black line in front of the white forehead; chin, throat, and sides of neck black; back grey; centre of belly nearly white.
Female. Above dull brown; underparts *paler*; breast shaded with chestnut and white.
Male in autumn much as adult female.
Young. Spotted. Length 5¼ inches.

17. Ruticilla titys (Scopoli). The Black Redstart.

Spanish. Culirojo, Tintorero.

"This species is the most common Redstart about Tangier, remaining throughout the winter among rocks and old buildings. They arrive during October, and depart in March. The old birds are solitary; but the immature birds keep together. They shake their tails incessantly, and, holding their heads erect, are difficult to get a shot at" (!).—*Favier*.

The Black Redstart is seen at Gibraltar, as at Tangier, arriving in November, and never being seen after March. They nest, however, a little way north of San Roque.

A specimen I killed at Gibraltar had been eating very small ants.

Tail and rump chestnut-red; two centre tail-feathers dark; axillaries *black*, or greyish black.
Male. Cheeks, throat, and breast black; primaries and secondaries edged on outer webs with white; centre of belly nearly white.
Female and young male. Above entirely sooty brown; underparts nearly as dark as the upper. Length 5¾ inches.

18. Ruticilla cyanecula, Wolf. **The White-spotted Bluethroat.**

Spanish. Soldiya, Gargantiazul.

"Found near Tangier only on passage, and then very rarely. I only obtained them four times—in 1839, 1844, 1866, and 1867. They cross to Europe in February and March, returning in October."—*Favier.*

Capt. Savile Reid saw many among reeds and rushes in the marshes of Meshree el Haddar in the winter of 1884–85 (Ibis, 1885, p. 242).

The greater number of this species must pass further to the east, as about Gibraltar I only saw one, which I shot on the 1st of March, as it was perched on some rushes in an old "salina" near Palmones; another, shot in November 1873 at the same place, was in the possession of Capt. Reid. They are fairly common on passage in the provinces of Seville, Granada, and Málaga, but are not known to breed.

This Bluethroat, in 1760, was called by Brisson the "Gorge bleue de Gibraltar."

Tail brown, with basal two-thirds of all but two centre feathers chestnut. *Male.* White spot in centre of the blue throat.

Female and young male. Below buffish white; a dark band across throat, with occasionally faint marks of blue and chestnut. Length 6 inches.

19. Ruticilla suecica (Linnæus). **The Red-spotted Bluethroat.**

Recorded by Arévalo from Malaga and Valencia. This form, which ranges furthest north, resembles the last, except in having a red instead of a white spot on the throat. The form with entirely blue throat is known as *R. wolfi*, and has been obtained at Málaga.

20. Erithacus rubecula (Linnæus). **The Robin.**

Moorish. Humar sidri. *Spanish.* Petirojo.

"Is resident near Tangier, and very common in all the

gardens around the town. Numbers also migrate, arriving during October and November, departing in February and March."—*Favier*.

Common throughout Andalucia in winter. The Robin only comes to Gibraltar from about the middle of October to the middle of March, but then in considerable numbers. They are resident in the Cork-wood, nesting abundantly in April, where, one day in May, my attention was attracted by the chattering and scolding of two Robins, evidently in a great state of alarm and excitement; close by them was a palmetto bush, to and from which they were flying, hovering over it, but not settling. At first I thought a cat, or perhaps an ichneumon, was lying up; but on peeping quietly into it, saw a snake, some three feet long, in the act of swallowing a half-fledged Robin at the edge of its nest. I drew back a pace, and fired a small charge of dust-shot into the reptile's head, cutting it nearly in half. The snake, however, had disposed of all the young birds; so, though too late to save them, the parents were rescued, as no doubt they would have shared the fate of their progeny but for my interference; the snake I hung up in the nearest bush, "*pour encourager les autres*," the old Robins all the time watching my proceedings; and it is to be hoped they were able to understand that their loss was partially avenged. The quantity of young birds—Robins, Nightingales, and similar ground-nesting Warblers—which are destroyed by snakes and lizards must be very great; but many of these birds in Andalucia build their nests in bushes at some distance from the ground, no doubt to avoid the reptiles.

Chin, throat, and breast *orange-chestnut*.

Young in first plumage mottled, each feather orange-buff tipped with black. Length 5¾ inches.

21. Daulias luscinia (Linnæus). The Nightingale.

Moorish. Mula el hasán (Owner of Beauty, *Favier*), Umm el hasán (Mother of Beauty). *Spanish.* Ruiseñor.

"This bird is very common around Tangier, arriving during March and April, passing on across the Straits to return in August and September. Great quantities remain to breed about the thick bushy places, chiefly constructing their nest with the fibres of the palmetto, the same material used by the Arabs in making their tents."—*Favier*.

The Nightingale is equally abundant on the Spanish side. The number heard singing in the Cork-wood and elsewhere is perfectly surprising, every clump of bramble-brakes having its pair, though in some seasons they are more numerous than in others; but there are always a great many. They are to be heard on the Rock for about ten days or a fortnight after their arrival, but nearly always pass on, though they have been known to nest, as in 1871. My earliest dates of their arrival are the 8th of April 1868, 2nd of April 1869, 7th of April 1870, 1st of April 1871, 21st of March 1872, Tangier; 30th of March 1874, Tetuan; noticed by Mr. Meade-Waldo on 22nd of March 1892, Tangier; 31st of March, 1894, Sierra Retin. Verner's dates of arrival are 5th of April, 1876; 3rd of April, 1877; 1st of April, 1879. The majority arrive about the 12th of April.

They begin to lay about the 1st of May, and usually build on the ground; but sometimes the nest is placed in ivy or rubbish some two or three feet high. In swampy jungles it is built at the bottom of a bush, and has the lower half constructed of dead leaves, the upper part being made of dry sedges, like that of Savi's Warbler (*Locustella luscinioides*); only it is much neater, and lined with fine grass, hair, and occasionally feathers. As a rule there are young Nightingales in the Cork-wood by the 24th of May. Verner found young as late as the 3rd of July, 1879.

General colour russet-brown above; upper tail-coverts and tail chestnut-brown; underparts buffish white.

First primary longer than primary-coverts.

Young in first plumage spotted like a Robin. Length $6\frac{3}{4}$ inches.

Subfamily ACCENTORINÆ.

22. Accentor modularis (Linnæus). **The Hedge-Sparrow.**

M. Favier did not include this bird in his list of Moorish birds, merely mentioning it as occurring near Gibraltar, having met with some during his "triste séjour" in that place, in November. I have seen specimens from the African side of the Straits. On the Spanish side they are found in winter, but not commonly, and I have shot them in the Cork-wood in January; whilst Arévalo records them as breeding near Málaga and Granada.

Above reddish brown, streaked with blackish brown; chin, throat, and breast bluish grey; belly whitish.

Young. Streaked above and below; no grey or white. Length 5½ inches.

23. Accentor collaris (Scopoli). **The Alpine Accentor.**

Spanish. Serrano (Mountaineer).

I have only seen this bird at the back of the Rock at Gibraltar in winter, and shot one on the 1st of February, seeing others on the 26th of the same month in 1870. Mr. J. H. Gurney, jun., who was passing through Gibraltar, was the first to notice it at the signal-station. Arévalo records them breeding in the sierras of the Provinces of Málaga and Granada; and they are no doubt found on all the high rocky ground, though I did not meet with any on the Sierra del Niño or elsewhere.

Chin and throat dull white, with black spot on each feather; wing-coverts tipped with white; tail dark brown, with pale buff tips. Length 7 inches.

Subfamily SYLVIINÆ.

24. Sylvia cinerea, Bechstein. **The Common Whitethroat.**

"Arrives about Tangier and crosses to Europe in April and May, returning to winter further south in September and October. Is nearly as abundant as the Blackcap, and seen on passage in small flights. On their return they have the top of the head the same colour as the back, like the females in spring."—*Favier*.

Mr. Meade-Waldo observed this bird's first arrival near Tangier on the 22nd of March, 1894.

I never saw the Common Whitethroat near Gibraltar in winter. Their first arrival was noticed in 1870 on the 7th of April, in 1871 on the 7th of April, in 1872 on the 11th of April, many passing on the 19th and 20th, and in 1874 on the 8th of April, in 1894 on the 30th of March. They nest abundantly in the Cork-wood, and also in quantities in marshy places, building their nests in thick leafy plants, often in those of the willow-herb (*Epilobium*); the average time for their laying is the 7th of May. When looking for Savi's Warbler, we sometimes found a dozen nests in the day.

Back reddish brown; legs *pale brown*; chin and throat much whiter than the rest of the underparts; quills and wing-coverts edged with pale rufous; iris *reddish brown*. Length 5½ inches.

25. Sylvia curruca (Linnæus). **The Lesser Whitethroat.**

This bird is, as far as my observations go, rare. A specimen was obtained in my garden at Gibraltar in April, and another on the 19th of April, 1872. It does not appear to have been noticed by M. Favier near Tangier.

Head and *back bluish grey*, back suffused with brown; legs *lead-colour*; iris *yellowish white*. Length 5¼ inches.

26. **Sylvia conspicillata,** Marmora. **The Spectacled Warbler.**

Favier merely says of the Spectacled Warbler, that about Tangier they are not common, and only seen on passage north in March. He gives no date of their autumnal migration, but states that they pass the winter somewhere further south.

The earliest date on which they were obtained near Gibraltar was on the 10th of March. Is a conspicuous, scrub-haunting bird, frequenting dry and more open ground than the Whitethroat, often being seen among cactus bushes. A sure place for finding them is on the Cartcian hills. They remain during the breeding-season, but I did not myself find the nest.

Chin and upper throat white, axillaries rosy rufous.
Male. Brown-grey; eyelid red; secondaries and wing-coverts broadly edged with chestnut; below pale rosy rufous; centre of belly white.
Female. Duller in plumage. Length $8\frac{1}{4}$ inches.
Irides very light brown; inside of mouth pale yellow.

27. **Sylvia hortensis,** Bechstein. **The Garden-Warbler.**

"Found near Tangier, on passage to Europe, in April and May, returning in October, when it is nearly as plentiful as the Common Whitethroat."—*Favier.*

The Garden-Warbler mostly arrives during the middle of April, and was first observed on the 10th. The latest I saw was on the 7th of October. They nest around Tangier and in the Cork-wood, laying about the 10th of May, and are brought into the market at Gibraltar as "beeafigos;" for later in the season, like most of the family, they are great devourers of figs.

General colour above and tail olive-brown; underparts greyish white. Head same colour as back; axillaries and under wing-coverts *buff*; chin and throat not whiter than rest of underparts. Length $5\frac{1}{4}$ inches.

28. **Sylvia atricapilla** (Linnæus). **The Blackcap.**
Moorish. Sherrir el Kebir.

"Is nearly as common as *S. melanocephala* about Tangier,

being seen on all sides during migration, passing north in January and February, returning in October. Many remain to nest."—*Favier*.

The Blackcap is to be seen during every month in the year, but is, of course, most common in February and October. They sometimes nest on the Rock, always plentifully in the Cork-wood. The young have been seen fully able to fly on the 24th of May. Verner found a nest with three eggs on the 15th of March, 1877, in the Convent Garden, and a nest with four hard-set eggs on the 16th of March, 1880, in the Mount Garden. They chiefly fed in my garden for some time on the seed of the so-called "pepper-tree" (*Schinus molle*), in company with Black-headed Warblers, and, to my surprise, with the Black Redstart; at least the latter were seen pecking at the seeds.

The species may be distinguished at a glance from the other black-headed Warblers met with near Gibraltar by the absence of white on the tail.

General colour above ashy brown; chin and throat *bluish grey*; tail *without any white*.
Male. Head black. Length 5¾ inches.
Female. Head rufous. Length 6¼ inches.

29. Sylvia orphea, Temminck. The Western Orphean Warbler.

Andalucian. Canaria.

"This Warbler passes by Tangier in April and May to return in September, travelling in company with the Whitethroats. Is not common, and in some years scarcely met with."—*Favier*.

The Orphean Warbler did not appear to be common near Gibraltar, and I could not get any till the 17th of May, 1871, when I found a nest on a branch of a pine-tree in the "Second Pine-wood," and shot both the old birds, which were very fearless, especially the female, who contained an egg ready for exclusion. The nest had only three eggs in it, and was badly built, being composed of grass and lichens. Verner found this Warbler on

8th of May, 1875, breeding in the cork-woods along the base of the Retin Hills; the nests were on the tops of branches of small cork-trees, about ten feet from the ground.

It would seem that this Warbler must chiefly pass further to the east. They nest around Seville and are common about Madrid; but I did not ascertain that they bred near Tangier.

Male. General colour above ashy grey; chin, throat, and underparts white; outer pair of tail-feathers with outer web *white*, inner web brown; next pair white only at tips; head *black*; legs bluish; irides yellow.

Female. Like male, but the head only slightly darker than back. Length 6¾ inches.

30. Sylvia subalpina, Bonelli. The Subalpine or Chestnut-breasted Warbler.

Favier merely states that " this species occurs near Tangier on passage in March and April, and again in October."

They are not often noticed near Gibraltar; but I shot one on the 20th March, 1870, and at Tangier on the 26th of March and 27th of April, 1874. Mr. L. P. Irby obtained one at Tangier on the 18th March, 1894. On the 27th of March, 1871, I saw eight or ten among the flowers and trees on the Alameda de Apodaca at Cadiz; they were exceedingly tame, and I watched them for a long time hopping about in and out among the flowers like a common Wren. One or two were very bright-coloured males. We also saw this Warbler on the 25th of April, 1869, in the Coto del Rey. Lord Lilford informs me he found a nest early in May, built in a gum-cistus bush in the Coto del Donaña, the eggs being very hard sat-on.

I never had the good fortune to discover a nest; but they build much in the same manner and situations as *S. melanocephala*, the eggs being also very similar to those of that bird.

Owing to the chestnut colour of the throat and breast of the male, this species is very apt to be confounded, when flying and hopping about, with the Dartford Warbler, but the length of the tail, shorter than the wing, easily distinguishes them from that bird.

Male. Above slaty grey; chin, throat, and breast chestnut; narrow white line from base of bill to shoulder.

Female. Above dull brown; buffy white where chestnut in the male. Eyelids red in both sexes. Length 5 inches.

31. Sylvia melanocephala (Gmelin). The Black-headed Warbler.

Moorish. Shorrir (*Favier*). *Spanish.* Palmera.

"This Warbler is resident and very abundant near Tangier; some migrate, crossing the Straits during February and March, returning in September. They are to be seen everywhere, nesting in small thorny bushes. The nest is not well built, and is made of strips of plants and blades of grass, without roots; rarely there is a little wool. It is lined with the down of some cotton-like plant, fine fibres of roots, and a few horse-hairs." They lay from April to July."—*Favier.*

The Black-headed Warbler, equally common around Gibraltar, is found in all scrub, gardens, and in the midst of woods, scolding with a chattering noise much like that of our common Wren. They might well be named the Gibraltar Warbler, being almost the only species which is a regular resident on the Rock. In habits they much resemble the Blackcap, but are more restless and obtrusive, and consequently more conspicuous; the contrast between the jet-black head of the adult male and the white throat also renders them more liable to be noticed. There were in different years several nests in my garden, which were carefully preserved; but what with cats and inquisitive human beings, they seldom succeeded in rearing their young. The earliest egg laid was on the 12th of March; this was built in a small rose-bush, and was spoiled by a gale of wind, which blew all the eggs out of it, being the only one I ever saw in what could be called an open bush. All the others were placed in thick bushes, generally box, about two to four feet from the ground, and were formed of grass with a few bits of cotton-thread, lined with hair; but they also nest at some height on boughs of trees. The eggs vary in number from three to five. The male assists in incubation.

This bird is, like the Blackcap and Garden-Warbler, very fond of figs and grapes and all kinds of fruit. The feathers at the base of the bill and the throat are often much coloured with the pollen of cactus, aloe, and other flowers, also with the seed of the "pepper-trees."

Tail longer than wing; claws and throat pure white; eyelids brick-red.
Male. General colour above slaty grey; nape and head black; below greyish white.
Female. Above brownish; head nearly black. Length 4½ inches.

32. Sylvia undata (Boddaert). The Dartford or Furze Warbler.

Spanish. Colorin, Caganchina.

"Is resident but not abundant near Tangier. Some migrate to Europe in March, to return in August. It is solitary in habits. They make a clumsy nest of grass and roots, lined with very fine coils of palmetto-fibre, laying in April."—*Favier.*

The Dartford Warbler is resident and not uncommon in all the scrub-covered hills on the coast near Gibraltar, particularly about San Roque, but is most abundant on the sides of the sierras, nesting in the heather about the 8th of April, on which date Mr. Stark found a nest near Algeciras with three eggs. There is no doubt they nest at Gibraltar, as they occasionally remain there through the summer.

Upper parts blackish brown; throat, breast, and sides *chestnut-brown*; feathers of chin and throat tipped with white; tail long and graduated, half the length of the bird; eyelids and iris red in adults, yellow in young. Length 5 inches.

33. Aëdon galactodes (Temminck). **The Western Rufous Warbler.**

Moorish. Houmeira. *Spanish.* Alzacola, Rubita, Viñadera.

"Abundant in the vicinity of Tangier, arriving in April and May, returning during September, many remaining to breed. Their habits are the same as those of the Nightingale. The nest, large and well built, is placed at some height from the ground, in thick foliage. The eggs, from five to six in number, only differ from Sparrow's eggs in the spots being more reddish. The males assist in incubation."—*Favier.*

On the Spanish side, this "Cocktail" Warbler, as they may well be called from their well-known habit of continually jerking their tails up, is very plentiful, frequenting sandy lanes hedged with aloes and prickly pears, such as those close to the First Venta, near Gibraltar. As Favier remarks, they resemble the Nightingale very much in some of their habits, and are at first sight very likely to be mistaken for that bird; only the Nightingale comes some three weeks or a month earlier.

The Rufous Warblers mostly arrive near Gibraltar between the 1st and 5th of May. The earliest I noticed in 1869 was on the 28th of April, in 1870 on the 29th, in 1871 on the 22nd, and in 1872 on the 28th of that month, the migration lasting for weeks. They nest about the last fortnight in May.

In places where there are many vineyards (which they frequent) they are known as *Viñadera*. *Alzacola* is the local name about Gibraltar; and "Cocktail" is very nearly a translation of it. "Rufous *Sedge*-Warbler," as this bird has been called, is most inappropriate, as they are never seen near either water or sedges.

Upper parts pale chestnut-brown. Tail long and graduated; the *two centre* feathers rich reddish buff; the others reddish buff, except the ends, which are black, tipped with white. Length 7 inches.

34. Acrocephalus turdoides (Meyer). **The Great Reed-Warbler.**

Spanish. Carrizalero; from "carrizo," reed-grass (*Arundo phragmites*).

This large species, though occurring in Morocco, is not included in Favier's list.

They are exceedingly plentiful in Andalucia, arriving in April, and chiefly frequenting tall reed-beds: they are very noisy, and, like other aquatic Warblers, conceal themselves at the slightest alarm. However, by ensconcing one's self and remaining quiet among the rushes, they are easily obtained, as they soon come out and sit singing and chattering on the top of some tall reed. They nest late in May, and build a nest interwoven with and suspended between reeds, resembling that of the Reed-Warbler (*Acrocephalus streperus*), only of course much larger. I have seen them building during the first fortnight in May, picking and carrying away the down of the "bulrush" (*Typha latifolia*) to use in constructing their nests.

Inside of mouth orange-yellow. Upper parts and tail olive-brown, below pale buff; centre of belly whitish; tail graduated and long; legs pale brown. Length 8 inches.

35. Acrocephalus streperus (Vieillot). **The Reed-Warbler.**

Not mentioned by Favier as occurring in Morocco; nor doc Mr. Drake appear to have observed any in that country.

On the Spanish side they appear in spring. The exact date of arrival I could not ascertain; but it is somewhere about the end of March. I never met with the Reed-Warbler during the winter months; but in the marshes at Casas Viejas, about the first week in May, we found them breeding in abundance. They keep among the sallow-bushes, but build their beautiful nests suspended on the dead stems of the *Epilobium hirsutum* or willow-herb, which grows in luxuriant tufts in the swampy jungle. These nests are constructed externally of strips of the rind or peel of the dead *Epilobium*-stems interwoven with sallow-cotton, the interior being composed of fine grass lined with the same material. The usual number of eggs was four, of a pale greenish colour, marked all over with ashy spots. One nest we found contained a Cuckoo's egg.

Upper parts olive-brown; below pale buff; both distinctly diffused with rufous, most so on rump and upper tail-coverts; legs and feet slaty brown. Length 5½ inches.

[*Acrocephalus palustris* (Bechstein). The Marsh-Warbler is said to occur near Granada, but I have never seen a specimen: it nests in drier places than the Reed-Warbler, though near water; the song and eggs also differ from those of that bird, which it resembles, except having the upper parts *olive-greenish* without any rufous tinge; legs and feet pale brown.]

36. Acrocephalus phragmitis (Bechstein). The Sedge-Warbler.

Favier says this is a very rare species near Tangier, that he seldom saw more than one or two on passage, in March or in September.

On the Spanish side I only noticed one in April 1894; but this common English migratory bird is reported from Málaga and Granada.

Upper parts brown, each feather having a dark centre; crown blackish brown, streaked with lighter brown; broad buffish-white eye-stripe.
Young. More yellow; a few dusky streaks on chest. Length 4¾–5 inches.

37. Acrocephalus aquaticus (J. F. Gmelin). The Aquatic Warbler.

This species, mentioned by Mr. Drake as having been met with in Morocco, is found in Andalucia, breeding near Málaga; but I only saw it once near Gibraltar. Verner found a nest, in

May 1875, near Casas Viejas, built on the ground amidst the roots of some flags.

Much as last, but is yellower in tint of plumage and has *two* broad dark bands along the crown, with conspicuous *pale line* down the centre of crown.

38. Locustella nævia (Boddaert). The Grasshopper Warbler.

Is recorded from Morocco and also from Málaga in winter; but I did not observe any near Gibraltar.

Above olive-brown, obscurely spotted on back, "like a Lark." Tail brown, indistinctly marked with transverse bars of darker brown.

Young. Feathers on throat with dark centres. Length 5¼ inches.

39. Locustella luscinioides (Savi). Savi's Warbler.

Recorded by Mr. Drake as met with in Morocco.

In Andalucia, I only found them in one situation where once, when snipe-shooting in winter, having noticed some old nests in the sedges which apparently belonged to this species, I made up my mind to try the next spring for them. However, for two years I was unable to do so; but in 1874 I went to this place in May with two friends, Mr. Stark being one, and we succeeded in finding thirteen nests.

The first nest was found by Mr. Denison, on the 4th of May, and contained four fresh eggs; the others as follows:—on the 6th, one nest with four fresh eggs; on the 7th, three nests—one empty (deserted), two with four eggs each, one lot fresh, the other hard sat-on; on the 8th, one nest procured with three eggs slightly sat-on, and one nest with five fresh eggs; on the 9th, two nests with four eggs each, all hard sat-on, and one nest with three young fully fledged; on the 11th, one nest with five fresh eggs; and on the 13th, one nest with two fresh eggs.

By this it will be seen that the time of their breeding is rather variable. I do not like to give the name of the exact locality where these birds nest, as Savi's Warbler might suffer in consequence.

The precise time of their arrival I could not ascertain; but it is about the 1st of April; and they are all gone by September. The nests, sometimes very near to one another, were most difficult to find, and, without exception, built in places where the mud and water varied in depth from two or three inches to perhaps two feet. All but one were in sedges, so well concealed as only to be found by accident. We spent sometimes the whole day in these marshes, looking in vain, with a gun in one hand and a sickle in the other, the latter used to open the sedges with, as it cut one's fingers severely to try and move them with the hand. What with the hot sun and the stink of the mud, we used to despair utterly after hours of fruitless search, but generally found a nest in the evening. The whole marsh was trodden down by us as if a herd of cattle had been wandering about; but perhaps the next day, going over the same ground, we would find a nest in a bunch of sedges which had been passed by within a yard. The nests were all alike, loosely and clumsily built, solely constructed of dead sedge, often placed so close to the water that the base was wet; they were always in the open marsh, none, that we saw, under bushes or in tall rushes or reeds, and the single nest that was not in sedges was in a tuft of the spiky rush so common in wet ground. In this case (the first one, found by Mr. Denison) the bird flew off—the only instance in which it did so, as they creep off generally like a mouse. On one occasion I cut away all the sedge round the nest, except just the patch in which it was built, as I wanted to shoot the bird from the nest to make certain of the identity of the eggs; but even then, after watching the old bird go in to the nest she would not fly off, but ran across the open space which had been cut away till she gained the shelter of the uncut sedges. Much more frequently seen than Cetti's Warbler, the great difficulty is in finding them when shot. If killed on the wing, it is almost hopeless to look for them; and those that I did obtain I had to thank my dog for finding, though he spoilt one or two. They are most easily to be got in the morning and evening, when the male perches on a sallow bush or tall reed and sings his grasshopper-like song, or rather whir.

We only found them in one particular locality: in other marshes, very similar in appearance, we failed to hear or see them; and they probably require a very large extent of sedge (*Cladium mariscus*).

The eggs are of a whitish ground-colour, marked all over with minute spots of brown, thicker at the larger end, often forming a well-marked zone. Sometimes the ground-colour is buff; but there were only two or three of this hue.

Savi's Warbler has been obtained near Seville by Ruiz, and Arévalo records them on passage near Málaga.

Above uniform russet-brown; chin whitish; underparts light brown. Tail slightly cuneiform, indistinctly barred with dark brown.

Legs and feet pale brown, the claws darker; irides olive-brown; lower mandible dirty white, with dusky tip; upper one blackish; inside of mouth of adult pale salmon-colour, that of young bright yellow. Length 6 inches.

40. Lusciniola melanopogon (Temminck). The Moustached Swamp-Warbler.

Has been obtained near Málaga; is common and breeds near Valencia. Inhabits rushy and reedy swamps.

Marked on back much as Sedge-Warbler: crown nearly black, broad white eyebrow, and blackish stripe through eye. First primary half the length of the second. Length $5\frac{1}{4}$ inches.

41. Cettia cettii (Marmora). Cetti's Bush-Warbler.

Favier states that "this Warbler is rare near Tangier, and seen on passage in February and March, to return in October." This, however, is quite different from my own observations. They certainly are not rare in spring near Tangier, where, as on the Spanish side, wherever there are thick bushes (generally bramble-brakes close to water) Cetti's Warbler is to be heard. Perhaps many migrate; but at Casas Viejas they are quite as common during the winter months as at any other season, and, somewhat like our own Robin, may be heard singing at all times. Very difficult to see in the breeding-season, in the winter months they do not skulk so much. They are excessively restless, being ever on the move; and often in the winter, when hidden up in the sotos near Casas Viejas, have I watched them quite close to me; but the slightest movement on my part sent them off to the thickest depths of the jungle. In the breeding-season it is almost impossible to catch a glimpse of one.

The only chance of shooting them is at the nest, which is always placed some distance from the ground, generally at a height of about two or three feet, and is either situated in a thick bush or (when in a bushy swamp) constructed, somewhat like the nest of the Reed-Warbler, on the stalks of reeds and *Epilobium*. These nests, extremely difficult to find, are built of bits of small sedges, intermingled with willow-cotton, and chiefly lined outside with strips of the stems of the *Epilobium*, inside with fine grass, a few hairs, and bits of cotton at the top. Those nests built in bushes are chiefly constructed with grass and cotton, and are entirely lined with hair. All the nests are deep and cup-shaped, largest at the base, measuring about $4\frac{1}{2}$ inches in height, the inside depth being $2\frac{1}{4}$, the internal diameter $2\frac{3}{4}$ inches. The beautiful pink eggs, which lose much of their beauty when blown, are laid about the end of April, and are usually five in number; but I have known only three.

The birds are rather irregular as to the time of nesting, as I have seen nests nearly on the point of hatching and others with fresh eggs on the same day (13th of May).

Tail much graduated and of *ten* feathers, with indistinct bands of dark brown.

Sexes alike, males slightly larger.

Head and upper parts rusty brown. Chin, throat, and centre of belly white. Inside of mouth yellowish. Length $5\frac{1}{4}$ inches.

42. Phylloscopus sibilatrix (Bechstein). **The Wood-Warbler.**

This species is not mentioned by Favier as occurring near Tangier, where, however, they are found, though not commonly. On the Spanish side of the Straits it is the scarcest of the four species of *Phylloscopus*, and was first seen on the 22nd of April. I killed one in my garden at Gibraltar, and some remain during the nesting-season in the Cork-wood, where Verner found a nest on the 25th of June; but we did not observe them in winter, and were unable to notice the date of their departure south.

Nest domed, but not lined with feathers, like those of *P. rufus* and *P. trochilus*, and is always placed on the ground.

The bird is easily distinguished by the streak of bright yellow over the eye and the white colour of the underparts, and is the largest species of the genus found near Gibraltar.

Distinct light streak from base of bill over eye to crown; white belly, contrasting with yellow breast and throat. Length 5¼ inches.

43. Phylloscopus bonellii (Vieillot). **Bonelli's Willow-Warbler.**

"Found during migration near Tangier, in company with *P. rufus* and *P. trochilus*, but is not so numerous. They return in September."—*Favier*.

This species, about the size of the Chiffchaff, is found in plenty near Gibraltar, nesting in the fern in the Cork-wood; the earliest I noticed arriving was on the 1st of April. Verner, on 2nd May, 1877, found a nest in a genista-bush about three feet from the ground.

They are not found in winter.

Head and back olive-brown, with green tinge; rump yellow; breast and belly white; chin and throat tinged with yellow; eye-streak greyish white. Length 4¾ inches.

44. Phylloscopus rufus (Bechstein). **The Chiffchaff.**

Spanish. Mosquilla.

According to Favier this bird is nearly as common as the

Willow-Warbler, crossing to Europe in February, March, and April, returning in October and November.

The Chiffchaff is to be seen throughout the year in the Cork-wood, but is most common from November to March. I found a nest on the 21st April in a bush about six inches from the ground.

The four Spanish species of *Phylloscopus* all build domed nests, usually on the ground, but occasionally in bushes or fern at an elevation of sometimes two feet or more above the ground; this is particularly the case with Bonelli's Willow-Warbler.

The Chiffchaff is difficult to tell from the common Willow-Warbler, but is always smaller and the legs are darker, being almost black, the eyebrow is not so well defined, and it is a more dull-coloured bird than *P. trochilus*. The note is also very different and distinct. The young of all the species are more highly coloured than the adult birds; but the genus is a very troublesome and perplexing one to the student, and only to be elucidated by observing the different species in a wild state, and listening to their notes. The skins shrink and the colours fade so much that a table-naturalist is much the most puzzled by them.

Above olive-green, below yellowish white. Smaller than next, and duller in plumage. *Legs nearly black.* Length 4¾ inches.

45. **Phylloscopus trochilus** (Linnæus). **The Willow-Warbler.**
Moorish. Simriz. *Spanish.* Mosquilla.

"The most common of Willow-Wrens near Tangier; crosses the Straits in April, returning in November."—*Favier.*

There is no doubt, although I did not find a nest, that this species breeds near Tangier. In the vicinity of Gibraltar they are to be found throughout the year in the Cork-wood, where they breed, and I have seen the young able to fly on the 8th of May. Although universally distributed in winter, they are most common when on passage in March and October.

Much as last, but larger and brighter. *Legs light brown.* Length 5 inches.

46. **Hypolais polyglotta** (Vieillot). **The Short-winged Yellow Tree-Warbler.**

Spanish. Almendrita de verano.

"Arrives and crosses to Europe in April, returning in August and September, many remaining to nest around Tangier."—*Favier.*

This Yellow Warbler is exceedingly plentiful near Gibraltar, being one of the latest of the spring arrivals; the first observed was on the 25th of April, and the earliest date on which eggs were found was on the 14th of May. The birds frequent trees and bushes, especially willows and sallows; and the nest, neatly built and cup-shaped, in a great measure composed of sallow-cotton and thistle-down, is placed in bushes, and usually contains four pinkish-tinged eggs, marked with blackish spots.

This bird was figured by Yarrell as the Melodious Willow-Warbler (*H. icterina*), a slightly larger species.

First primary small, but longer than the primary coverts; in *H. icterina* it is scarcely as long, but the wing is longer.

Above olive-green; below lemon-yellow; lores yellow; secondaries broadly margined with buffish white. The inside of the mouth bright orange-yellow. Length 4¼ inches.

47. **Hypolais opaca** (Lichtenstein). **The Western Pallid Warbler.**

"This Warbler is nearly the same in size as *H. polyglotta*, but somewhat larger, and identical with that bird in habits, times of arrival and departure, and also in manner of nesting. They build on trees, bushes, and small plants, laying in May or the beginning of June."—*Favier.*

This Pallid Warbler is the latest of all the spring migrants that arrive in Andalucia, being a little later than *H. polyglotta*. They are much more plentiful eastward of Gibraltar than in the immediate vicinity, where they are rare. Another species,

H. olivetorum, is stated to have been met with at Tangier and Fez, but did not come under my observation, and, being found in S.E. Europe and Asia Minor, is not likely to occur.

<small>Above olive-brown; tail darker brown; throat and centre of belly white; the rest below buffy white. Length 5¼ inches.</small>

Subfamily REGULINÆ.

48. Regulus cristatus, K. L. Koch. The Gold-crested Wren.

I have never met with this bird in Andalucia, where they have been recorded as common, and Lord Lilford informs me that he never obtained an Andalucian specimen. Possibly they may occur irregularly, like the Siskin—that is to say, not in all winters consecutively. Arévalo says they have been found near Málaga and Granada.

<small>*Male.* General colour above olive-green, a black streak on each side of the orange-coloured crown.
Female. Less bright than male. Length 3½ inches.</small>

49. Regulus ignicapillus (C. L. Brehm). The Fire-crested Wren.

This species is resident and common in the Cork-wood and in the wooded valleys at the back of Algeciraz, coming as near to Gibraltar as the Málaga Gardens, close to San Roque. They nest rather early, the young being able to fly on the 15th of May.

<small>*Male.* Much as last, but whitish streak over the eye, and a *third* black streak through eye to the olive-green nape; crown flame-coloured.
Female. Less bright than male. Length 4 inches.</small>

Family **TIMELIIDÆ.**   Subfamily BRACHYPODIINÆ.

50. Pycnonotus barbatus (Desfontaines). **The White-vented Bulbul.**

Moorish. Bou lág-lág.

"Is very abundant and resident around Tangier. When the oranges are ripe, they are always to be heard and seen chattering and fighting in the gardens. They nest in May, June, and July, laying from three to four eggs, which are very thin-shelled and tender, of a greyish-white colour, marbled or spotted with reddish spots of two or three shades of brown and purple. The nest is built in the branches of fruit-trees (orange-, apricot-, pear-, &c.), and is shaped like those of the Woodchat Shrike, coarsely interlaced outside with ends of small roots and with creeping plants. They feed on all kinds of fruit and different flowers, are very fond of oranges, and prefer them to anything else.

"This species is subject to variations, as I have seen two which had the head, breast, and neck brown, with white spots, while the wings, back, and tail were brownish red, the rest being dirty white."—*Favier.*

In accordance with Favier's statement, this Dusky Bulbul was found in great plenty about the gardens just outside Tangier. They were shy; but one day in March I stalked up to and watched for some time a lot of seven or eight in the Belgian Consul's garden. They were squabbling and playing with one another on a Persian lilac or common bead-tree, the seeds of which they were pecking at; and they reminded me much of some of the Indian Babblers (*Crateropus*), particularly in their flight and garrulous chattering. Besides this noise they have a melodious whistle, which I took down at the time and tried to note thus—*Pwit, Pwit, Qüitĕrä, Qüitĕrä,* rather in the tone of a Blackbird. This song, if it may be so called, and their chatter are so remarkable as to attract attention at once.

I took a good deal of pains to ascertain the correct local Arabic name, which is "Bou lág-lág"; and as no one could tell me the meaning of the latter part, I conclude it is suggestive of their cry, or rather clacking: one of the Arabic names of the White Stork is "Bou lák-lák," from the noise made by the clacking their bills.

Among the Jews, who speak Spanish, they go by the name of "Naranjero" (*litt.* "The orange-man"), from their orange-eating propensities. They make a small hole in the side of an orange and completely clean it out, leaving nothing but a shell of orange-peel, which remains hanging on the tree. I have more than once pulled these husks down, thinking them to be sound fruit. Owing to the mischief they thus do, they are not favourites, and consequently are more timid near Tangier than about Larache, where we shot some of them.

We were informed that they do not breed till the end of May, and so had no opportunity of studying their nesting-habits. In the end of April, near Larache, they were evidently not then nesting; and, as at Tangier, all those which we saw were near gardens and villages.

Mr. Meade-Waldo found them in February 1892, out in the open, feeding on the flower of the Asphodel.

This Bulbul certainly does not occur in the western part of Andalucia; I have tried everywhere for it. If found anywhere, the coast near Tarifa would be the most likely ground; but in the orange-groves there, the Spaniards, when asked if there was a bird like the "mirlo" which ate oranges, simply looked on me as more "loco" than the generality of "los Ingleses," who, in their opinion, are all mad, and disclaimed any knowledge of a "naranjero" in the shape of a bird of such size. The Great Titmouse, however, they say eats oranges, but not unless the skin is broken.

Sexes alike. General colour dull brown, except the white belly and under tail-coverts, the latter sometimes faintly tinged with yellow. Length 8 inches, tail 4 inches.

Subfamily CISTICOLÆ.

51. Cisticola cursitans (Frankland).   The Fantail or Grass-Warbler.

Moorish. Bou-fesúha (Father of eloquence).   *Spanish.* Cierra-puño, Tin-Tin, Biutrecillo, Trepatorres, Buitron.

"Is the most common of the aquatic Warblers around Tangier, and seen migrating in lots of from ten to twelve during March and April, returning in October, November, and December. Many remain to breed, nesting twice in the season."—*Favier.*

This diminutive Grass-Warbler is resident near Gibraltar, and exceedingly plentiful in the winter, frequenting marshy ground wherever there is any herbage, such as grass, sedges, or short rushes. In the spring they go to the corn-fields as well, never, however, being found away from water. I do not recollect ever seeing them perch on a bush or tree, but always on some plant. Their note and jerky flight somewhat remind one of the Meadow-Pipit; during the nesting-season in particular they will fly darting about high overhead for several minutes, continually uttering their squeaky single note (whence the name of Tin-Tin), all the time evidently trying to decoy the intruder from their nest. They undoubtedly breed twice a year—according to the Spaniards, three times. I have found the young well able to fly, and a nest with eggs ready to hatch, on the same day, the 19th of April; an unfinished nest on the 8th of May, and a nest with eggs very hard sat-on on the 10th of that month.

The nest much resembles the caterpillars' webs which are common on pine-trees in some parts of Andalucia; any one would take them for the web of an insect; but they are very troublesome to find, and made of the cotton of plants and thistle-down, with small bits of grass beautifully sewn and interwoven with the corn or grass in which the nest is built; the entrance is at the top, the bottom being the broadest part, the whole length about five inches. The usual number of eggs is five, generally of a pale blue; but, as is well known, they vary strangely in colour.

Sexes alike. Tail much graduated. Inside of mouth black; irides very pale brown. Crown and back streaked with black and buff. Below buffish white; flanks rufous. Length 4½ inches, tail 1¾ inches.

CRATEROPODES.

52. Argya fulva (Desfontaines). The North-African Babbler.

This Babbler is mentioned by Mr. Drake as occurring in the southern part of Morocco, but does not appear ever to have come under Favier's notice in the northern part.

Sexes alike. Bill stout and strongly curved.
General colour rufous fawn. Chin and throat white. Length 10 inches, tail 5 inches.

PANURIDÆ.

53. Panurus biarmicus (Linnæus). The Bearded Reedling.

This reed-frequenting bird is found at the Albufera near Valencia, but I have no certain evidence of its occurrence nearer to Gibraltar.

Tail *fawn-coloured*, about three inches long, graduated, and slightly curving downwards.
Male. Bill yellow; head grey; black moustachial stripe. General colour above tawny buff.
Female. Paler; no moustachial stripe; head fawn-colour.
Young. Like female, but head and back slightly striped with black. Length 6 inches.

PARIDÆ.

54. Acredula irbii, Sharpe and Dresser. **The Spanish Long-tailed Tit.**

Spanish. Mito.

This little bird, a climatic race of our British *A. caudata* (or, as separatists have it, *rosea*), is only to be found around Gibraltar in the Cork-wood of Almoraima, chiefly keeping to the sotos and to the district round the Mill, the Long Stables, and the second venta. Similar in its habits to the British form, the nest and eggs are also exactly the same as those of that bird. I found the young able to fly by the middle of April, and on the 12th of that month found a nest with seven young fully fledged; this would make the date of laying about the 20th of February. The nests, without exception, were all built in the thorny creeper, a species of *Smilax*, called *Zarzaparilla* by the Spaniards, which forms regular net- or lattice-work walls from the ground to the lower branches of the trees, and are usually placed about 15-16 feet from the ground and very difficult to get at, the only way being either to cut or shoot away the creepers above them—often no easy matter. The only eggs obtained were addled ones, left in nests from which the young had flown.

The adults differ from the British and North-European races in having the entire back *bluish grey*.

Crown black, with whitish stripe along the centre. Length 5½ inches, tail 3½ inches.

55. Parus major, Linnæus. **The Great Tit.**

Spanish. Quive-vive, Carpintero, Carbonero, Cerrajero, Guerrero.

Favier considers this species to be extremely scarce near Tangier, but specimens have been obtained there in winter, and Mr. Meade-Waldo saw plenty on the 27th of February, 1892.

On the Spanish side of the Straits they are extremely plentiful, and to be heard wherever there are any trees, nesting in April in holes of the cork-trees. There is a great increase of their numbers in winter, when they visit the Alameda and gardens at Gibraltar, being the only observed Calpeian representative of the Tits.

Male. Crown bluish black; cheeks white; *black stripe* along the *middle* of the greenish-yellow breast and belly.

Female. Similar, but black stripe below not so extended. Length 6 inches.

56. Parus cæruleus, Linnæus. The Blue Tit.

Spanish. Herrerillo (Little smith).

The Blue Tit is very common in Andalucia, being resident and particularly abundant in the Cork-wood of Almoraima, generally nesting (about the middle of April) in the decayed hollow branches of the cork-trees.

In April 1894, at Retin, I saw a pair of these birds going in and out of a dome-shaped nest, constructed externally of small sticks, which they had either built or enlarged, at the end of a horizontal bough of a cork-tree. It looked like a miniature Magpie's nest, and I could, when it was first found, see the light through: unable to reach it without a ladder, I left for Gibraltar, and Verner, who remained behind for a few days, reported that ultimately they began to dismantle the nest and carry the materials to some more usual situation.

Spanish specimens are very bright in colour—one or two so much so that, until I had seen a specimen of *Parus teneriffæ*, I imagined them to be that species.

Crown and wing-coverts azure-blue. Length 4½ inches.

57. Parus teneriffæ, Less. The Ultramarine Tit.

Moorish. Bou rezizi (Father of the little turban).

" Is resident near Tangier, but less frequent in December and

January than during other months. They nest in holes of trees, in April, laying from four to five eggs, white, with very small red spots, similar to those of *Parus cæruleus*, which they replace in Morocco, and appear to be a variety of that bird constant to this climate."—*Favier*.

I have never been able to detect the Ultramarine Tit on the Spanish, nor seen the Blue Tit on the Moorish side of the Straits, where the present species is plentiful, their habits &c. being identical.

The African bird is easily recognized by the greyish-blue back and the deep blackish blue on the crown of the head, as well as on those parts which are cobalt-blue in the European species.

58. Parus ater, Linnæus. The European Coal-Tit.

I never met with this species, which, however, is recorded from Granada, Cordova, and Málaga by Arévalo.

The Algerian Coal-Tit (*Parus ledouci*) in all probability is to be met with in Morocco. This bird has those parts of the head and nape of the neck lemon-yellow which are white in *P. ater*, the under surface being also lemon-yellow.

Head black; nape and cheeks white; wing-coverts tipped with white, forming two bars on the wing; back *bluish grey* in winter. Length $4\frac{1}{4}$ inches.

59. Parus palustris, Linnæus. The Marsh-Tit.

I did not observe this bird near Gibraltar, but Mr. Saunders, Mr. Stark, and Arévalo all report it from near Granada.

Back greyish brown; crown, chin, throat, and nape glossy black. Length $4\frac{1}{2}$ inches.

60. Parus cristatus, Linnæus. The Crested Tit.

Spanish. Capuchino.

The Crested Tit is resident and common in the Cork-wood of Almoraima, in all the neighbouring pine-woods, and in the valleys and on the hill-sides at the back of Algeciraz up to near

Tarifa, wherever the cork-tree grows; but singularly is not found in the Sierra Retin, or in the Sierra Bartolomé. They nest about the 10th of May, in the hollow ends of boughs of the cork- and pine-trees, the eggs being about five in number, much spotted, and resembling strongly those of the Creeper (*Certhia familiaris*).

There is reason to think the species occurs in Morocco, but this is only mentioned with the view of directing the attention of future collectors there, in order that they may look out for them.

General colour greyish brown; throat black; crown dull black, all the feathers tipped and edged with white, and the hinder feathers *long* and *pointed*, forming a conspicuous *crest*. Length 4¾ inches.

61. **Ægithalus pendulinus** (Linnæus). **The Penduline Tit.**

Spanish. Pajaro moscon.

Specimens of this bird have been procured near Málaga; further east they are more common, building their retort-shaped nest at the extremity of boughs, generally of poplars.

Bill short, straight, and much pointed.
Crown and nape greyish white; forehead and sides of head black.
Above chestnut-brown; throat white; rest of underparts creamy. Length 4½ inches.

SITTIDÆ.

62. **Sitta cæsia**, Wolf. **The Common Nuthatch.**

This bird, our British Nuthatch, was not mentioned by Favier, but Capt. S. Reid mentions five or six having been obtained by Olcese near Tangier about 1883.

On the Spanish side, Mr. Saunders records them to be common near Granada, as also does Arévalo, stating them to be resident. We did not meet with any near Gibraltar.

Bill longer than head. Above slaty grey; throat whitish; rest of underparts *cinnamon-buff*, lightest next the throat; legs dull brown. Length 5¼ inches.

CERTHIIDÆ.

63. Certhia familiaris, Linnæus. **The Tree-Creeper.**

Spanish. Barba-jelena, Trepa-troncas, Arañero.

The Tree-Creeper is resident and common in the Cork-wood and in the valleys near Algeciraz, nesting in April.

A single specimen was shot near Tangier about the 20th of April, the only one I heard of on the African side.

Bill slender, curved downwards, and pointed. Above brown, spotted with paler brown; below white. Tail graduated or cuneiform, reddish brown, with stiff points. Length 5 inches.

64. Tichodroma muraria, Linnæus. **The Rock-Creeper.**

I have never met with this bird, which is recorded from near Antiquera, Gaitan, and the Sierra Nevada, and is stated to have been seen at Gibraltar many years ago.

General colour slate-grey; all the primaries, except the first three, crimson on the basal half of the outer web; throat black in summer, white in winter; bill as in last, but longer in proportion. Length 6 inches.

TROGLODYTIDÆ.

65. Troglodytes parvulus, K. L. Koch. **The Wren.**

Spanish. Cucito, Ratilla.

"Resident near Tangier, and numerous, nesting from March to June. Some are migratory, arriving in November, and leaving again in February."—*Favier*.

The above remarks equally apply to the Wren on the Spanish side, where they are most abundant, nesting very early; and I have seen young fully able to fly on the 26th of April, and they are resident on "the Rock."

It is very curious that this little bird should be a resident in the scorching sun of Morocco and Andalucia as well as in the bitter cold of the hills in Inverness-shire, where they are one of the very few birds which remain to brave the winter.

Above reddish brown; breast whitish brown; tail closely barred with black, and much more rufous than back. Hind toe as long or longer than middle toe. Length 4 inches.

CINCLIDÆ.

66. Cinclus albicollis (Vieillot). **The Grey-backed Dipper or Water-Ouzel.**

Spanish. Tordo de agua, Pechiblanco.

Occurs in the streams of the Sierras, and is resident. I have seen them near the waterfall beyond Algeciraz, where Mr. Stark found a nest about the 17th of May; but they are not abundant anywhere.

Resembles the English Chestnut-breasted Dipper, *C. aquaticus*, except that the back is paler and the head lighter, and it can only be considered a climatic race of that species. Length 7 inches.

ORIOLIDÆ.

67. Oriolus galbula, Linnæus. **The Golden Oriole.**

Moorish. Tair es sfar (Yellow bird). *Spanish.* Oropendola.

According to Favier the Golden Oriole "crosses the Straits in great numbers during April and May, returning in July, August, and September." These dates much agree with my own observations on the Spanish side, I having first seen them in 1869 on the 21st of April, in 1870 on the 18th, in 1871 on the 4th (one only), and in 1872 on the 11th: many passed on the 16th in that year. The spring migration lasts up to the 14th or 15th of May. Some few pairs remain to breed in the vicinity of Gibraltar; but the majority pass further north and resort to fruit-producing districts, where they get the credit of doing much damage to cherries, mulberries, &c., but at the same time they eat caterpillars and other insects.

Almost entirely a fruit-eating bird; those who have kept them alive informed me that they could not preserve them through the winter—nor, indeed, longer than fruit was to be obtained.

When the Japanese loquats (*Eriobotrya japonica*) were ripe in my garden at Gibraltar in May 1870, Golden Orioles remained about as long as the loquats lasted, but would not admit of much observation, as they were very shy and difficult to watch. They are more often heard than seen; and I have spent hours in trying to get a shot as they skulked in the thickest foliage of tall trees, continually piping their flute-like note.

Some are always to be heard during May near the Mill and the "Second Venta" in the Cork-wood; and a pair usually frequented the lower part of the First Pine-wood. I found one nest in the middle of May, built at the very extremity of a bough at the top of a high oak tree, which was impossible to obtain without cutting the branch off. Verner remarks also that the Golden Oriole has a habit of, when disturbed, flying into the thickest green-foliaged tree, not settling on cork-trees, in which the foliage is scanty.

Male. Head and general colour golden yellow. Black spot between crimson eye and dull red bill; wings black, with yellow tips to secondaries. Tail: outer feathers with more than terminal half yellow.

Female. Greenish yellow above; outer tail-feathers tipped with yellow. I have never seen a female Golden Oriole in same plumage as male.

Young. Greenish yellow above; below whitish tinged with yellow; breast slightly streaked with brown; the black parts of adult male replaced by greenish brown. Length 9 inches.

STURNIDÆ.

68. Sturnus vulgaris, Linnæus.   **The Common Starling.**

Moorish. Zarzor.   *Spanish.* Estornino.

" This bird arrives about Tangier in large flights from October to January, departing in March. During the autumnal migration the flights are often mixed up with *S. unicolor*. In October, 1842, a Moor brought to Tangier about three hundred and fifty Starlings, which he affirmed he had caught at one time in a net; about half of these birds were *S. unicolor*."—*Favier*.

In Andalucia, the Common Starling may be said, roughly speaking, to come and go with the Golden Plover. The earliest date noticed of their arrival was the 15th of October, the latest date on which any were seen being the 1st of March. I have a note of seeing many thousands passing southwards in successive flights on the 28th of October. During the winter months they are seen in swarms about low ground; and the Spaniards shoot immense numbers at their roosting-places in the reed-beds near Vejer and Casas Viejas. Consequently, during their stay, Starlings form a very cheap and, it may be fairly said, nasty dish in all the ventorillas in the vicinity.

Male. Black, with purple and green gloss, small buff tips to feathers above. Head, throat, and breast with green gloss.
Female. Similar to male, but less brightly marked.
In winter, all the feathers of upper parts tipped with buff, those below tipped with whitish.
Young in first plumage. Uniform greyish brown; throat dull white; lower parts clouded with white. Length 8½ inches.

69. Sturnus unicolor, Temminck. The Spotless Starling.

Moorish. Zarzor kahal (Black Starling). *Spanish.* Tordo.

"This Starling is very abundant around Tangier, passing north in March and returning during the month of September, many, however, remaining to breed."—*Favier*.

The Sardinian Starling, as the species has been termed, Spotless Starling being a more appropriate and distinctive name, is almost entirely migratory in Andalucia; but I have seen them there in December. Not so abundant as the Common Starling, they resemble that bird in their habits and note, nesting about the end of April in roofs of houses in towns, and they make use of the old Moorish towers, besides building in holes of trees; the eggs exactly resemble those of *S. vulgaris*. They are more common some sixty miles north of Gibraltar than in the immediate vicinity. Three or four pairs used to frequent the Venta at Casas Viejas, and during November and December nearly every morning assembled on the roof, whistling and pluming themselves before going forth for the day. The *amo*, or landlord, well known as "old Bernardo," begged me not to molest them— a request I most scrupulously complied with; but on my return there in 1874, they were absent, probably killed by some of the shooting visitors from Gibraltar. Whether the death of the old man caused them to lack protection I cannot say. This old fellow, who had served as a sergeant in the Spanish army, and was present at the defence of Tarifa in 1811, was a fine specimen of the Spaniard, and used to tell wonderful stories of his soldiering days. I regret that since his decease the Venta has changed for the worse, both in prices and accommodation.

Head and back uniform. No spots in breeding-plumage, but in winter all the body-feathers are tipped with arrow-shaped spots of greyish white. Length 8¼ inches.

70. Pastor roseus (Linnæus). The Rose-coloured Starling.

The Rose-coloured Pastor, as it used to be termed, is an occasional wanderer from the East to Andalucia, and has been obtained near Seville and Málaga.

Male. Head black, with crest of pointed and elongated feathers; back, scapulars, rump, breast, sides, and belly rosy pink; wings, tail, and *thighs black*; bill rose-coloured, black at base.

Female. Crest smaller and less bright.

Young. Crest absent; colour greyish brown, where rosy in adults. Length 8½ inches.

CORVIDÆ.

71. **Pyrrhocorax graculus** (Linnæus). The Red-billed Chough.

Moorish. Narrar. *Spanish.* Graja.

This species is stated by Favier to be found in large flights near Tetuan—a statement we can fully corroborate. We also saw a great many about the cliffs of Abyla, or Apes' Hill, opposite to Gibraltar.

In the rocky sierras of Andalucia the Red-billed Chough is plentiful, particularly about Ubrique. They are, of course, resident; but I am unable to state the time of nidification.

Jet-black, with steel gloss; the curved bill, eyelids, legs, and feet *red*. Length 14–17 inches.

72. **Pyrrhocorax alpinus**, Vieillot. The Yellow-billed Chough.

Although there is no record of the occurrence of this Chough on the African side, at Apes' Hill, in 1877, a bird flew so close to us that we thought we could distinguish the yellow bill.

On the Spanish side they occur near Granada, and at the Tajos del Gaitan, Málaga.

Plumage and size as last, but bill *yellow* and slightly shorter.

[**Nucifraga caryocatactes** (Linnæus). **The Nutcracker.**

I never met with this pine-forest bird on either side of the Straits, though there was one in a collection at Cordova; but from what locality was not stated; so, until further evidence be obtained, the species cannot with certainty be included as an Andalucian bird. It has been recorded from Estremadura by Captain Cook Widdrington, and possibly may be found in some of the high ranges, where *Pinus cembra* grows.]

Head dark brown; general colour clove-brown, most of the feathers of breast, sides, and underparts spotted with a triangular white mark. Rump and upper tail-coverts uniform brown. Tail blackish, tipped with white. Length 14 inches.

73. Garrulus glandarius (Linnæus). The West-European Jay.

Spanish. Arrendájo.

This British Jay is not recorded by Favier from Morocco; nor did I obtain any species of Jay on the African side; but Captain Savile Reid, in February 1883, brought home a specimen, one of three obtained by Olcese near Tangier. The Editors of the 'Ibis,' 1885, p. 246, examined this bird, and considered it a cross between *G. glandarius* and *G. cervicalis*. We may reasonably assume that they sometimes cross the Straits, as they occasionally appear at Gibraltar in winter. Four frequented the Alameda and other gardens in the south from about the 10th of November, 1870, to the 4th of April, 1871; and I saw another in March, 1872; this last bird did not linger about for more than a few days.

This Jay is very plentiful near Gibraltar in the Cork-wood, and in the wooded valleys and hill-sides up to a considerable elevation. At the same time it is rather local; and though many are resident, they are more abundant in the winter months.

They nest in some numbers in the Cork-wood, laying their eggs early in May; and, at that season particularly, they are easily decoyed within shot by secreting one's self in thick cover and imitating either their call or the squeal of a wounded rabbit.

Throat white; crown with black streaks; feathers of forehead and crown edged with white; back vinaceous; outer web of wing-coverts *barred with blue and black*, inner web black; tail often barred slightly at the basal end in the same manner as the outer web of wing-coverts (this is not the result of age, birds in first plumage occasionally being so marked); iris pale blue. Length 14 inches.

74. Garrulus cervicalis, Bonaparte. **Algerian Black-headed Jay.**

Mr. Meade-Waldo found this bird on the Moorish side of the Straits, and brought home several; he describes it as chiefly a mountain bird, with a voice different to that of *G. glandarius*.

<small>Crown with thick black crest; nape and fore part of back vinous rufous; space round eye white. Length 14 inches.</small>

75. Pica rustica (Scopoli). **The Common Magpie.**

Spanish. Urraca, Marica.

Our British Magpie is extremely local in Andalucia; but where met with is very abundant; they do not, however, occur to the south of Seville, except on the banks of the Guadalquivir to below Coria, as far as there are any trees and bushes. Great numbers frequent the Coto del Rey, where they breed in the beginning of May, accommodating the Great Spotted Cuckoo with their nests. The Spanish bird undoubtedly runs into the African form *P. mauritanica*.

<small>Long graduated iridescent green tail; rump greyish white. Length 16–18 inches, tail 10–11.</small>

76. Pica mauritanica, Malh. **The North-African Magpie.**

Arabic. Akâka.

This species, which, however, I failed to meet with in Morocco, is the Magpie of the country, and perhaps is very local, for Mr. Drake describes it as abundant in parts he visited.

<small>Is distinguished from *P. rustica* by the bare space behind the eye and by the black rump, both species being otherwise identical in size and markings.</small>

77. Cyanopica cooki, Bonaparte. **The Spanish Azure-winged Magpie.**

Spanish. Mohino rabilargo, Mohino.

This species is peculiar to the Peninsula, but does not occur in the vicinity of Gibraltar. The nearest locality to that place

where they are to be found is about Coria del Rio, below Seville; thence, as far as the Coto del Rey, they occur in tolerable numbers, but are much more common towards Cordova, and are reported to be very numerous in some parts of Estremadura, being, however, a very local bird.

The nests which I have seen were built on boughs at no great height from the ground, rather clumsily constructed with small sticks, grass, moss, and wool—containing five eggs; but as many as seven are frequently found. They are well figured in 'The Ibis' (1866, p. 382, pl. x. figs. 3–8), from specimens obtained by Lord Lilford in 1864, and vary a great deal in colour and markings, the commonest form being of a stony-buff colour marked with purplish and brown spots. I kept four of these birds, reared from the nest, for some time alive, feeding them on grapes, figs, bread, beetles, and grasshoppers. Always placing the insects under their feet, they picked them to pieces much as a Hawk or an Owl tear their prey. They became very tame and amusing; but during my temporary absence, unluckily, all died.

I never heard of this bird on the Moorish side of the Straits.

The sexes are alike in plumage.

78. **Corvus monedula**, Linnæus. **The Jackdaw.**

Spanish. Grája.

Mr. Drake mentions having met with the Jackdaw near Tetuan, where I did not see any, nor find them anywhere on the African side. Favier also omits the bird from his list.

On the Spanish side of the Straits they are extremely local, the only locality in which I have seen any being the Coto del Rey, near Seville, where, in 1870, they were common, nesting about the end of April in holes of trees, one or two pairs building in the roof of the Palacio. Jackdaws are also said to be abundant near Granada.

Black; ear-coverts, nape, and sides of neck grey; belly leaden black. *Young.* Little or no grey on nape. Length 14 inches.

79. Corvus corax, Linnæus. The Raven.

Spanish. Cuervo.

The Raven is found sparingly but very generally distributed on the Spanish side of the Straits, but does not seem to be found on the Moorish side. They are resident, and usually commence to lay about the middle of March, thus, very curiously, breeding later in Andalucia than in England or further north. Verner found, on the 24th of May, 1878, a nest with young just hatched, a few days earlier one with fledged birds, whilst in 1886, at Crete, he took fresh eggs of Ravens on 26th of March, when other nests had eggs or were ready for eggs.

One pair nest at Gibraltar, and, as customary with Ravens, are the terror of all birds that approach their domain. Another pair nest at Casas Viejas, in the old quarry called La Cima, just outside the village.

In no case that I have seen have their nests been in anything like proximity to one another, the reverse being the case with *Corvus tingitanus*.

General colour glossy steel-black; throat-feathers pointed; tail slightly cuneate. Length 24 inches.

80. Corvus tingitanus, Irby. The Tangier Raven.

Moorish. Grâb.

This species or race appears to me to be quite distinct from *C. corax*, and was noticed and described in 'The Ibis,' 1874 (p. 264).

Smaller than the Common Raven, *C. corax*, its note is different, while its very gregarious habits are opposed to those of our common Raven; and it is the Raven of the Canary Islands.

Many specimens are very much marked with rusty brown on the wings and tail, others very slightly so. In all that I have seen there is a tinge of brown on the wings—not that this coloration is of any consequence in determining it as a distinct species. They also breed later than *C. corax* does on the Spanish side.

This Raven is exceedingly abundant around Tangier and along the coast as far as some distance south of Larache. We did not observe any in the high parts about Apes' Hill. Outside Tangier, flocks of them may be seen feeding on the refuse which is carried from the town and thrown on the sea-shore. They are exceedingly tame to the natives, being viewed with superstitious awe by the Moors, but are wide awake to the European, especially if he carries a gun, and if once fired at are not likely to give a second chance. The only way to be sure of getting them is at their nest, which, constructed of sticks, neatly lined with grass and small roots, is built in clefts of rocks, on trees and in low bushes; one nest which I saw was fixed in the crook or angle formed by a dead flowering stalk of the aloe (*Agave americana*), which had fallen across another stalk in full flower.

The eggs are usually laid about the 20th of April, and vary in number from five to seven, and, like those of others of the Crow tribe, differ much in the markings. Favier in his MS. says of this Raven, under the head of *C. corax*, "This species is another of those birds for which the Mahometans evince a superstitious feeling, the liver, tongue, brain, and heart of the Raven being considered antidotes against the effects of the evil one; the same virtues are attributed to the feathers and heart of the Hoopoe. The Raven is the only species of Crow found in the neighbourhood of Tangier, and is very abundant."

It seems that this African Raven crosses the Straits, as Verner reports having, near Gibraltar, taken a nest, apparently of this bird, but was unable to trap or shoot an old bird. He also reports having seen "small Ravens," and "forty small Ravens were seen together near Tarifa." "fifty Ravens were seen together" on the 29th of April, 1880, near the 1st River; while another officer noticed forty-two together near Palmones on 23rd of April.

Resembles the Common Raven, but has the throat-hackles not so long, and is much smaller in size. Length 18·5 inches, wing 14·5, tail 8, tarsus 2·5, bill from gape 2·5.

81. Corvus corone, Linnæus. The Carrion-Crow.

Spanish. Gragilla.

Not mentioned by Favier, but is included by Mr. Drake in his list of the birds of Morocco; I never met with any on the African side. On the Spanish side the Black Crow is scarce, and I only remember one nest, which was taken near Utrera during the month of March; another pair nested near Motril in 1893 (*Mena*).

Black, with metallic gloss; nostrils covered with bristly feathers; base of body-feathers *whitish*. Length 18–19 inches.

82. Corvus cornix, Linnæus. The Hooded or Grey Crow.

Not recorded from the Moorish side of the Straits. Saunders mentions the Hooded Crow as having been met with in Andalucia; there was one in a museum at Seville, but upon inquiry it proved to be from France. I never observed any, and the Grey Crow must be a very rare straggler, as Arévalo does not mention it as Andalucian.

Head, throat, wings, thighs, and tail-feathers black; the rest of plumage dull grey. Length 18–19 inches.

83. Corvus frugilegus, Linnæus. The Rook.

On the Moorish side of the Straits I can find no record of the occurrence of the Rook. I never met with any near Gibraltar, or, indeed, further south than the Coto del Rey, in the neighbourhood of Seville, where there were several large flocks in January; and they appear to be there regular winter visitants.

Black, with blue gloss.

Adults. With bare scurfy skin on forehead, lores, and throat.

Young in first plumage have these parts feathered, and resemble young Carrion-Crows, but the bases to the body-feathers are *grey* and the bill is slender. Length 18–20 inches.

LANIIDÆ. Young barred below.

84. Lanius meridionalis, Temminck. **The Spanish Grey Shrike.**

Spanish. Alcaudon real.

This Shrike is scarce in the neighbourhood of Gibraltar, the few specimens I have seen there having occurred in autumn only. Further north, though rather local, they become common in many places, being abundant and resident in the scrubby jungle near Seville. They nest, about the 15th of April, in bushes and low trees, building a large nest, the internal diameter measuring some five inches. When placed on a bough, the lower half is sometimes made of mud, the upper half being constructed with rough grass lined with fine grass, the whole covered outside with lichens and bits of Cudweed (*Gnaphalium luteo-album*)—the same plant so much used by the Woodchat and many other birds. The eggs are from four to five in number. At one time I was under the erroneous impression that these birds were migratory, from having seen one or two near Gibraltar in autumn; but, never having seen or heard of them on the African side, must have been mistaken; besides, they were more numerous about the Coto del Rey in winter than in May. However, this tends to show that they shift their ground in Spain, though not migrating out of the country.

Sexes alike. Above bluish grey; below with rosy tinge, except the grey flanks; narrow white stripe from forehead over eye. Length 9 inches.

85. Lanius algeriensis, Lesson. **The Algerian Grey Shrike.**

Moorish. Bou-scrund (*Favier*).

Favier's remarks, which under the synonym "*meridionalis*" refer to this species, do not add anything to the following notes.

This Shrike, which would be more fitly named the North-west-

African Shrike, as it is not peculiar to Algeria, is not common in the immediate vicinity of Tangier; but a little further south, near Larache, and towards the Fondak on the road to Tetuan they are very abundant. Their habits, nests, and eggs are identical with those of *L. meridionalis*, their Spanish representative, and they are only met with in scrubby jungle. On the 18th of April we found one nest in a thick lentiscus bush, with five eggs, which were hard sat-on, and another on the 20th, with only three fresh eggs.

This species is distinguishable from the Spanish Grey Shrike by the grey colour of the underparts.

Plumage black, white, and grey.

Above dark bluish grey; *below grey*; no white streak over eye. Length 9½ inches.

86. Lanius minor, J. F. Gmelin. The Lesser Grey Shrike.

This small migratory Shrike is said to have been obtained at Lanjaron (*Arévalo*), but Lord Lilford informs me (1894) that he never met with it in Andalucia and that his record of the bird there was an error. It is reported to occur in the east of Spain.

First primary *very short*, less than one third of second; tail even.

Male. Above grey; forehead and feathers from bill, round eye to ear-coverts, black; breast and flanks with a roseate blush. Wing-bar white.

Female. Less black on fore part of head.

Young. Has only black round and behind eye. Length 8–9 inches.

87. Lanius collurio, Linnæus. The Red-backed Shrike or "Butcher-bird."

Mr. Meade-Waldo observed this Shrike near Tangier on the 10th of April, 1892, and it has been obtained there, though very rarely in Andalucia; so we may reasonably assume that their line of migration is not across the Straits of Gibraltar; and it would be interesting to know the reason of this, as in 1876 Lord Lilford and myself found them common in the Province of Santander.

Male. Scapulars dull brick-red, uniform with the back; crown, hind neck, and rump grey; chin white; breast with roseate tinge.

Female. Above brownish grey; tail brownish red. Underparts white; sides of neck, breast, and flanks barred with brown.

Young. Above reddish brown; below pale brown; above and below barred with blackish brown. Length 7½–8 inches.

88. Lanius pomeranus, Sparrman. The Woodchat Shrike.

Moorish. Aisha el kra (*Favier*)*. *Spanish.* Alcaudon.

As common in Morocco as in Andalucia, the Woodchat arrives in March and April, leaving in August and September. The first arrival noticed at Gibraltar in 1868 was on the 3rd of April, in 1869 on the 3rd of April, in 1870 on the 29th of March, in 1894 on the 28th of March; the passage ceases about the 20th of April. The latest seen was on the 14th of October, 1871; in 1869 I observed them returning south on the 26th of August.

The Woodchat is one of the most abundant and conspicuous birds in spring on both sides of the Straits. Very tame and confiding, unlike their big cousins *L. meridionalis* and *L. algeriensis*; their pied appearance and the bright chestnut-coloured head of the adult males cause them to be noticed even by the most unobservant. They are to be seen in every direction in woods and on plains, perched on tops of trees, bushes, aloes, and tall plants, making their larders on the spikes of the aloes, and impaling on the thorns, beetles, bees, and all kinds of insects, and are extremely mischievous among bees.

The nest, which usually contains eggs by the 10th of May, is a small edition of that of *L. meridionalis*, but more covered outside with the greyish-white flowers and stalks of Cudweed (*Gnaphalium luteo-album*), and usually placed low down in trees.

---

* "Kra" is a kind of ringworm, and no doubt given as a name to the Woodchat owing to the supposed resemblance the chestnut head of the males has to the head of a Moor afflicted with this disorder, which is common in Tangier, and causes a rusty mangy baldness. "Aisha" is a female name: why applied to pied birds?

The eggs, four or five in number, sometimes six, are subject to great variation, many resembling those of our English Butcher-bird, *L. collurio*.

Male. Forehead black; centre of crown and nape chestnut; scapulars white, forming a large white patch on each side; rump and underparts white; white alar bar, or speculum, formed by the white outer web of base of primaries.

Female. Like the male, but markings ill-defined and not so bright.

Young. Much like young of last, but lighter. Scapulars and rump paler; plumage vermiculated with dark brown. Length 7½ inches.

89. Telephonus erythropterus (Shaw). The Hooded Shrike or Tchagra.

Moorish. Abermat (*Favier*).

"This Shrike is nearly as common as *Lanius algeriensis* near Tangier, and is resident, nesting in bushes twice a year—in May or June, and again in November. Their note, which is a kind of whistle, harmonious and well sustained, and very like that of a Blackbird, is usually heard from the middle of some thick bush (where they have a habit of hiding themselves), as well as in the thickest part of trees. They lay about three eggs, of the same shape as those of other Shrikes, but white marked with lines and small spots of ash-brown and russet, mostly at the thick end. The sexes are alike in plumage, and undergo no change."—*Favier*.

According to my limited experience, the Tchagra is rather scarce near Tangier, but more plentiful about a day's journey south. On the 25th of April we took a nest in a small tree close to the ground, containing three slightly incubated eggs, which is, we were informed, the usual complement. The nest was not so compact as that of the Woodchat, containing less grass and dried flowers, being chiefly built of fibrous roots. Mr. Meade-Waldo writes that "when beating for pigs, and these birds are hustled, they dart into a thick bush and sit perfectly still, so that you can look at them from a yard's distance or less; when undisturbed in the early morning, they have a most beautiful wild rich song." It is an easy bird to recognize when once seen on the wing, the chestnut of the wing-coverts and the long tail being very conspicuous.

Favier states that they cross the Straits; all I can say is, I never saw a Spanish specimen: if they do occur in Spain, they are as yet unobserved by any competent ornithologist.

Crown black; broad white eye-stripe, with black stripe below. Wing-coverts chestnut; below dark ash-grey. Tail much graduated, all the feathers, except the two light brown centre ones, black, tipped with white. Length 9 inches, tail 4 inches.

MUSCICAPIDÆ. Nostrils more or less covered by bristly hairs.

90. Muscicapa grisola (Linnæus). The Spotted Flycatcher.

Spanish. Papamoscas, Piñata.

"This Flycatcher is very common near Tangier, where they arrive in April and May in pairs and small flights, some remaining to nest, the others passing across the Straits to return in September, when they disappear. Near Rabat they are called *Sorsh* by the Arabs."—*Favier.*

The Spotted Flycatcher is exceedingly numerous near Gibraltar, chiefly nesting in the pine-woods, and was first seen on the 11th of May, 1870, on the 3rd of the same month in 1871, and on the 8th in 1874. The first egg obtained was on the 24th of the same month. Verner found a nest with fully-fledged young on 3rd of July, 1879. I regret not to have any note of their departure; but it is previous to the middle of September, and Verner informs me that they leave about the end of August.

Ashy brown above; forehead lighter than head, which is mottled with streaks of darker brown; breast white, with brown streaks; axillaries fawn-coloured.

Young. Spotted. Length 5½ inches.

91. Muscicapa atricapilla, Linnæus. The Pied Flycatcher.

Spanish. Cerrojillo.

"Very abundant near Tangier on passage, crossing to Europe in pairs and small flights during April and May, returning in September and October."—*Favier.*

In Andalucia the Pied Flycatcher only appears during migration; and I was never able to detect them remaining to nest. The earliest date of arrival noticed was the 8th of April; from then till the 1st of May they pass in great numbers, returning late in September. The latest date on which they were observed was the 17th of October, 1870, when I found one in an owl's disused cage, where there was a lot of carrion which attracted flies; and, again, in 1871 I noticed them on the 16th of October.

Male in spring. Above black, except white forehead and white wing-bar; axillaries and underparts white; quills brownish black. Tail black, three outer feathers on each side having two-thirds of the outer web from the base white.

Female, male in winter, and young. Above brownish grey; underparts dirty white. Tail as in male, but duller. Length 5 inches.

92. Muscicapa collaris, Bechstein. The Collared Flycatcher.

This Flycatcher is recorded by Mr. Saunders as having been once seen by him at Seville. Is said to be common in Portugal, therefore it is somewhat singular that the bird should not be more frequently noticed in Andalucia.

The adult male differs only from *M. atricapilla* in having a white collar on the back of the neck.

HIRUNDINIDÆ.

93. Hirundo rustica, Linnæus. **The Common Swallow.**

Moorish. Khotaifa. *Spanish.* Golondrina.

"Great flights of Swallows pass in January and February to Europe, returning in September and October to join those which remain near Tangier to nest, all leaving to go further south for the winter. The Moors believe that it offends God to kill these birds, in the same way as they believe it pleases or soothes the Evil One to kill the Raven. The stories on which this superstition is founded are too long to relate; but I was informed by one person that the Swallows and White Storks were inspired by Allah to protect the harvest and the country from noxious insects and reptiles, and that the birds themselves (knowing the benefits they confer on man) ask in return protection for their offspring by building their nests on the walls of towns and houses, and that therefore any one who kills them must be a Kaffir, *i. e.* not a true believer of the Prophet, especially as the birds would only be killed for mischief, being useless when dead."—*Favier.*

I wish this belief could be instilled into the minds of English people, who kill and destroy every rare bird they see, through ignorance, love of destruction, and to gratify the cupidity of private collectors.

About Gibraltar the Swallow generally arrives about the 13th of February, although a straggler is occasionally seen in December and January. I have observed them crossing the Straits in considerable numbers up to the 15th of April; the latest passing were noticed on the 24th of that month. Their migration, like the nest of the Hirundinidæ, is spread over a considerable period; I have observed the nest finished on the 23rd of February, and young birds able to fly on the 24th of May. One of each pair, when they first arrive, is tinged with a rufous-buff colour on the underparts; and as these are slightly larger in size, I think they are the male birds; but did not, even for the sake of proving this, kill one. I remember, on a very cold day (the 13th of March, 1874), Mr. Stark particularly drawing my attention to this difference in the pairs of birds, which, driven by the cold into the stables and outhouses of the venta at Pulverilla, were sitting side by side, touching one another, allowing us almost to touch them. The contrast in their colour was then most conspicuous; but they appear gradually to lose this rufous tinge as the season advances, and by the end of April it is not apparent.

In the month of March, during the time of the northern migration of Swallows, a small butterfly, *Thestor ballus* (one of the Lycænidæ, between the Hair-Streaks and the Coppers), is out in great abundance on the plains. When walking across the grass, the Swallows, which keep flying very close to leeward of you, instantly catch any unfortunate *ballus* that flies up; but they seem unable to take them on the ground, perhaps from the protective colouring of their green under-wings they cannot see them when at rest; but any way the Swallow is an annoyance to the butterfly collector.

Head, back, and rump steel-blue. Throat and forehead chestnut-red, with complete blue-black band across the lower part of the throat; underparts buff to creamy white. Tail strongly forked; two outer feathers greatly prolonged. Length 8½ inches.

94. Hirundo rufula, Temminck. Red-rumped Swallow.

Arévalo mentions this Eastern Swallow as having nested near Málaga, and it is also recorded from Valencia.

Above glossy purple-blue, with whitish streaks on back. Below white, tinged with buff and streaked with dark brown.
Nape and stripe over eye (forming a broad collar) and rump brick-red. Lower part of tail-coverts white. Length 7½ inches.

95. Chelidon urbica (Linnæus). The House-Martin.

Spanish. Vencejo.

"As common as the Swallow near Tangier, this species is seen in flights on passage, crossing to Europe in February, returning in September and October, frequently travelling in company with *Hirundo rustica*, and, as in their case, remaining to breed in some numbers. They often make their nests touching one another, as many as sixty being joined together; the entrance-hole is sometimes at the side, sometimes in the centre, according to the position of the nest. They are named 'Khotaifa' by the Arabs, indiscriminately with the Swallow."—*Favier*.

The above notes equally apply to the House-Martin in Andalucia. The earliest date of arrival noticed at Gibraltar was the 5th of February. Verner gives notes of great numbers passing on 15th of April, 1875, and many passing on the 17th of February, 1879.

Both this bird and the Swallow frequently nest in caves and on overhung rocks.

Rump *white*; under surface pure white; tail much forked; toes *feathered*. Length 4¾ inches.

96. Cotile riparia (Linnæus). The Sand-Martin.

"Migratory, and the least abundant of the Swallows about Tangier, arriving to cross the Straits in March and April, returning in October to disappear for the winter."—*Favier*.

We found the Sand-Martin at Ras el Doura, in Morocco, in small numbers, and have no doubt that they were nesting in the vicinity. They breed in the neighbourhood of Seville, but near Gibraltar are only met with on passage. The first seen by me was on the 24th of March 1870, 22nd of March 1871, 24th of February 1872, 28th of February 1874; they were seen passing as late as the 24th of April. On the 13th of May I saw, in the evening, over some marshes near Vejer, a flight of Sand-Martins numbering many hundreds—I might say, thousands. I noticed them on the 14th of October on their southward journey.

Above mouse-coloured; underparts white, except greyish band between chest and throat. Minute tuft of feathers just above hind toe.

Young. Feathers above edged with buffish white. Length 4¾ inches.

97. Cotile rupestris (Scopoli). The Crag-Martin.

Spanish. Vencejillo.

"Nearly as common as the House-Martin about Tangier. Sometimes they pass in large flights, crossing the Straits in February and March, returning in October and November."—*Favier.*

The Crag-Martin, though universally distributed during the breeding-season in the rocky sierras, is to a great extent migratory. Those which do not quit the country appear during the daytime in low ground near the coast about the middle of October, great numbers being then seen at Gibraltar. In March they return to their breeding-haunts, some nesting in inaccessible places at the "back of the Rock."

They commence about the 10th of March to build their nests, which resemble those of the Swallow, *H. rustica*, but being placed on the roofs of caverns are very difficult to reach; and I did not succeed in examining the inside of one. The birds were sitting by the 30th of April. One locality for nests near Gibraltar, and the most accessible that I have seen, was a cave in a patch of rocks at the entrance of La Trocha, on the road from Algeciraz to Ojen, where it passes by the side of the ravine called la Garganta del Capitan.

At the back of the Rock, at Gibraltar, is a cave almost under the Osprey's eyry, which can only be entered by landing from a boat in fair weather. This cave is very large and open, with sand at the bottom sloping upwards for a considerable distance at a sharp angle, and at the end, judging from the tracks of divers Genets or Striped Cats (*Viverra*), seems to be the regular dining-room of these animals; for whenever we visited the place it was covered with the tail-feathers and pinions of numbers of Rock-Martins mingled with those of a good many Swifts, Rock-Doves, and a few Lesser Kestrels.

Above mouse-coloured; underparts buffish brown. Oval white spots on all but the centre and outer tail-feathers. Length 5 inches.

FRINGILLIDÆ.

98. Coccothraustes vulgaris, Pallas. **The Hawfinch.**

Spanish. Cascanueces (Nutcracker), Piñonéro, Pico gordo.

Favier states the Hawfinch to be "very rare near Tangier, having only met with two—one in 1836, the other in 1849." Olcese obtained one since then (Reid, 'Ibis,' 1885), whilst Mr. Meade-Waldo saw several near Tangier in the spring of 1892.

On the Spanish side of the Straits this bird is very common, and most plentiful in winter. Some nest in the Cork-wood in May; and during the season of migration they often frequent pine-woods, and are then rather shy and difficult to approach. About Cordova they are most abundant, and are there and at Seville exposed alive for sale at about one real apiece. I kept a pair, purchased at Seville, for some time; but never could tame them. The hen bird at last killed her mate, having previously at regular intervals plucked him while living.

I gave this amiable and domestic female to a bird-fancier at Gibraltar, much to his delight, but ultimately to his sorrow, as she vented her temper upon some other pet birds with which she was caged, and, in consequence, justly suffered capital punishment.

Bill very large. Fifth and next four primaries shaped like a bill-hook.

Adult male. General colour above chestnut-brown; crown reddish brown, lightest on forehead; hind neck grey; black patch on chin; larger wing-coverts tipped with white; sides of body and flanks vinaceous brown; bill bluish; iris greyish white.

Female. Head ashy brown; secondaries edged with bluish grey; flanks as in male.

In winter. Bill fleshy white.

Young. Spotted, no grey at back of neck or black patch on chin; lower breast and flanks spotted and barred with brown; iris brown. Length 7 inches.

99. Ligurinus chloris (Linnæus). The Greenfinch.

Spanish. Verdon.

"Found near Tangier as a common resident; others migrate in immense flights, which pass north in February and March, returning in October and November."—*Favier.*

This species, another of our common British birds, is extremely abundant on both sides of the Straits. Many are resident, nesting during the month of May; and hundreds are caught in August and September and brought into the markets, where they are exposed for sale in large bunches. The Greenfinch is also a very common cage-bird, for sometimes as many as twenty may be seen, each in a separate cage, hanging outside the wall of a house. What their merits as a cage-bird are it is difficult to understand, as their song, if it can be dignified with the name, is to me positively unpleasant.

Greenfinches from Morocco and the south of Spain are rather smaller and more brightly coloured than English birds.

Adult male. General colour above olive-yellow, shaded with ashy grey; crown more ashy than back; axillaries bright yellow; primaries edged with bright yellow reaching to the shaft; tail black at ends, yellow at the base; outer tail-feathers yellow at the base of *both* webs.

In winter. Browner.

Female. Browner than male; primaries *only margined* with yellow; outer tail-feathers edged with yellow on *outer* web only.

Young male. Like female, but has primaries and tail as in adult male. Length 6 inches.

100. Carduelis elegans, Stephens. The Goldfinch.

Moorish. Mouknin. *Spanish.* Gilguéro. *Andalucian.* Silguéro.

"Exceedingly plentiful near Tangier, and resident; but numbers migrate, arriving from about the month of August, to depart again for the north in the month of March."—*Favier.*

The Goldfinch is, without doubt, the most common and

abundant bird in the west of Andalucia. Always plentiful in every direction, they appear in countless flocks when the seed of the various thistles becomes ripe; and Spain is the country *par excellence* both of thistles and donkeys. The former, in some of the vegas and plains, grow in almost impenetrable thickets, in places covering acres of ground; for when the land is left fallow for a season, all weeds are allowed to run riot, and they do so with a vengeance. Some of the thistles (and there are many different kinds) are very handsome—a large, yellow, carline species being perhaps the most attractive to the eye. The stalks, heads, and leaves of a species of *Cynara*, very like the garden artichoke, are a staple vegetable (*cardo*) with the Spaniards. The dried stalks of another thistle are much used as tinder in the rural districts, and known as *yesca de cardo*, which takes light well from the sparks made by a flint and steel, most of the peasants using no other method of lighting their *papelitos*.

To return to the Goldfinches, at the time of their thistle-harvest they are caught in vast quantities in clap-nets; and it is not unusual to see a man with bunches of several hundreds, which are sold at a ridiculously low price. Though perhaps rather dry, they are not to be despised as morsels; but one feels as if committing a sin when devouring such a charming and useful little bird.

The Goldfinch in Andalucia breeds about the beginning of May, and occasionally nests at Gibraltar in the Alameda and various gardens at the South.

Bill nearly conical and sharp-pointed.

Adult. General colour above ruddy brown. Forehead, upper throat, and cheeks *crimson*; hinder crown and sides of neck *black*; outer web of basal half of primaries, except the first, and the larger wing-coverts, brilliant yellow.

Young. Mottled, no red or black on head, that part being greyish brown. Length 5 inches.

101. Carduelis spinus (Linnæus). The Siskin.

Spanish. Lúgano.

On the African side of the Straits, Mr. Meade-Waldo found the Siskin, in the early spring of 1892, abundant near Tangier. Neither Favier nor Mr. Drake mention the bird.

In Andalucia they are very irregular in appearance, in some winters not being noticed at all. The Spaniards say they only come every seventh year. This idea is prevalent about Seville, as well as near Gibraltar; but, it is needless to say, is a popular error.

In the winter of 1870–71 they were plentiful wherever there were any alder trees; and I saw some as late as the 4th of April. In the two previous winters, and during the one following, none were obtained by the birdcatchers, who are always looking out for them, as they are much desired and fetch a good price as cage-birds. In 1874, I saw four on a white poplar tree in the Alameda of Gibraltar, on the 24th of March; they were so tame as to allow of my approach within a yard of them, and remained for a long time close to me.

Adult male. Above yellowish green; cheeks, throat, and breast bright yellow; flanks streaked with black; crown and small patch on chin black; tail blackish, all but the two centre feathers yellow at the base.

Female. No black on head or chin; throat uniform dull white. Length 4½ inches.

102. Chrysomitris citrinella (Linnæus). The Citril Finch.

Reported by Mr. Saunders to be found on the coast, and Arévalo says they are of irregular occurrence in autumn near Granada and Málaga. I never met with any near Gibraltar, and Lord Lilford informs me that he never handled a Spanish specimen; while Major Verner, who knew the bird well, tried in vain to obtain or even see one during six years at Gibraltar, none even being brought into the market.

Male. Back dull olive-green, each feather striped with dark brown.

Crown, cheeks, rump, and underparts greenish yellow. Nape, hind neck, sides of neck, and flanks *ashy grey*.

Female. Duller in plumage. Length 5 inches.

103. Serinus hortulans, K. L. Koch. The Serin Finch.

Spanish. Chamaris.

"This bird is very abundant near Tangier, both as a resident and on migration, when they are seen passing north in immense flights during February, returning in October and November."—*Favier.*

The Serin Finch is found on the Spanish side in accordance with the above note. During the breeding-season they greatly frequent the Cork-wood, and their hissing unpleasant song is to be heard all around. They seem to keep very much to the banks of rivers, nesting in May on trees and bushes, like the Goldfinch, resembling that bird both in their nest and eggs.

Bill conical, short, stout, and blunt.

Adult male. General colour above pale brown, each feather edged with yellow, and streaked with black on the centre; crown like the back; *forehead*, nape, eye-stripe, throat, and breast yellow; flanks streaked with black.

Female. Like male, but duller; throat, breast, and flanks streaked with dark brown. Length 4½ inches.

104. Passer domesticus (Linnæus). The House-Sparrow.

Moorish. Bertal. *Spanish.* Gorrión.

Common on both sides of the Straits, being the Sparrow of the district.

Adult male. Crown, nape, and rump *ashy grey*, with a chestnut streak on each side of head; throat black; ear-coverts white; general colour above chestnut, streaked with black on back.

Female. Lacks black throat of male; above dingy brown, streaked with black; pale eye-stripe; rump ashy brown.

Young. Like female, but can always be known by the yellowish skin at angle of gape. Length 6 inches.

105. Passer montanus (Linnæus). The Tree-Sparrow.

Spanish. Gorrión serrano.

This Sparrow occurs sometimes in Andalucia, as I have seen specimens obtained in the country; but I did not observe any near Gibraltar.

Sexes alike. Smaller than last. Always nests in *holes* of trees, thatch, and buildings.

Adult. Crown and nape uniform vinaceous chestnut; throat black; ear-coverts ashy white, with black patch on lower part; rump ashy brown.

Young. Duller, but show indistinctly markings of adults. Length 5½ inches.

106. Passer hispaniolensis, Temminck. The Spanish Sparrow.

This is another of the chestnut-headed Sparrows, and is local in distribution on both sides of the Straits. In some places they are very abundant; and, as is well known, often build under the nests of the larger birds of prey. I found a nest built underneath one of *Buteo desertorum*.

Male. Crown and nape chestnut; cheeks whitish; back black, each feather streaked with white; *flanks streaked* with black; throat and chest black.

Females resemble those of the Common Sparrow. Length 5½ inches.

107. Petronia stulta (Gmelin). The Rock-Sparrow.

Spanish. Gorrión montes.

Neither Favier nor Mr. Drake mentions having seen this Sparrow in Morocco, where, however, it is found, as on the Spanish side, commonly in the sierras and rocky ground, nesting in May in holes of rocks.

The adult male has a yellow spot on the throat; in the female this mark is much fainter, and absent in the young. Length 6 inches.

108. Fringilla cœlebs, Linnæus. The European Chaffinch.

Spanish. Pinzon.

This Chaffinch crosses in winter to the African side of the

Straits, as Capt. S. Reid in 1884–85 found many in the Tzelatza Valley; whilst Mr. Meade-Waldo informs me that in the spring of 1892 he saw immense numbers, far more than of the next species. Throughout Andalucia where there are trees this bird is as common as in England, being most abundant in winter, when the residents are outnumbered by the migrants. They appear on the Rock as early as the 12th of August, but I did not detect them remaining to nest, although quantities breed in the Cork-wood and all the wooded valleys of the neighbourhood, usually laying about the end of April; but in 1894 I found a nest touching the ground on the Sierra Retin, which contained young about a week old, on the 25th of March.

Adult male. Forehead black; head slate-grey; back *rufous*; ear-coverts and underparts vinous red; rump olive-green. Two white bars on wing.
Male in winter. Duller, the slate-grey feathers having brown tips, and the white on wings is tinged with yellow.
Female. Head and back ashy brown; below pale brown; rump yellowish green.—*In winter* is browner, and the white on the wings has yellow tinge. Length 6 inches.

109. Fringilla spodiogenys, Bonaparte. The North-African Chaffinch.

Moorish. Birdôn, Birdûl.

This Chaffinch is common and resident in Morocco. The nest and eggs resemble those of our Common Chaffinch, but the harsher note is very distinct.

Mr. Meade-Waldo found them fairly common in evergreen scrub, and says that they frequented more wooded ground than the last species, in the spring of 1892. There is no record of their occurrence on the Spanish side of the Straits.

The adult male is to be distinguished from *F. cœlebs* by the back being *yellowish green*, and by the throat and breast being light yellowish buff. Length 6 inches.
The females are similar to those of the Common Chaffinch.

110. Fringilla montifringilla, Linnæus. The Brambling.

Spanish. Montañes, Millero.

This species "has been once obtained near Tangier, in 1845, when I killed a female from among a lot of Linnets; the male escaped."—*Favier.*

The Brambling, on the Spanish side of the Straits, is of very irregular though not unfrequent appearance near Gibraltar in winter; during that of 1870-71 they, as well as Siskins, were abundant. Near Seville they are more regular in appearance, and are sufficiently well known about Cordova to bear the local name of "Millero."

Rump *white*, intermixed with black; axillaries and smaller inner wing-coverts *pale yellow.*
Male in summer. Head and upper back blue-black; throat and chest orange; flanks spotted with black; bill bluish.
Male in winter. Black parts edged with buff; throat duller, shaded with sandy buff; bill yellow.
Female. Head and upper back dark brown; rest of plumage much as male in winter, but less bright. Length 6½ inches.

111. Montifringilla nivalis (Linnæus). The Snow-Finch.

This Alpine Finch is found in the Sierra Nevada. Mr. Stark, in letter, says: "This bird is very common in Sierra Nevada, at from 3000 to 6000 feet, in small flocks."

Head and nape ashy grey. Back brown, centre of feathers darker; wing-coverts and axillaries white. Below creamy white. Black patch on throat in summer. Bill black in summer, yellow in winter. Two centre tail-feathers blackish, the rest white, all but the outer tipped with black. Length 7 inches.

112. Linota cannabina (Linnæus). The Common Linnet.

Moorish. Sharif (*Favier*). *Spanish.* Camácho, Jamas.

"Abundant around Tangier, many being resident and nesting from March to June. They are mostly migratory and cross to

Europe in March and April, returning in large flocks during September and October."—*Favier.*

The Common Linnet is very plentiful on the Spanish side, especially during the winter months. Great numbers remain to breed, nesting in April, mostly in scrub on the sides of the hills. Upon one occasion a pair built on an olive-bush in my garden at Gibraltar.

The adult males are, as a rule, far more brightly coloured than English specimens.

Adult male. General colour above reddish brown ; forehead and breast rich crimson ; rump paler than back ; wing-coverts uniform *chestnut-brown,* like the back, without *white edging* ; throat *whitish.* In winter the red colour is obscured by pale edgings to breast-feathers, which wear off.

Female. Has no red on head or breast ; sides of face dark ashy, like the head ; bill dusky.

Young. Like female, but spotted. Length 5¼–6 inches.

113. Linota rufescens (Vieillot). The Lesser Redpole.

This bird is not mentioned by Favier, but is included by Mr. Drake in his list of the birds of Morocco.

On the Spanish side of the Straits it can only be considered a very rare and irregular winter visitant like the Twite.

Adult male. Above light brown, *streaked* with blackish brown ; fore crown carmine ; chin *black* ; throat and breast pink ; rump dusky brown, tinged with crimson and *streaked* with brown ; wing-coverts tipped with rufous buff, forming a *double wing-bar.*

Female. Like male, but only red on the head. In winter the pink colour is much hidden by pale edges to the feathers.

Young dull coloured, without any red or pink. Length 4¾ inches.

114. Linota flavirostris (Linnæus). The Twite or Mountain-Linnet.

I have no record of the occurrence of this Linnet on the Moorish side. In Andalucia it is a rare winter straggler.

No red on forehead or breast ; bill yellow in adults, dusky in young.

Adult male. Above ruddy brown, feathers streaked with black down the centre, those on the back with pale margins; rump purplish red; throat and fore neck *clear reddish brown*, the latter streaked with dark brown; axillaries *reddish brown*, with black centres.

Female. Like male, but lighter and without the rosy rump, which is uniform with the back. Length 5–5¼ inches.

115. Pyrrhula erythrina, Pallas. Scarlet Grosbeak.

Three immature specimens of this Eastern Finch have been obtained in October, near Málaga.

The females and young males of this species are at first sight very likely to be mistaken for immature Greenfinches (*C. chloris*), but are to be distinguished by the form of the bill and the two distinct yellowish-white bars on the wing. In this plumage it is doubtless the *Fringilla incerta* of Risso.

Wings shorter than tail.

Adult male. General colour rosy or crimson; head crimson; rump brighter than back.

Female. General colour above olive-brown; feathers with dusky centres; rump same colour as back; middle and greater wing-coverts tipped with yellowish white, forming a *double wing-bar*; throat dull white, streaked with brown. Length 5½ inches.

116. Erythrospiza githaginea (Lichtenstein). The Desert Rosy Bullfinch.

This species is mentioned by Mr. Drake as being seen in the south of Morocco, and has occurred accidentally near Málaga. Several were caught in 1877.

Adult. General colour rosy. Female duller than male. Young sandy brown. Length 5 inches.

117. Loxia curvirostra, Linnæus. The Common Crossbill.

Spanish. Pico cruzado, Pico tuerto.

Favier only mentions having obtained this conifer-frequenting bird once near Tangier, "a specimen being picked up in a dying state in 1855."

Although never having myself met with the Crossbill on either side of the Straits, I have seen undoubted Andalucian specimens.

Points of bill crossing each other.

Adult male. General colour red, brightest on rump; but sometimes breeds in yellow plumage of female, very faintly streaked with red in a few places.

Female. Olive-yellow where red in male, brightest on rump.

Young. Like female, but streaked above and below with dark brown. Length 6 inches.

The so-called Parrot Crossbill (*L. pityopsittacus*) is a Northern form of the Common Crossbill, with the bill very much stouter, and is usually a larger bird.

118. Emberiza miliaria, Linnæus. The Corn-Bunting.

Moorish. Dorrais (*Favier*). *Spanish.* Triguéro; Ave tónta.

This well-known bird is exceedingly numerous on both sides of the Straits, and, being to a great extent migratory, is perhaps least plentiful in winter. From their fearless stupidity and conspicuous habit of perching on the top of some small bush or plant, vast quantities are killed by the Spaniards and exposed for sale in the markets, being excellent food, while during the winter months a great many are caught roosting on the ground by the aid of the lantern.

The Common Bunting commences to lay about the first week in May, often placing the nest at the edge of marshes; and I have taken it in the midst of a swamp, placed on a dry tussock, within a yard of a nest of Savi's Warbler. Verner remarks that eggs of this Bunting "appear to undergo extraordinary variations in S. Spain. I have found many about the vega of La Janda, totally unlike any I have ever seen in England, but of the authenticity of which I had no doubt."

There is a country fable to the effect that the Hoopoe on first arrival in Spain had no place to go to, and bought or hired some land from the Bunting; but when the time for payment arrived, "Poo, poo," said the Hoopoe, and flew away repeating his cry. Ever since then the Bunting is continually and monotonously complaining of the Hoopoe, and in vain asking for his money.

Sexes alike. General colour greyish brown, streaked with dark brown; light eyebrow; tail brown, with edges and tips of buffy white; no other colours in plumage. Length 7 inches.

119. Emberiza citrinella, Linnæus. The Yellow Hammer.

Our well-known "Yellow Hammer," so common in the north of Spain, is only found in Andalucia as a winter straggler. I have seen specimens from Granada and Málaga, but never observed any near Gibraltar.

Male in summer. Head lemon-yellow; back rufous, streaked with dark brown; rump *chestnut*; under surface yellow.

In winter. Head marked with brown, and generally less bright.

Female. Head less yellow, crown streaked with black; throat and breast striped with blackish. Length 6¾–7 inches.

120. Emberiza cirlus, Linnæus. The Cirl Bunting.

Spanish. Linacéro.

According to Favier's notes, this Bunting is equally common around Tangier as near Gibraltar, migrating northwards in March returning in October and November, remaining during the winter months; many also stay to breed during April.

The Cirl Bunting is very frequent all along the road from Algeciras to Tarifa, and from its tameness, and the bright colour of the males, with their conspicuous black throats, is sure to attract attention. They appear to be more a tree-frequenting bird than the Yellow Hammer (*Emberiza citrinella*), and are especially fond of the glades and open patches of cultivation in the Cork-wood.

Least wing-coverts *olive-green*; rump *olive-brown*.

Male. Chin, throat, and line from bill through eye to nape black; eyebrow yellow; yellow crescent under the black throat; upper chest dull olive, bordered below by chestnut; belly dull yellow.

Female. Much like female of Yellow Hammer, but wanting the yellow colouring.

In winter, colours of male less bright, the black parts obscured by light margins. Length 6 inches.

121. **Emberiza hortulana**, Linnæus. **The Ortolan.**

Moorish. Merskezan (*Favier*).   *Spanish.* Hortoláno.

"The Ortolan is, next to the Common Bunting, the most abundant of the genus near Tangier. Some remain to breed; while the rest pass on during April, returning in September. Migrating in large flocks, they prefer wet ground, and are not observed in the winter months."—*Favier.*

Curiously enough, I never succeeded in obtaining the Ortolan nearer to Gibraltar than the vicinity of Casas Viejas, where I found them in May. In the vicinity of Seville they are plentifully met with, but do not occur during the winter.

Male. General colour above pale reddish brown; head greenish olive; cheeks, throat, and axillaries pale yellow; neck and chest greenish olive; rest below cinnamon; bill reddish brown.

Female. Paler than male; lower throat streaked with brown. Length 6 inches.

122. **Emberiza schœniclus**, Linnæus. **The Reed-Bunting.**

Included by Favier in his list as "rare near Tangier; met with in December." Capt. Savile Reid found them common in winter at Meshree el Haddar. They are most abundant near Gibraltar from December to February, and were seen on passage as late as the 7th of April. They do not remain to nest in the sotos at Casas Viejas; but near Seville, where they are often sold in cages under the name of "Hortoláno," I have seen them in May, and have no doubt that they there remain throughout the breeding-season.

Male in spring. Head and throat black; cheeks white; eye-stripe white; white collar from bill round nape; rump bluish grey; lesser wing-coverts chestnut.

In autumn the black is hidden by rufous edgings, and the white by sandy-brown edgings.

Female. Head and ear-coverts reddish brown, streaked with black; breast and flanks white, streaked with blackish. Outside web of second tail-feather white. Length 6 inches.

123. Emberiza pusilla, Pallas. **The Little Bunting.**

Nine specimens of this north-eastern Bunting were obtained near Málaga on the 28th of December, 1874.

Male in spring. Centre of crown vinous chestnut, with black band on each side; eye-stripe, lores, sides of face, and *throat* vinous chestnut.
Female. Like male, but not so richly coloured on throat.
Young. Throat white, no chestnut on breast or flanks. Length 4¾ inches.

124. Emberiza cia, Linnæus. **The Rock-Bunting.**

Spanish. Escribáno.

Although not mentioned by Favier as found in Morocco, I have seen specimens obtained there, and met with a pair in April near Jebel Musa.

On the Spanish side of the Straits is a common and, like most of the Buntings, a stupidly tame bird, as far as my experience goes, living about stony, rocky, and hilly ground. Till 1874 I never noticed them perching on trees; but in the spring of that year saw three different birds, when disturbed, settle on trees and bushes. At Gibraltar they are met with in winter, but disappear in the spring. I have shot them at the back of the Rock when looking for Alpine Accentors, in company with which birds have seen them feeding on the refuse-heap at the signal-station. In April they frequent the slopes and tops of the sierras, nesting during that month.

Male. Centre of crown bluish grey, sides of crown blackish. White eyebrow; black stripe through eye; ear-coverts *bluish grey*; black moustachial stripe from bill to round ear-coverts. Middle and greater wing-coverts tipped with white, forming distinct wing-bars.
Female. Paler. Length 6 inches.

125. Emberiza saharæ, Tristram. **The House-Bunting.**

This bird is found in the city of Morocco and other Moorish towns.

Back nearly uniform rufous; breast and axillaries sandy rufous; head grey, with blackish streaks; throat and fore neck light grey; ashy-grey streak through eye and upper edge of cheek. Length 5 inches.

126. Plectrophenax nivalis (Linnæus). The Snow-Bunting.

The Snow-Bunting has only been recorded once from the Moorish side of the Straits; and this occurrence was mentioned by Mr. Drake. This specimen, lately in the possession of Olcese (Favier's successor at Tangier), was a female, and in fine plumage.

In Andalucia is a very rare straggler in winter; a male, which I have seen, was shot near Málaga on the 18th of November, 1872.

Tail: six centre feathers black, fringed externally and round tip with white; three outer pairs white, with black at end of outer web; claw of hind toe *elongated*, but *not longer* than hind toe.

Male in summer. Head, neck, and under surface white; above black; wing-coverts white; bill black.

Female. Dark brown and white; secondaries white.

Male and female in winter. Crown reddish brown; feathers on upper parts broadly edged with reddish brown; bill yellowish, with dark tip. Length 6½–7 inches.

MOTACILLIDÆ.

127. Motacilla alba, Linnæus. The White Wagtail.

Moorish. Emzizi. *Spanish*. Pispita.

"This is the most abundant of the Wagtails, and passes the winter near Tangier, arriving during September and October, leaving in March. They are to be seen in large flocks following the plough, twittering incessantly."—*Favier*.

The above notes apply equally to the White Wagtail in Andalucia; but it was never seen by me after the 24th of March; though Mr. Stark found a nest at Alora, near Málaga, and they are recorded by Arévalo as breeding near Granada. They roost together in great numbers on the short rushes and grass in the marshes at Casas Viejas, where I have often seen them on the backs of horses and cattle, picking off vermin and catching flies, doing the work of Starlings and Buff-backed Herons.

Male. Crown, nape, throat; and breast black; back from nape ash-grey; front and sides of head white.
Female. Like the male.
In winter. Resembles the next (*M. lugubris*), but has lighter back.
Young. Undistinguishable from the young of the next. Length 7–7½ inches.

128. Motacilla lugubris, Temminck. The Pied Wagtail.

"This is the most rare of the Wagtails near Tangier; they are found at the same times and places as *M. alba.*"—*Favier.*

I obtained a specimen in summer dress at Tangier; it is scarce enough in Andalucia in that plumage, but probably in winter dress escapes unnoticed.

Male in spring. Crown, nape, *back*, chin, and throat black, the latter uniting with the black on the back and nape; forehead and sides of the head white.
Female. Like male, but has the back slaty grey, with blackish feathers here and there.
Both sexes in winter have the back ash-grey; chin and throat white; back of the head and nape black, with a black crescent on front of neck.
Young. In first plumage have entire head ash-grey; face washed with yellow; the black crescent on front neck gradually developing from a small spot to a full crescent. Length 7–7½ inches.

129. Motacilla melanope, Pallas. The Grey Wagtail.

This Wagtail is stated by Favier to be a common winter visitor near Tangier, appearing in September and October, departing in February and March.

In Andalucia they are most abundant on passage and during the winter months, but many pairs nest along the mountain-streams of the sierras—three or four pair particularly on the rivulet which runs down the Garganta del Aguila, the valley in which is situated the "waterfall" of Algeciraz; and they build usually in holes of the brickwork of the water-mills, sometimes close to the wheel. A pair also regularly nest at the mill in the Cork-wood; and Mr. Stark, when with me on the 9th of April, found a nest built in a hole of a large rock overhanging the

Guadalmalcil, a mountain-torrent between Tarifa and Algeciraz. This nest was placed out of reach of either man or beast; the hen bird was visible from the opposite side, and apparently sitting close. On the 19th of April, the nest at the mill in the Corkwood contained one egg, while another nest found on the 24th of May had four fresh eggs in it, which tends to show that they breed more than once in the season. The nest is constructed of grass and small roots lined with hair.

Some only of the males had the black throat on the 8th of March; but all had assumed it by the 1st of April. The females do not always exhibit this mark, some not having it at all, and in none is it so well defined as in the males.

It is the longest of the Wagtails found in these parts, with the tail-feathers much longer in proportion to the body than in other species.

Under tail-coverts *brighter yellow* than belly.

Male in summer. Above bluish grey; white eye-stripe; rump and upper tail-coverts *greenish yellow*; underparts yellow; throat black.

Female. Resembles the male, but has the throat white, or white with very rarely a few black feathers.

Young. Above tinged with brown; throat and eyebrow buff.

In winter. Both sexes are alike, having a white throat. Length 7–7¼ inches, tail about 3½.

130. Motacilla flava, Linnæus. The Blue-headed Yellow Wagtail.

Spanish. Nevadilla.

This species is found on both sides of the Straits in great abundance; the earliest seen was on the 20th and 24th of February (in different years), many appearing on the 25th. From that time till the 20th of April they continued to pass; and on that day I saw great numbers at Gibraltar, resting on the "flats" at Europa after their flight across the sea. They leave in August and September. Exactly resembling our English Yellow Wagtail (*M. raii*) in habits, they keep to marshes, nesting in grass and herbage at the edge of water, sometimes among the sedges, and lay in the end of April.

I

Male. Above yellowish green; underparts, except *white* chin, bright yellow; broad *white stripe* over eye from bill to nape; head, nape, and ear-coverts *blue-grey*.

Female. Head brownish and duller in colour. Length 6-6½ inches.

131. Motacilla borealis, Sundevall. The Grey-headed Yellow Wagtail.

Occurs on passage; passing later than the preceding, of which it and the next can only be considered races.

Like the last, but head slaty grey and has *no eye-stripe*, and only the *chin is white*.

The race *Motacilla cinereocapilla*, Savi, has throat white and partly defined white eye-stripe. I shot specimens in spring, and they were nesting near Casas Viejas in May.

132. Motacilla raii (Bonaparte). Yellow Wagtail.

This, the English race of Yellow Wagtail, occurs on passage in spring, but not commonly, and has been obtained at Tangier and Málaga. We saw many about 12th April, 1894, at Tapatanilla.

Male. Head canary-yellow; upper parts olive-green; nape yellowish green; all underparts, eye-stripe, and axillaries bright yellow.

Female. Eye-stripe buff; plumage much less brilliant.

Young. Eye-stripe and underparts buffish white, with no yellow except a tinge on lower belly. Length 6½ inches.

133. Anthus trivialis (Linnæus). The Tree-Pipit.

According to Favier this Pipit is common near Tangier during migration, crossing the Straits in March and April, returning in October and November. On the Spanish side they are found on passage only: the 9th of April is the earliest date on which I noticed them, but I saw many about the 20th.

Above clear brown, distinctly streaked with dusky; spots on breast small; flanks streaked with black, like the breast; middle and greater wing-coverts tipped with white, forming a double wing-bar; light part of outer tail-feather white or smoky white; axillaries sandy buff. Hind claw *curved*, shorter than hind toe. Length 6½ inches.

134. Anthus pratensis (Linnæus). The Meadow-Pipit.

The Meadow-Pipit is equally common in Morocco and Andalucia from October to the end of March.

Head and upper parts olive-brown, mottled with black centres; rump uniform; throat, chest, and flanks streaked with black; light pattern of tail-feathers white; axillaries edged with olive-yellow. Hind claw *nearly straight*, longer than hind toe. Length 5½ inches.

135. Anthus cervinus (Pallas). The Red-throated Pipit.

I obtained two Pipits in 1870 on the 10th of March, which I took home to England; and they were identified as belonging to this species by Mr. Sharpe and Captain Shelley. In 1874, on the 8th of March, I shot among a lot of *A. pratensis* another bird, which appeared to be *A. cervinus*; but as the rufous throat is not developed, though it showed signs of that mark of the breeding-plumage, to determine with certainty to which species it really did belong is impossible; so I mention and include the species in my list with a view to some future collector paying attention to the subject. For my own part I have little doubt that *A. cervinus* does occur on passage in Andalucia and Morocco.

Male in spring. Much resembles last, but has eye-stripe, cheeks, throat, and breast deep *vinous red*.

Female. Only the throat vinous.

In winter the difference between the two species is hardly distinguishable; but it is said that in this species the rump is spotted like the back, and the under tail-coverts have dark centres. Length 5½ inches.

136. Anthus obscurus (Latham). The Rock-Pipit.

Favier states that this species occurs in winter near Tangier, and may be always seen on the sea-shore. I think (not having seen any of his specimens) that these remarks apply to *A. spipoletta*, which he does not mention in his MS.; but Mr. Dresser, in his 'Birds of Europe,' examined a specimen obtained by Olcese at Tangier, and I brought home a Pipit shot on the mud at Palmones, near Algeciraz, in March 1870, which was identified by Mr. Sharpe as *A. obscurus*.

Axillaries and light pattern on outer tail-feathers *smoky brown*. Hind claw *much curved*, and equal in length to hind toe.
Males in spring have a rosy tinge on breast, chiefly southern birds. Length 6½ inches.

137. **Anthus spipoletta** (Linnæus). **The Water-Pipit.**

Found on mud-flats near Algeciraz and near Málaga in winter.

White eye-stripe; below pale rosy; chest uniform, without streaks. Light pattern of outer tail-feathers *white*. Hind claw long and straightened.
Young. Undistinguishable in plumage from those of *A. obscurus*. Length 6½ inches.

138. **Anthus campestris** (Linnæus). **The Tawny Pipit.**

Moorish. Solist (*Favier*).

"Found near Tangier on passage in April, returning in August, but is not very common. They migrate in pairs and keep close together, so that it is very easy to shoot both at one shot."—*Favier.*

The earliest date on which I saw one was at Tangier on the 31st of March. On the Spanish side they appear to frequent high ground, as on the 1st of May we saw many on the open spaces about Ojen, and thence all along to the Venta de Subalbarro. We never met with them on low ground, and there is no doubt they breed high up on the sierras.

General colour of upper surface dull greyish brown, darker on centre of feathers; broad buffy-white eyebrow; throat whitish; underparts *uniform pale buff*; wing-coverts edged with pale buff, varying much in depth of colour; light pattern of outer tail-feathers white. Hind claw stout and slightly curved, about equal in length to hind toe. Length 6¼-7 inches.

139. **Anthus richardi**, Vieillot. **Richard's Pipit.**

I shot one specimen of this large eastern Pipit on the 1st of March on the shore, evidently just arrived, and obtained others on the 20th of April, 1870, not noticing any again; but Verner reports that he shot one on the 9th June, 1877, at the stream between the Pine-woods, and Arévalo records them on passage near Málaga.

Above dark brown, with sandy-buff edges to feathers; throat and breast streaked; axillaries sandy rufous; light pattern of outer tail-feathers white. Hind claw long and nearly straight. Leg about 1½ inches long. Length 7¾ inches.

ALAUDIDÆ.

140. Certhilauda bifasciata (Lichtenstein). Desert Curved-billed Lark.

This Desert-Lark is recorded from Málaga by Arévalo.

Hind toe very short. Bill long and curved. General colour above and centre tail-feathers isabelline. Below creamy white; thin collar of blackish spots on breast; eyebrows white. Length 8 inches.

141. Certhilauda duponti (Vieillot). Small Curved-billed or Dupont's Lark.

Specimens of this Algerian Lark were obtained near Málaga by Francisco de los Rios, and others since his death.

Those found in Portugal have been described as a distinct species, *C. lusitanica*, Bocage.

Bill long, slightly curved, and slender. First primary very short. General colour sandy brown, with "lark-like" back, dark spots on back with a vinous sheen. Length 6½ inches.

142. Alauda arvensis, Linnæus. The Skylark.

Spanish. Zurriága, Terréra.

" Found near Tangier during winter, arriving in October and November, departing in March. They are found in immense flocks during their stay."—*Favier*.

The same is to be said of the Skylark in Andalucia, where in some localities quantities are caught at night with a bell and a lantern, and I have known a boy bring in six or seven dozen birds at a time. Calandras, Buntings, Larks, in fact any birds that sleep on the ground can be thus taken.

Breast spotted. Outer tail-feathers *white*, except inner edge of inner web; next pair white only on outer web. Hind claw long and straight. Bastard primary very small. Length 7¼ inches.

143. Alauda arborea, Linnæus. The Woodlark.

Spanish. Alóndra de monte (Lark of the scrub).

According to Favier, this species "occurs near Tangier on passage during March." Some were obtained by Capt. Savile Reid near Larache in the winter of 1884–85.

On the Andalucian side the Woodlark is sparingly and locally distributed during the winter months up to as late as the 21st of April, frequenting scrub where not very thick, a favourite locality near Gibraltar being the *chaparales** in the Cork-wood. Well known to the Spanish birdcatchers, and highly valued as a cage-bird; they assured me that the Woodlark never remains to nest near Gibraltar, but they are known to breed near Málaga.

Light streak over eye; primary-coverts tipped with white, showing small white spot on closed wing. First primary long, third primary longest. Tail short; outer feather greyish white at end, and outer web bordered with white, next three tipped with triangular white spots; hind claw curved. Length 6 inches.

144. Alauda cristata, Linnæus. The Crested Lark.

Moorish. Kubaa (hooded one—as hood of jellabia, or crest of a helmet). *Spanish.* Carretera.

The Crested Lark is one of the most abundant birds both in Morocco and Andalucia, though never seen in any great numbers together. They are distributed in pairs on every road-track and open plain, often at intervals of only some twenty yards. Excessively tame and fearless, they have acquired the name of *Carretera*, from their habit of frequenting roads, to which they

---

* "Chaparal," *lit.* a plantation of ilex. The "chaparales" here mentioned are simply ground covered with brushwood or scrub.

resort as much on account of the horse- and mule-dung, at which they are to be seen pecking, as for the purpose of dusting themselves; and they are often to be noticed on the sea-shore, running about like a Sanderling within a yard of the water. They have no song worthy of the name, and are altogether rather vulgar and uninteresting birds. This species is one of those which I could not detect migrating in the slightest degree.

The Crested Lark usually commences to lay about the 20th of April, placing the nest in some tuft of grass or under shelter of a small stone or clod of earth—constructing it, like those of other Larks, with bits of grass, bents, &c., lined with hair.

One nest which we found was placed between the tracks of a much frequented road near Tangier, in such a position that every passing animal must have touched the small clump of grass under cover of which the nest was built. Now, was this site chosen because snakes, lizards, and other vermin would be less likely to come on the beaten track? I cannot help thinking that birds in many instances have instinct enough to breed close to houses and roads with a view to obtain protection from some of their enemies through the presence of man, who is perhaps their worst foe.

The Crested Lark is subject to great difference in the tints of the plumage. The difference of colour varies according to the soil and climate, and has been very puzzling to cabinet or table naturalists, as the enormous list of synonyms will testify. Mr. Dresser, in his article on this bird, gives no less than thirty-seven different names, which have for the greater part been manufactured on account of the variations of plumage and size noticed in this species.

Mr. Sharpe (Catalogue of Birds, British Museum, vol. xiii. p. 633) has *Galerita (Alauda) theeklæ* as a distinct species, giving S. Spain and N.E. Africa as the habitat. Exactly similar in habits and note, it appears to be only a small local race of *A. cristata*.

Galerita macrorhyncha, Tristram, mentioned by Mr. Drake as occurring near Morocco, is only another local race of the Crested Lark.

General ground-colour varies much from greyish brown to buffish brown. Conspicuous occipital *crest*; axillaries buff; outer web of outer tail-feathers *buff*. Length 6¾ inches.

145. Alauda brachydactyla, Leisler. The Short-toed Lark.

Spanish. Terréra.

"This bird is found on passage near Tangier, crossing in very large flights during March and April, returning in August and September. Many remain to breed, frequenting the same localities as the Calandra Lark."—*Favier.*

On the Andalucian side of the Straits the spring arrival commences about the middle of March; and the passage continues for a month later, at which time nests with eggs may be found near Gibraltar. Excessively abundant, as above stated, in the same situations as the Calandra; they prefer fallow ground, nesting under shelter of some clod or in any slight depression of the ground. I never could find the nest, except by putting the old bird off. A very good way of finding the nests of all the Larks and ground-breeding birds is, with the assistance of a man to hold it at the other end, to drag a rope about a hundred yards long across the ground, being careful that it drags *on* the ground; directly a bird flies up, drop the rope, go to the spot, and in all probability a nest will be found.

Below buffish white; *no spots on underparts*; but sometimes a streak or two and brownish patch on each side of upper breast. Outer tail-feathers buffish white, except the brown basal half of inner web; the next feather has outer web with buffish-white edging. Front claws *very short* and curved; hind claw straight and rather elongated. Length 5½ inches.

146. Alauda bætica, Dresser. The Andalucian Short-toed Lark.

Spanish. Cujáilla.

This small Lark was discovered by Lord Lilford in the cornland on the banks of the Guadalquivir below Seville, where they are known to occur from February to the summer. Major

Verner found them about the vega of La Janda, and obtained several nests there; the eggs were much like those of the Crested Lark. They also occur in the vicinity of Málaga throughout the year.

Marked much as *A. brachydactyla*, but the secondaries very much shorter than the primaries. More ashy in colour; throat, breast, and flanks very broadly marked with black. Length 5½ inches.

147. Alauda calandra (Linnæus). The Calandra Lark.

Spanish. Alóndra, Calandria.

The Calandra is extremely abundant and resident on both sides of the Straits, gathering together in flocks during the winter.

Frequenting all the vegas or plains in Andalucia, they are, from their numbers, size, note, and peculiar varying flight, very conspicuous, and in some localities positively swarm. At times their flight is very like that of some of the smaller Waders; and often when flying in the breeding-season they utter notes which very much resemble the cry of the Green Sandpiper, only of course not so loud. In spring they soar to a great height, singing on the wing, but not hovering like the Skylark. At this season, when the garbanzos (*Cicer arietinum*) are sprouting, they are very troublesome, picking the shoots off, so that the farmers have to scare these and other Larks away.

They consort much with the Short-toed Lark, and nest sometimes close together on cultivated as well as pasture land, laying about the second week in April.

The Calandra is a very common cage-bird at Gibraltar, and they are as much prized for their song as for their lively habits.

Bill short and stout, arched above. Large triangular black patch on each side of throat extending to the neck forming an interrupted collar. Outer tail-feather almost entirely white. Length 8 inches.

148. Otocorys bilopha (Temminck). The Horned Desert-Lark.

This species is mentioned by Mr. Drake as having been

obtained at Morocco; and has been found as a straggler near Málaga.

<small>Hind claw long and nearly straight. Back pale fawn-colour, the adult male having a black gorget and two long black ear-tufts. Length 6 inches.</small>

Order **PICARIÆ**.   Family **CYPSELIDÆ**.

Tail of ten feathers.

149. Cypselus apus, Linnæus.   Common Swift.

Moorish. Tair abila (*Favier*).   *Spanish.* Avión.

"This Swift arrives at Tangier, *en route* for Europe, during March and April; vast numbers remain to nest here, and return south in September and October."—*Favier.*

Mr. Meade-Waldo saw a Swift near Tangier as early as the 22nd of February, 1892.

The above notes equally apply to the Common Swift in Andalucia, the earliest date of arrival noted being the 4th of March, the main body passing during the last fortnight in that month, some as late as the 24th of April. The majority leave by the end of August, some staying on into the middle of September, the last being seen on the 16th of October. The number in some towns, particularly Algeciras, is perfectly marvellous, and the noise they make morning and evening quite annoying.

Verner writes :—" In order to compare nests of this Swift with those of the next species, I visited great numbers of nests of the Common Swift on the Rock. In the Casemate Barracks a large number nest yearly in the verandahs, and there, as elsewhere, I found all the nests, if there were any, to be only a heap of castings and insects' wings, and now and then the remnants of a Sparrow's nest. In most cases the eggs were laid on the bare mortar and there was no attempt to weld the castings &c. together with mucilage. I caught and released a number of old birds, all of the blackest hue. Every nest contained two eggs, except one, which held three.

General colour blackish brown, except small whitish chin-patch; four toes all directed forwards. Length 7½ inches.

150. Cypselus murinus, A. and E. Brehm. Mouse-coloured Swift.

"This Swift is found near Tangier on passage, crossing to Europe in April and May. Some remain to breed; but it is the least common of the family, being seen alone or in pairs in company with *C. apus*. I found a pair in July 1861, nesting in company with some House-Martins (*Chelidon urbica*); the nest was simply an old nest of that Martin, which the Swifts had appropriated, and contained two eggs of the usual *Cypselus* shape."—*Favier*.

They are abundant at Gibraltar, and are said to arrive at Tangier somewhat earlier than the Common Swift, though there appears to be no difference in the time of their arrival. Easily noticed on the wing by their light colour, they mix both with the Common and White-bellied Swifts.

In May 1874, when near Vejer with two ornithologizing friends, we found this species to be more abundant than *C. apus*, while, curiously enough, at Algeciraz (where, as mentioned, there are countless swarms of Common Swifts) we never could detect one single *C. murinus*. They are common around Málaga; and Mena, in 1882, noticed their first arrival on the 14th of March. He also told me that this Swift does not, like *C. apus*, enter the nest direct, but settles or hangs outside before entering.

Verner writes:—"In spite of this Swift having been considered only to be a subspecies, I am convinced that in many cases the Mouse-coloured Swifts nest in separate colonies apart from the common species, and, as far as my experience goes, they differ considerably in their nidification.

"A small colony used to breed in the weep-holes in the sea-wall of the New Mole Parade. Many black Swifts nested in close vicinity, but from continued observation it appeared that the light-coloured Swifts nested in adjacent holes and kept apart from their dark congeners. These holes being far in, it was difficult to be certain, since nests and old birds were out of reach. However, another colony nested in 1878 in the Patio of the Convent, and I was able to watch them daily and hourly for some weeks from the A.D.C.'s room which I occupied. I soon found that there were not any dark Swifts, and after making sure of this I inspected their nests. On the 12th June I found five nests —one with two eggs, three with three eggs, and one with two young birds nearly fledged; some of the eggs were fresh, others much incubated. The nests (placed on the tops of rafters and on a wall, and two between a rafter and the wall) were solidly built of castings of insects' wings, thistledown, and bits of paja, glued together by mucus so strongly as to require much force to separate them from the rafters: those on the tops of the rafters were much smaller than the others, and little more than a saucer-shaped rampart. In all cases I caught the old birds and examined them carefully before releasing them. It is curious that the black Swift usually lays two eggs, rarely three, whilst three out of four of the pale Swifts' nests contained three eggs."

151. Cypselus melba, Linnæus. White-bellied Swift, Alpine Swift.

Moorish. El namera. *Spanish.* Avión real, Avión de pecho blanco.

"Found near Tangier on passage, crossing the Straits from March to May, returning from August to October. It is not so common as *C. apus.*"—*Favier.*

The White-bellied Swift breeds sparingly at Gibraltar in the inaccessible crevices of the rocks on the Mediterranean side; they seem to arrive, if anything, a little later than the Common Swift. The earliest dates of arrival noticed were the 24th of March

1871 and 24th of March 1894, Mr. Irby, 60th Rifles, having shot one at Tangier on the 18th. On the 4th of April, 1871, near San Roque, I noticed a flock of about two hundred passing in a northerly direction, with a gyrating flight, making a great noise, though they were very high up. A few Common Swifts (their cry attracted my attention to them) were with the flock. On the 5th of November, 1871, at Casas Viejas, I saw six hawking about over the marshes for about an hour, when they disappeared in a westerly direction. An officer who was at Fez told me that he saw a great many Alpine Swifts there in large flights about the 23rd of February.

Although far out of the range of this book, it is interesting to record that Major Verner, when at Crete, noticed numbers of this Swift passing north on the 24th of March, 1886.

The sexes are alike in plumage, except that the female is marked or striated with a faint black line on the centre of the feathers of the white breast. The brain of this, as in all Swifts that I have examined, is small for the size of the bird.

Above greyish brown; chin and belly white, with band of greyish brown across upper breast; toes as in last. Length 8¾ inches.

CAPRIMULGIDÆ.

Mouth very wide, extending behind the eyes; tail of ten feathers; claw of middle toe serrated on the inner edge.

152. Caprimulgus europæus, Linnæus. Nightjar or "Goatsucker."

"Occurs near Tangier, but is less numerous than the Rufous-naped Nightjar, some, however, remaining to nest. The others pass on across the Straits during May and June, returning from September to November to pass the winter further south."—*Favier.*

The Nightjar is found in Andalucia, as near Tangier, the earliest date of arrival noticed being the 5th of May.

Male. White spot near end of inner web of three first primaries of each wing, and the two outer tail-feathers on each side tipped with white.

Female. Like male, but without the white marks on wings and tail. Length 10½ inches.

153. Caprimulgus ruficollis, Temminck. Rufous-naped Nightjar.

Moorish. Terref el rayan. *Spanish.* Zumaya, Chota Cabras, Engaña-pastores.

"This Nightjar is very abundant near Tangier, arriving to cross the Straits in April and May, to return in October and November. Many remain to breed, nesting on the bare ground among scrubby brushwood, and laying two eggs, which are to be found from May to August."—*Favier.*

The Rufous-naped Nightjar is extremely plentiful near Gibraltar. I knew one instance of its occurrence on the 16th of February near Málaga; the earliest date of arrival near Gibraltar was on the 15th of April, the latest date of departure the 5th of October.

Much resembles the last, but larger, with *rufous* nape and more ruddy chin.

Sexes alike, both male and female having white spots on wings and tail. Length nearly 12 inches.

PICIDÆ. Two toes in front, two behind.

Subfamily PICINÆ. Tail-feathers stiff and pointed: nostrils covered with bristles.

154. Dendrocopus major (Linnæus). The Great Spotted Woodpecker.

This Woodpecker is very local, and is always to be seen or heard among the old alder trees in the Soto gordo of the Corkwood of Almoraima. They are found all over that wood, up the valleys (*gargantas*) of the sierras, particularly along that one down which runs the river Palmones. They are common near Ojen, also abundant about Pulverilla on the road between Casas Viejas and Gibraltar. Further than this I never noticed them; nor did I ever see them where oak and alder trees were absent. The local name is *Pito real.* They nest about the 1st of May in holes of decaying trees, and do not appear to be in the slightest degree migratory.

Black and white; scapulars white; *back* and *rump black*; under tail-coverts scarlet; iris red.
Male. Nape scarlet.
Female. No red on head and nape.
Young. Crown of head red. Length 9½ inches.

155. Dendrocopus numidicus, Malherbe. **The Algerian Pied Woodpecker.**

Moorish. Nakab.

"Resident and common in the vicinity of Tangier, being found only in large woods, where they nest in holes of trees, laying from five to six eggs, similar to those of *Picus major.*"—*Favier.*

I did not find this bird "common" near Tangier; and as for the "large woods," there are none close to that town; about Tetuan this Woodpecker is plentiful, similar in habits to *D. major.* Favier states that they migrate across the Straits.

Mr. Hargitt, in his 'Catalogue of Woodpeckers in the British Museum,' vol. xviii., gives the Pied Woodpecker of Morocco as a distinct species, *D. mauritanus,* Brehm, resembling the Algerian *D. numidicus,* except that the black stripes which border the throat and extend to sides of the chest do not form a complete band tipped with scarlet on the chest, as in *D. numidicus*; further that the lateral tail-feathers are more broadly marked with black, and the bill and legs less powerful. Andalucian specimens of *D. major* often have traces of crimson and black crescent on the chest; and until a larger series of specimens are examined, I think *numidicus* and *mauritanus* are only climatic races of *D. major.*

[Dendrocopus medius. **The Middle Spotted Woodpecker.**

This Pied Woodpecker is stated by Arévalo to be resident in

the Province of Granada. At Pótes, near Santander, in 1876, we found this species at a higher elevation than *D. major.*

Both sexes have the crown vermilion, the abdomen and tail-coverts rose-colour. Length 8½ inches.]

156. Gecinus sharpii, Saunders. The South Spanish Green Woodpecker.

Spanish. Pito real.

This Green Woodpecker, in habits, note, and manner of nesting, is exactly similar to the British *G. viridis*; they are abundant in some localities near Seville, particularly in the Cotos and towards Cordova and Granada. I never met with any nearer Gibraltar than the vicinity of Seville, and it is very singular they should not occur in the Cork-wood or in the wooded gargantas or valleys in the vicinity of Gibraltar.

Resembles *G. viridis*, but has the side of the face grey and the red moustache of the male not bordered with black. Length 11½–12½ inches.

157. Gecinus vaillanti (Malherbe). The Algerian Green Woodpecker.

Moorish. Nakâb el tebak (the borer of the wood).

"Resident near Tangier, but not so common as *Picus numidicus*; like the latter avoiding the haunts of men and living in large woods. They nest in holes of trees in April and May, and lay from five to eight shining white eggs. The males assist in incubation."—*Favier.*

We found this Green Woodpecker to be common near Tetuan and in the province of Angera, especially among the short stunted trees which grow in the valleys about Jebel Musa; they are rare near Tangier, the scarcity of trees accounting for their absence; in habits and note they exactly agree with *G. viridis* and *G. sharpii*, but both the latter and the present bird, in my humble opinion, are only climatic or local races of *G. viridis.*

The characters given are:—Face grey, with whitish stripe across from base of upper bill to end of moustache, which is black in both sexes; but I have seen male specimens from Morocco with the moustache red.

Male. Crown and nape red.

Female. Crown grey, striped with black; nape only red. Length 12 inches.

158. Gecinus canus, Gmelin. The Grey-headed Green Woodpecker.

I have never met with this species in Andalucia; but there was a specimen in an Instituto at Seville, stated to have been obtained in the neighbourhood. Lord Lilford records them from the vicinity of Madrid, and Arévalo from Valencia.

The note of this Green Woodpecker is quite distinct from that of *G. viridis*.

Nape and head grey. Below uniform; moustache black in both sexes.

Male. Fore crown red.

Female. Crown grey. Length 8 inches.

Subfamily IYNGINÆ. Nostrils partly covered by a membrane.

159. Iynx torquilla, Linnæus. The Wryneck.

Spanish. Torcecuello, Hormiguéro, Lililo.

"Rather scarce and seen only in pairs near Tangier during passage, crossing the Straits in March and April, returning in August and September, but occasionally observed up to December."—*Favier.*

Mr. Meade-Waldo saw one near Tangier at the end of January, 1892.

On the Spanish side of the Straits the Wryneck is occasionally heard in March, April, and September; probably their line of migration lies further to the east.

General colour greyish brown, vermiculated with blackish; below dull white; throat and breast tinged with buff and crossed with blackish bars. Tail *soft and rounded*, with six blackish bars; the outer feather on each side so extremely short as to give the appearance of only ten feathers. Length 7 inches.

ALCEDINIDÆ.

160. Alcedo ispida, Linnæus. **The Kingfisher.**

Moorish. Kandil el behar (lamp of the sea). *Spanish.* Martin pescadór.

"This bird, only found from August to March, is not numerous near Tangier, but is more abundant near Rabat."—*Favier.*

The Kingfisher is common in winter and spring near Gibraltar, being frequently seen among the rocks on the coast, and often the "inundation" at the North Front; and they have bred near Gibraltar, where the majority arrive in October, leaving in March. Arévalo says they are resident in Spain.

Male. Above greenish blue; middle of back, rump, and upper tail-coverts cobalt-blue; throat and patch on each side of neck white; lores black; rest below rich chesnut; bill black. Length 7½ inches.

Female. Lower mandible reddish at base.

CORACIIDÆ.

161. Coracias garrula, Linnæus. **The Roller.**

Moorish. Sharrakrak. *Spanish.* Carlánco, Carráca.

"This bird is seen in numbers near Tangier on passage, migrating in pairs and crossing the Straits in April and May, returning in August to retire further south. Their food is all kinds of insects, even scorpions."—*Favier.*

The Roller breeds at Larache, nesting in holes of the walls of the ramparts at the end of April. I did not observe any elsewhere in Morocco, except about the ruins of "old Tangier."

In Andalucia they are also very local, and arrive during the latter end of March, leaving by September. I have seen one or two in May near Casas Viejas, one 12th April, 1894, Sierra Retin, while Verner saw one at Pulverilla, August 20, 1878; but they are not common nearer to Gibraltar than the vicinity of Seville. Thence along the valley of the Guadalquivir they abound, nesting in holes of trees, walls, and ruins; they lay about the 14th of April, from four to six shining white eggs.

Back, scapulars, and tertials cinnamon-brown; inner web of end of primaries blackish brown. Neck, throat, breast, and underparts bluish; rest green or purplish green. Length 13 inches.

MEPOPIDÆ.

162. Merops apiaster, Linnæus. The Bee-eater.

Moorish. El Leeamoon. *Spanish.* Abejarúco.

"The Bee-eater is seen on passage near Tangier in great flights, which attract notice from their cry. They arrive and cross over to Europe during March and April, returning in August, many remaining to breed. They nest in May, the eggs varying in shape, being some oval, some oblong."—*Favier.*

This bird did not appear to me to be quite so common in Morocco at the end of April as on the Spanish side of the Straits, where, during April, May, June, and July, it is one of the most conspicuous birds in the country; at that season Andalucia without Bee-eaters would be like London without Sparrows. Everywhere they are to be seen; and their single note, *teerrp*, heard continually repeated, magnifies their number in imagination. Occasionally they venture into the centre of towns when on passage, hovering round the orange-trees and flowers in some patio or garden. Crossing the Straits for the most part in the early part of the day, flight follows flight for hours in succession, always exactly in the same direction, due north. When passing at Gibraltar they sometimes skim low down to settle for a moment on a bush or a tree, but generally go straight on, often almost out of sight; but their cry always betrays their presence in the air.

My dates of their first arrival noticed are:—the 7th of April, 1868; 4th of April, 1869; 1st of April, 1870; 29th of March,

1871; 26th of March, 1872; 28th of March, 1874; 29th of March, 1876 (*Verner*); 28th of March, 1877 (*Verner*); 29th of March, 1894. None were seen on the 30th, many on the 31st of March, 1894; none on the 1st, 2nd, 3rd of April, many on the 6th; some on the 7th, many on 8th and 9th, most on the 10th; numbers on 11th, 12th, 13th, and 14th. They were observed passing in great numbers from the 10th to the 14th of April in three consecutive years, the greatest quantity arriving on the 10th; so, in Spanish fashion, I christened that date "St. Bee-eater's day." The latest flight I ever saw going north was on the 7th of May.

Having remained at Gibraltar once only during July and August, I had but that opportunity of watching the return migration, which appeared during the last week in July and also on the 11th and 12th of August, the last being noticed on the 29th of that month, all with few exceptions being heard passing at night. Verner noticed the return migration at Gibraltar on the 20th of July and on the 18th of August, earliest and latest dates. The first arrivals, as is the case with all migrants, are those which remain to breed in the immediate neighbourhood. Commencing their labours of excavation almost immediately they arrive, the earliest eggs that I know of were taken on the 29th of April; but usually they do not lay till about the second week in May, often not so soon.

In some places they nest in large colonies; in others there are perhaps only two or three holes. When there are no river-banks or barrancos in which to bore holes, they tunnel down into the ground, where the soil is suitable, in a slightly vertical direction, on some elevated mound.

The shafts to these nests are not usually so long as those in banks of rivers, which sometimes reach to a distance of eight or nine feet in all; the end is enlarged into a round sort of chamber, on the bare soil of which the usual four or five shining white eggs are placed; after a little they become discoloured from the castings of the old birds, the nest being, as it were, lined with the wings and undigested parts of bees and wasps. Vast quantities of eggs and young must be annually destroyed by snakes and lizards: the latter are often seen sunning themselves at the entrance of a hole among a colony of Bee-eaters; and frequently have I avenged the birds by treating the yellow reptile to a charge of shot. The bills of Bee-eaters, after boring out their habitations, are sometimes worn away to less than half their usual length; but as newly arrived birds never have these stumpy bills, it is evident that they grow again to their original length. It has often been a source of wonder to me how they have the strength to make these long tunnels; the amount of exertion must be enormous; but when one considers the holes of the Sand-Martin, it is perhaps not so surprising after all.

During my stay at Gibraltar, Bee-eaters decreased very much in the neighbourhood, being continually shot on account of their bright plumage to put in ladies' hats. Owing to this vile fashion, we saw no less than seven hundred skins, all shot at Tangier in the spring of 1874, which were consigned by Olcese to some dealer in London. However, the enormous injury these birds do to the peasants who keep bees, fully merits any amount of punishment; but at the same time they destroy quantities of wasps. After being fired at once or twice, they become very wary and shy at the breeding-places; and the best way to shoot them is to hide near the *colmenares*, or groups of cork bee-hives (*corchos*), which in Spain are placed in rows sometimes to the number of seventy or eighty together; and it is no unusual thing to see as many Bee-eaters wheeling round and swooping down, even seizing the bees at the very entrance of their hives.

The reason of their early departure in August is to be accounted for by the simple fact that bees cease to work when there are no flowers, as by that time all vegetation is scorched up.

Bill long, pointed, slightly curved downwards; iris red. Forehead white next bill, then a bluish tinge; crown rich chestnut; chin and throat rich yellow, bordered below by a black line. Tail green, long; two centre feathers an inch longer than others. Length 10–11 inches.

UPUPIDÆ.

163. Upupa epops, Linnæus. The Hoopoe.

Moorish. Hudhud, Tair ababil, Kubaa deen Nasara (the Christian's Crested Lark). *Spanish.* Abubilla, Gallo de Márzo, Cajonéra, Cagajonéra, Sabubilla.

"Seen in great quantities near Tangier on passage, crossing to Europe during February, March, and April, returning, to retire altogether for the winter, in August, September, and October. In some years the vernal migration is earlier, and they are seen at the end of January. They rarely remain to nest near Tangier. The females have a nearly white throat. The superstitious Jews and Mahometans both believe that the heart and feathers of the Hoopoe are charms against the machinations of evil spirits."—*Favier.*

Hoopoes seldom remain to nest in the vicinity of Gibraltar: Verner, in 1875, found a nest in a hollow tree in the Sierra Retin, which contained four fresh eggs on 31st May, and a few breed about Casas Viejas, and thence northwards, where there are trees; towards Moron and Seville their "hood, hood" may be frequently heard in spring and summer. They begin to lay about the 1st of May, in holes of trees.

My dates of their earliest arrival at Gibraltar are:—the 17th of February, 1870; 18th of February, 1871; 16th of February, 1872; 17th of February, 1894; but on the 11th of January in 1872 I saw a single Hoopoe in the Coto del Rey. Verner first noticed them in 1875 on 17th of February; 1876 on the 18th; in 1879 on the 21st; Mr. Irby, 60th Rifles, on 17th of February, 1892; whilst Capt. Savile Reid informed me of one appearing as early as the 16th of January in 1874. They mostly pass in March, whence their local name *Gallo de Márzo*, March-cock.

Bill long, thin, slightly arched and pointed. Erectile rich buff crest, tipped with black; the hind feathers of the crest with white before the black tips. Tail black, of ten feathers, with broad white bar across the lower part. Length 10-12 inches.

CUCULIDÆ. Tail of ten feathers; two toes in front, two behind.

164. Cuculus canorus, Linnæus. **The Common Cuckoo.**

Moorish. Takouk, Ukouk.   *Spanish.* Cúco.

" More abundant near Tangier than the Great Spotted Cuckoo; seen during passage, in pairs, which cross to Europe in April and May, and return in August to winter, probably, in the interior of Africa. Some remain during summer, awaiting the return of the autumnal migration."—*Favier.*

The Cuckoo is very plentiful near Gibraltar, especially in the Cork-wood and on all hill-sides wherever there are any trees. I saw a great many at the top of the mountains at the back of Algeciras at the end of May, but not beyond the line of trees. First heard on the 7th of April in 1868, on the 22nd of March in 1870, on the 31st of March in 1871, on the 29th of March in 1872, and on the 30th of the same month in 1874; on the 11th of March, 1879 (*Verner*); 24th of March, 1894. They remain till the end of July.

A female shot in the second week in May had then two eggs remaining in the ovaries, nearly ready to lay. Verner found on 25th June, 1879, near Gibraltar, a Cuckoo's egg in a Wood-Warbler's nest.

Male. Above bluish grey; chin and neck ash-grey; below white, barred with black. Tail greyish black, graduated, slightly spotted and tipped with white; iris, eyelids, legs, and feet yellow.

Female. Like male, but usually with slight rufous tinge on breast. Females much less numerous than males.

Young. Upper surface and tail clove-brown, barred with pale brown, feathers tipped with white; white spot on nape; iris brown. Length 14 inches.

165. Coccystes glandarius (Linnæus). The Great Spotted Cuckoo.

Moorish. Teir el Keber (Bird of news) (*Favier*). *Spanish.* Cúco real, Cúco moñon.

"Occurs near Tangier on passage, always in pairs, but not in any great numbers. They cross to Europe in January, February, and March, returning in June, July, August, and September. Their food is entirely caterpillars, both smooth and hairy."—*Favier.*

The Great Spotted Cuckoo arrives in Andalucia much earlier than the Common Cuckoo; and though Favier states that they pass in January, the 25th of February and the 2nd of March are the earliest dates which I have for their arrival, and they mostly appear between the 7th and 28th of March. Verner records one on 8th March and another on 4th April, 1879, both near Gibraltar. The latest I saw was on the 7th of August, in the Alameda at Gibraltar; but they are seldom noticed near there, and pass on to districts further north, where there are Magpies (*Pica rustica*), as they lay in the nests of the latter, and occasionally, it is stated, in those of the Spanish Magpie (*Cyanopicus cooki*). The eggs can be easily distinguished by their elliptical form, those of the Magpie being pointed at one end. They vary a good deal in size and much in the markings, like those of the bird whose nest they use. As far as we yet know, this Cuckoo always places its eggs in nests of the *Corvidæ*. The majority of eggs I have seen, mostly obtained by Ruiz of Seville, came from the vicinity of Cordova; there are a good many in the Coto del Rey. A female killed on the 7th of March had the eggs so far developed as to show that the probable number of eggs she would have laid was four.

The Rev. John White mentions this Cuckoo as having been killed at Gibraltar about 1776.

Adults. Crested. Head and nape bluish grey; rest of upper parts greyish brown; wings, scapulars, and tail (except two centre feathers) tipped with white; underparts white. Sexes alike.

Young. Basal two-thirds of primaries *chestnut*; head blackish brown, without any crest. Length 15-16 inches.

Order **STRIGES**.   Family **STRIGIDÆ**.

166. Strix flammea, Linnæus. **The White or Barn-Owl**.

Moorish. Youka, Tair el mòt (Death-bird), Sehar, Bou tezaz. *Spanish.* Lechuza.

"This Owl, resident near Tangier, is nearly as abundant as the Little Owl, inhabiting ruins and holes in rocks, and nesting twice a year, between April and November. They lay from three to four eggs. The inhabitants of Tangier consider this bird the clairvoyant friend of the Devil. The Jews believe that their cry causes the death of young children; so, in order to prevent this, they pour a vessel of water out into the courtyard every time that they hear the cry of one of these Owls passing over their house. The Arabs believe even more than the Jews; for they think that they can cause all kinds of evil to old as well as to young; but their mode of action is even more simple than that of their antagonists the Jews, as they rest contented with cursing them whenever they hear their cry. Endeavouring to find out from the Mahometans what foundation there is for the evil reputation of this species, I was told this:—'When these birds cry, they are only cursing in their language; but their malediction is harmless unless they know the name of the individual to whom they wish evil, or unless they have the malignity to point out that person when passing him; as the Devil sleeps but little when there is evil work to be done, he would infallibly execute the command of his favourite if one did not, by cursing the Owl by name, thus guard against the power of that enemy who is sworn to do evil to all living beings.'

Having learned the belief of the Mahometans relative to this Owl, it was more difficult to find out exactly that of the Jews, who when questioned by me knew not how to answer, except that the act of pouring out water in the middle of the courtyard is a custom of long standing in order to avert the evil which the Owl is capable of doing; that is to say, the water is poured out with a view of attracting the Evil Spirit's attention to an object which distracts him, and so hides from him the infant which the Owl in its wickedness wishes to show him."—*Favier.*

On the Andalucian side of the Straits the White Owl is common and resident, nesting at Gibraltar in the Moorish Castle.

I must here digress to say a few words in favour of this most useful of birds. Almost exclusively feeding on rats and mice, they deserve every encouragement and support that can be afforded them; but from being in all countries regarded with superstitious awe and dislike, they are more or less persecuted on that account; and in England, through the ignorance and stupidity of gamekeepers, who fancy that they kill game (*i. e.* feathered game), they suffer most severely. This excuse is ridiculous; for the old birds they have not the power to kill, and young pheasants and partridges at the time the Owls are on the feed are safely being brooded by the parent bird.

Those who wish to encourage and increase Owls, and have not hollow trees or buildings where they nest, may always gratify their wishes by fixing an empty barrel (about an 18-gallon size) horizontally in the fork of any large tree, cutting a hole in one end large enough for the birds to enter; but the hoops of the cask should be screwed on, or it will soon fall to pieces. Not only the Barn-Owl, but the Tawny Owl (*Syrnium aluco*) also will use these barrels or "owl-tubs." The difficulty, however, is to keep out Jackdaws; but when once the Owls have established themselves, there is no fear of that intrusion.

In a barrel put up too near another in which was an Owl's

nest, a pair of Stock Doves took possession and reared their young. This same tub afterwards had a hornet's nest in it.

Facial disk complete and large, tuftless; skin covering orifice of ear (*operculum*) large.

Above pale orange-buff, speckled with grey and spotted with black and white; underparts and facial disk white, but these parts vary, the former being sometimes marked with black specks, and both are occasionally of a complete buff colour. Iris black. Toes without feathers, covered with a few bristles; middle claw serrated. Length 14 inches.

167. Asio otus (Linnæus). The Long-eared Owl.

Spanish. Cárabo.

This arboreal Owl is not mentioned by Favier, though Olcese obtained one near Tangier in 1884, where Mr. Meade-Waldo found it the most common Owl, except the Little Owl and Scops, and, as in the Canaries, frequenting rough scrub-covered ground.

I did not meet with any near Gibraltar, but shot one in winter in the Coto del Rey. They are found near Cordova and Granada and breed there.

Facial disk complete; ear-tufts *very long*, equal to hind toe and claw; operculum semicircular; iris orange. General colour orange-buff; above mottled with blackish brown, below streaked and faintly barred with brown. Length 14 inches.

168. Asio accipitrinus (Pallas). The Short-eared Owl.

Moorish. El hama (*Favier*). *Spanish.* Cárabo.

"This species occurs less abundantly than the Cape-Owl (*A. capensis*), being found on passage in small flights on open and wet ground. Some breed near Tangier; but the remainder cross to Europe in February and March, returning in November. This Owl interbreeds with the Cape-Owl, producing hybrids which only differ from that species in having the front of the facial disk, the throat and tarsi whitish, while the irides are *half* yellow. The Arab chasseurs confound the two species under the name of 'el hama'; but they are easily distinguished by the irides, which are yellow in the present species, and hazel in the Cape-Owl."—*Favier*.

The above story about the hybrids is difficult to believe, and is to my mind apocryphal; however, it is given for what it may be worth. I confess I am very sceptical as to the assertions made about the interbreeding of different species in an absolute state of nature, excepting only the Gallinæ; but most hybrids among these are produced under circumstances of acclimatization which can hardly be called a really wild state.

The Short-eared Owl may nest so far south, but, as far as my observations go, is in Andalucia only a winter visitor, and even then not very abundant. I should have omitted this story of Favier's but that it has appeared in print before.

Disk and operculum like last; ear-tufts very short.
Above tawny, each feather with dark brown down the centre; below buff, streaked with blackish brown; iris yellow. Length 14–16½ inches.

169. Asio capensis (Smith). Marsh-Owl.

Moorish. El hama.

"Is a common resident near Tangier, usually frequenting wet swampy ground, feeding chiefly on insects. Some pass over to Europe in March and April, returning in November and December. They nest on the ground in April or May, laying four, rarely five, round white eggs, sometimes marked with a few rusty spots. The young are not always hatched at the same time, as in the same nest may be found young birds of different growths."—*Favier*.

My experiences of this Owl in Spain are very limited, and as follows:—In October 1868, on my first visit to Casas Viejas, when looking for Snipe in one of the wettest parts of the Mill soto, two Owls rose at my feet, which I shot, winging one, which I carried home alive to take to Gibraltar, seeing at once from the bluish-black colour of the irides that I had got an Owl which I did not know. Afterwards hunting about, one more was seen, and killed. On the 10th of November following, during my second visit, I saw three more, two of which I winged and also carried off alive to Gibraltar, keeping them there for some time, till one got out and flew off as if nothing was the matter with it; so I sent the other at once to Lord Lilford, who had it alive till 1870. I met with no more till the 10th of November, 1870, when I shot one and picked up the remains of another. In October and November 1871 I repeatedly and carefully went over the same ground, but did not see any, while friends of mine there in August and September, whom I begged to look out for these Owls, did not come across one. All the eight birds above mentioned were found within a space of about a square mile; and, strange to say, I never saw any elsewhere. In December 1873, Capt. Savile Reid, of the Royal Engineers, shot one when snipe-shooting in the same locality. I was there in March and May in 1874, and, though I hunted all the likely ground over, failed to meet with even one; but they have since been obtained there, notably in the winters of 1882-83 and 1893-94.

General colour above earthy brown, indistinctly vermiculated with rufous. Ear-tufts barely visible. Iris *bluish black*. Length 13-14 inches.

170. Syrnium aluco (Linnæus). The **Tawny, Wood**, or **Brown Owl**.

Moorish. Lū Lūal, Bū-rū-rū, *Spanish*. Cárabo.

"This species is the scarcest of the Owls near Tangier, being met with on passage, crossing to Europe in February, returning in November and December. Some remain to nest in April, laying two eggs, of which often only one is hatched. They live in large thick woods."—*Favier*.

Mr. Meade-Waldo says the Tawny Owls which he saw in Morocco were very grey birds and very large; all specimens which I saw from that country were of the grey race. The Arabic name Bū-rū-rū is delightfully suggestive of their cry.

I never met with or heard one in Andalucia, and it is not

mentioned by Arévalo as an Andalucian bird; but Mr. Stark saw one in April, 1876, near Algeciras, and another was obtained by Mena in winter near Málaga.

Facial disk complete; no tufts; operculum large; toes feathered; iris blackish. Two phases of plumage occur: grey and rufous. Length 18–19 inches.

171. Scops giu (Scopoli). The Scops Owl.

Moorish. Maroof ("the well known"). *Spanish.* Cornéja, Cornéta, Cuquillo.

"Occurs near Tangier on passage, crossing to Europe in March, returning to winter further south in September and October. Many pass the breeding-season in Morocco."—*Favier.*

The Scops Owl is very plentiful, both in Morocco and Andalucia, but is almost entirely migratory. I was much surprised to hear one on the 13th of January, 1872, near the Coto del Rey, and another nearer Seville on the 15th; but from what I afterwards was told at Seville, there is no doubt a few sometimes remain there during the winter; I never observed them during that season at Gibraltar, the earliest date of the vernal migration noticed being the 4th of March, the first nest being on the 4th of May. This Owl always nests in holes of trees, at least I do not know of any instance of their nesting in rocks or ruins, like *Carine noctua*, which breeds by preference in those places.

Abundant in the Cork-wood; the nest is easily discovered by going round and hammering at the old cork-trees with a stick, when, if a Scops Owl flies out, ten to one there is a nest. They are strictly arboreal, and their monotonous single note may be frequently heard repeated at regular intervals by day as well as by night; they even frequent trees in the midst of towns, being often heard in the trees which fringe the Delicias, the drive and Rotten Row of Seville.

They chiefly feed on Coleoptera, and I believe are entirely insectivorous.

Facial disk incomplete above eyes, tufted; no operculum. General colour grey, with minute marks of brown and spots of dark brown. Legs feathered; *toes bare*. Iris yellow. Length 8½-10 inches.

172. Bubo ignavus, T. Forster. **The Eagle-Owl.**

Spanish. Bújo real.

This Owl is not included in Favier's notes on the birds of Tangier, though it is, no doubt, found in the mountainous districts of Morocco; indeed, we heard of a large Owl about Tetuan, but could not obtain a specimen.

They are resident in all rocky localities in Andalucia; and some frequent the "Rock," probably nesting in some of the numerous inaccessible caverns of the east side. One was caught in 1869 in a magazine near the Rock gun; having gone down into the narrow space between the outer and the main wall of the magazine, it was unable to rise. I had this bird alive for some time, and ultimately sent it to Lord Lilford, in whose possession it paired with another from Norway. I also had three young from a nest near Castellar, about eighteen miles from Gibraltar. While keeping these Owls, the wild ones used to come at night close to the cage and answer the call of those that were shut up. Its loud, melancholy, human-sounding note is sometimes to be heard all night long up the Rock, and is usually supposed to be the cry of the apes.

They breed very early: judging from the size of the young which were obtained, they would lay about the end of January; and such, say the cabreros, is the case. I never could succeed in discovering the nest, though I knew of several reputed nesting-places, but on examining them found nothing but bones of rabbits, rats, partridges, and small birds, never even seeing one of the Owls, though the charcoal-burners, *carboneros*, assured me that they had taken the young from these situations. One man, however, said that these Owls bring the young from their nests to these caves. Verner reports that on 1st of April, 1894, he saw an Eagle-Owl fly round a hill where he had seen a pair twenty years before; climbing up he discovered the nest, which was merely a basin-shaped hollow in the dry sand under an overhanging crag: round the nest was a great mass of bones and castings, and half a rabbit, a water-vole, and part of a peewit—not a common bird in those parts in April. The nest, which contained one young bird and an addled egg, was well concealed in the thick tall heather and most difficult to find. There was a second disused nesting-place within twenty yards.

The Rev. John White mentions the Eagle-Owl as occurring at Gibraltar during his residence there about 1776.

Facial disk incomplete above eyes; tufts very large; no operculum. General colour above blackish, mottled with tawny yellow. Toes so thickly feathered that the last joint is hidden. Iris orange-yellow. Length 26-27 inches.

173. Carine noctua (Scopoli). Little Owl.

Moorish. Mouka, Mouéka, Bouma. *Spanish.* Mochuélo.

"Is the commonest species of Owl near Tangier, being both resident and migratory. Those which migrate pass to Europe during March and April, returning in August and September. During passage they are met with in pairs or small flights; at all other times they are found singly or in pairs among large rocks and old buildings."—*Favier.*

The above was written by Favier under the head of *Athene glaux*, or, as he had it, "*Strix noctua meridionalis*"; but as that species has not yet been noticed in Andalucia, and as *C. noctua* is the Little Owl of Tangier, I have no hesitation in referring the above notes to that bird—not that it would have been much loss to have omitted them altogether, the only information of importance being that they migrate.

Near and at Gibraltar this Little Owl is common and resident, nesting, about the end of April, in holes of trees as well as in rocks.

BLACK OR CINEREOUS VULTURE.

Facial disk ill-defined; tuftless; no operculum.
Above greyish brown, spotted with white; below white, much *streaked* with brown; iris yellow; toes *without feathers*, but covered with bristles. Length 7½–8 inches.

174. Carine glaux, Savigny. Southern Little Owl.

This bird, which is only a light-coloured race of the last, does not appear to be met with in the immediate vicinity of Tangier, the only specimens I have seen having been obtained three or four days' journey on the way to Fez. The Little Owl of Tangier is undoubtedly *C. noctua*.

Resembles Little Owl, except is isabelline or pale fawn-colour where dark brown in that bird.

Order ACCIPITRES.   Family VULTURIDÆ.

175. Vultur monachus, Linnæus. The Black or Cinereous Vulture.

Spanish. Buitre négro.

This Vulture is mentioned by Favier as having once occurred near Tangier; and there is a specimen in the Norwich Museum from that locality, perhaps the identical bird. They are probably not so rare in Morocco as Favier implies. On the Spanish side of the Straits they are not often to be seen, and generally alone in winter and early spring.

They are more common near Seville than Gibraltar. Some breed in Andalucia, as I discovered one nest by watching the birds building or, rather, repairing it; for on examination it appeared to be an old nest, probably a Stork's, and was a vast pile of sticks placed on a half-decayed alder tree, about fifteen feet from the ground, in the midst of the thick jungle of the Soto Malabrigo, near Casas Viejas. This place is almost impenetrable, surrounded by open marsh, and is formed of a mass of huge tussocks placed far apart, on which grow wide-spreading sallows and brambles well interlaced. The space between these tussocks is covered with rushes and sedges, growing in mud and water, in places up to the waist. In my first expedition to the nest it took me more than half an hour to reach the tree, a distance of only about a hundred and fifty yards from the edge of this paradise of Water-Rails and aquatic Warblers. Upon climbing the tree it was very difficult to see into the nest, as it so overhung, owing to the great breadth; and, alas! there was no egg, not even any lining.

A few days after, on the 26th of February, I again examined the nest, only to find it lined with wool and a few dried rushes. Muster-day at Gibraltar, on the 28th, compelled our return to the Rock; so I engaged a man to take the nest and bring the egg to Gibraltar, which he never did, probably not liking the journey through the swampy jungle. The following year this nest was not used by any birds; but in 1874 a pair of White-shouldered Eagles took possession, repairing the nest and lining it with fresh green boughs. This was early in March; and with persistent bad luck, on our return there in April, my friend found nothing in the nest, although the Eagles were about; either they had been robbed of their eggs, or else had deserted owing to too frequent examination. Verner took a nest, in the spring of 1875, of the White-shouldered Eagle from this tree, which was subsequently burnt down, and he observed a pair of Black Vultures about the vicinity of the Malabrigo during that and the four following springs. He told me that once he came across a large flock of Griffons feeding on a dead horse, and among these birds was a single Black Vulture, which he watched and noticed was master of the situation and drove away any Griffon that attempted to feed too near.

The Black Vulture is said to nest near Utrera; but upon inquiry I could not ascertain such to be the case; they appear to go further north to breed, as Lord Lilford found them nesting towards Madrid, and in one season received no less than some seventy eggs. More solitary in habits than the Griffon, and unlike that Vulture, they build in trees and not in colonies—laying only one egg, about the beginning of April.

This Vulture is to be recognized when on the wing, within a short distance, by its dark appearance. The immature birds are very dark-coloured, becoming lighter with age, till they attain the adult plumage. The bare skin about the head and neck is of a *pale bluish* colour; nostrils rounded.

Adult. Ruff of brown down. Plumage much lighter than young.
Young. Ruff of lanceolated feathers, general colour blackish brown. Length 42 inches.

176. Gyps fulvus (J. F. Gmelin). Griffon Vulture.

Moorish. Niser. *Spanish.* Buitre, Pajaráco, Buitre franciscáno.

"This Vulture occurs commonly near Tangier, both as a resident and on passage, and is often seen feeding in company with the *Neophron* on the same carcass."—*Favier.*

I did not see many Griffon Vultures in Morocco, but there were a few pair about Jebel Musa in April. Near Gibraltar they are very plentiful, nesting in colonies, not exceeding thirty-five pairs, in holes or, rather, small caves in the perpendicular crags or "lajas," which are found in many of the Sierras; but occasionally a solitary nest will be found some distance from any other, while Mr. A. C. Stark mentions a nest "built on the ground near the top of a hill" in the Tarifa district.

The most important breeding-places near to Gibraltar are the Sierra de San Bartolomé, the Sierra de Plata, and la Laja del Ciscar, all near Taivilla. One egg only is the usual complement; and they lay about the 20th of February. Should the first egg be taken, it seems that they lay again about the 15th of April. Of course it is impossible to prove this; but eggs were laid at that time in nests which had been robbed in February. Stark says that in the neighbourhood of Gibraltar and Tarifa fresh eggs of the Griffon may be obtained, roughly speaking,

148   VULTURIDÆ.

NEST AND EGG OF GRIFFON ON OPEN LEDGE 200 FEET FROM
SUMMIT OF EL CISCAR.

from the 1st of February to the 1st of March, the majority laying between the 10th and 20th of February. Near Málaga they are somewhat earlier, many laying in the latter half of January. The egg is usually white, but is occasionally marked with buff-coloured blotches, the nest consisting sometimes merely of three or four bits of green bush laid on the rock, but being generally lined with green materials, mostly broom, esparto grass, rushes, and one with furze (*Stark*), and the birds, like other Raptores that use green stuff to line their nests, continually renew it.

Verner obtained "fifteen eggs on February the 25th, 1879, six of which he blew, and found two fresh, three slightly, and one much incubated. One of the fifteen was faintly spotted with rufous at the large end; the others were quite white." On 15th of March, 1878, he took "eight eggs, one spotted with rufous at the small end; the others were white: four of the eggs were fresh, four considerably incubated." On the 15th of April he got "two eggs, which contained perfectly-formed embryos, about size of newly-hatched Jackdaws, in which the shape of the bill, feet, and claws of the adult Griffons was clearly discernible." On May 14th, 1875, he got "two almost quite fresh eggs, no doubt laid by birds whose first eggs had been taken. As regards the colour of eggs: when first laid they are pure white, but soon become stained and often covered with mud and blood. Anyone who has seen a party of Griffons on damp soil, churning up the ground with their feet around a carcass, can easily understand the eggs becoming soiled. They are essentially cavern-haunting birds, and whenever possible construct their nests in cavernous situations—occasionally in isolated crags, very rarely on an open ledge, as shown in the illustration on p. 148; but the engraving of the young Griffon in the nest, and that of the cave (p. 150), where two pairs of birds were nesting, better exemplify their usual breeding-places "*.

* The Griffon was found nesting on an oak tree in Slavonia by the late Crown Prince of Austria.

CAVE WITH GRIFFONS' NESTS.

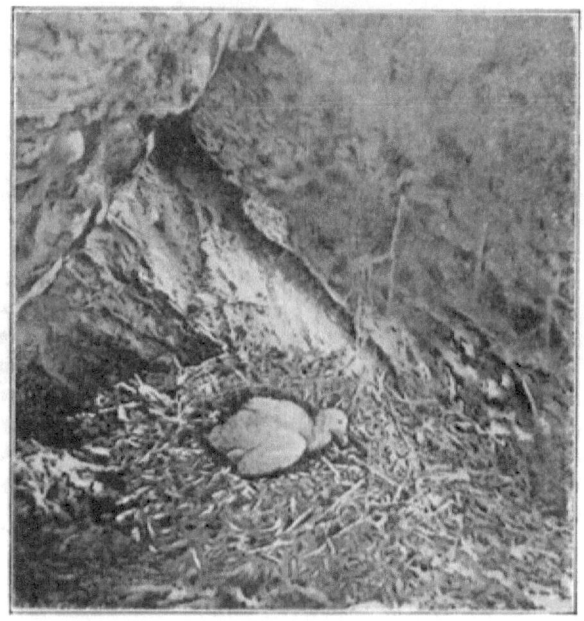

YOUNG GRIFFON IN CAVERN.

Stark also mentions that many castings, about four inches long by one inch in diameter, composed entirely of vegetable matter, such as long grass, fibres, and green leaves of the cork-tree, are to be found near their nests and roosting-places; these materials do not appear to have been "accidentally devoured with the intestines of animals, but are probably plucked and swallowed by the Vultures to cleanse their stomachs, for when freshly ejected they are coated with a tough glairy mucus."

It is a fine sight to see thirty or more of these gigantic birds fly out at once with a rushing noisy flight from their nests, which they do if a shot is fired at the bottom of the cliff in which they breed; and this is the only method of finding the exact position of their nests, as well as those of other rock-nesting birds, though later on each large crevice or hole where there is a nest is plainly visible, owing to the dung which covers the face of the rock below, looking as if a bucket of whitewash had been poured out of the cave. Vultures in Andalucia are far more wary than in other countries in which I have seen them, except, of course, during the breeding-season.

Griffons roost according to the wind, generally about rocks, and near their breeding-places; but we found in the Sierra Retin many roosting on cork-trees on the side of a sheltered valley. Some of these trees were nearly killed by the Vultures' droppings, and the ground all around strewed with their feathers, showing they must have used this situation for many years. Verner informs me that on the opposite side of the great cliffs where they breed on the Ciscar, he has seen as many as eight together taking shelter in one large sandstone cavern on the lee side of the mountain.

How the numbers which inhabit Andalucia at times find sufficient to eat is a puzzle to me; they must be able to fast for some days, or else travel immense distances for their food, as in the winter and spring it is unusual to see dead animals about; but in the hot parching summer months vast quantities of cattle die of thirst and want of pasture. A bull-fight is a sort of harvest to Vultures, which flock in great numbers to revel on the carcases of the unfortunate horses that have been so cruelly killed.

The Griffon Vulture may be distinguished on the wing by its light colour when within reasonable distance.

Nostrils perpendicular, slightly oval. General colour ashy fulvous; head and neck covered with whitish down; ruff of white down. Primaries and tail blackish; iris light yellow.

Young. Much darker; ruff of tawny lanceolate feathers; iris hazel. Length 40 inches.

177. Neophron percnopterus (Linnæus). **Egyptian Vulture.**

Moorish. Rekhama. *Spanish.* Monigéro (near Gibraltar), Relijéro, Alimocha, Pernetéro, Abanto, and, away from the Sierras, Quebrantahuésos.

"Appears near Tangier in flocks during migration, some remaining to nest in the vicinity, awaiting the return of the autumnal migration, to winter probably in the interior of Africa. Those which pass over to Europe cross from February to April, returning in August and September. They nest on rocks in April, generally laying two eggs, sometimes only one. These have a rough surface, and vary in shape. Sometimes there is an interval of two or three days in the hatching of eggs in the same nest. Fifty-four eggs have passed through my hands."—*Favier.*

Near Gibraltar, Neophrons, during their stay, are abundantly distributed. Two pair nest regularly on "the Rock," going by the name of "Rock-Eagle" among those who would call a Buzzard a Bustard, and *vice versâ*. One nest is below O'Hara's Tower, the other below the Rock gun on the North Front.

Many pass northwards at the end of February, the 23rd of that month in 1870, and the same day in 1892, at Tapatanilla, being the earliest dates on which they were observed by me; and the greater number, many hundreds, almost always in pairs, pass during March. On the 21st and 24th of that month, in 1872,

NEST OF NEOPHRON, SHOWING CRAG.

NEST OF NEOPHRON, NEARER VIEW.

great quantities crossed at the same time as flights of Booted
Eagles, Snake-Eagles, Common Buzzards, Red and Black Kites;
Verner noticed numbers passing at Gibraltar on the 25th of
March 1877, 31st of March 1878, and 28th March 1879.

The Neophron usually begins to lay about the 1st of April.

Verner found eggs on the 6th of April, slightly incubated, and
on the 13th of April two quite fresh; he says " the second egg
is always laid some days later than the first one; often the eggs
in same nest vary in depth of colouring, but there is no rule as
to whether the first or second egg has most colouring."

Two eggs seem to be the usual number; the pair are usually
alike, but those from different nests vary very much—some are
almost round, others much elongated; some blackish brown, and
others almost white.

I have known a third egg laid in a nest from which one had
been abstracted, one having been left; but whether the third
egg was laid by the same bird is of course " not proven."

Verner, on the 18th of April, 1879, found Neophrons laying in
an old nest of the Snake-Eagle (*Circaëtus gallicus*), from which I
had, in May 1877, shot an old bird; this nest was on a bough of
a cork-tree, about twenty feet from the ground. He took an egg
on the 18th, and on the 25th a second egg, snaring one of the
old birds, ultimately to liberate it. The Snake-Eagles constructed
a fresh nest close by. This is the only instance which I know
of the Neophron nesting in a tree in Andalucia, but the Indian
Neophrons usually do so.

The nest is often easily accessible from below, and, placed on
a ledge of some overhung rock, generally at the top of a sierra,
is composed of a few dead sticks, always lined with wool, rags,
and rubbish—such as a dog's head, boars' tusks, dead kittens,
foxes' skulls and fur, rotten hedgehogs, dead toads, dead snakes,
skeletons of snakes, lizards, mummified lizards, lizards' heads,
carapaces of the water-tortoise, rotten fish, excrement both of
man and beast, bones, bits of rope and paper. In one nest Verner

found, among a heap of filthy rags, a number of meal-worms. Probably the Neophron had picked up a bag with some flour in it. Naturally from the above-mentioned contents their nests are most offensively odoriferous.

NESTING-PLACE OF NEOPHRON.

Neither Verner nor myself ever knew a Neophron to take a lizard or any animal alive, and we imagine that the heads &c. found in their nests are the remains of those killed by other animals. They are probably among the foulest-feeding birds that live, and are very omnivorous, devouring any animal substance, even all sorts of excrement; nothing comes amiss to them. Sometimes they are seen feeding on the sea-shore on dead fish thrown up by the tide.

Neophrons in Andalucia, like Griffon Vultures, usually roost among rocks; but in March and April, 1894, Verner and myself noticed some twenty collect every afternoon to roost on some cork-trees on the side of a hill facing west. An intelligent cabrero told us this was their usual habit.

I never in the spring saw any Neophrons in the dark immature plumage, so we may infer that in a wild state they get the adult white dress, or nearly so, within eight months from their birth; but in captivity I have known them to take three years to assume the white plumage.

Adults. Whitish, primaries black; fore part of head and neck bare of feathers and yellow.

Young. Dark brown; front of head and neck dirty grey. Length 25 inches.

178. Gypaëtus barbatus (Linnæus). The Bearded Vulture or Lämmergeyer.

Spanish. Quebrantahuésos.

This Vulture is without doubt found on the mountains on the Moorish side of the Straits, as it is recorded from the Atlas ranges; but we did not notice any near Apes' Hill.

On the Spanish side the Bearded Vulture is well known in the sierras and used to nest within a short distance of Algeciraz.

Verner says that "Twenty years ago these birds nested regularly not far from Gibraltar, but owing to persecution have of late years disappeared or retired to less-frequented sierras. The four nests I have climbed to were all in caverns on isolated crags on the rocky sides of the hills, and they appear to prefer such situations to the great cliffs frequented by Griffons. The young do not leave the eyry till June, as the late Crown Prince Rudolf of Austria had on board his yacht a young bird about three-fourths fledged, taken by him about the 18th of May near Granada.

"The *cabreros* or goatherds near Tarifa hold these Vultures, right or wrong, responsible for any missing kids; and owing to this idea, and to their habit of nesting in crags which can often be approached without difficulty to within easy gun-shot, added to the great increase of guns carried lately, their disappearance in the districts near Gibraltar is easily accounted for."

Other causes of their decrease are attributed to poison laid for wolves and, more than all, ornithological collectors. The Griffons have not diminished about the Vega de la Janda, so poison can have done little damage, though in the provinces of Málaga and Granada many Vultures have been poisoned.

NEST OF BEARDED VULTURE.

The name of "Quebrantahuésos" is applied from their well-known habit of taking bones up to a great height and dropping them on the rocks, so as to break the bones small enough to be able to swallow the fragments. These bone-breaking places, which they regularly use on tops of the sierras, are well known to the cabreros, and one which I examined did not appear to differ from any other flat rock. The wedge shaped tail of the Bearded Vulture is very apparent when flying overhead; their flight and habits are those of a Neophron, and the stories of their taking live prey are doubtless erroneous and applicable to Eagles.

The following notes on the Bearded Vulture in Andalucia, as observed by Mr. Stark some ten years ago, have been kindly sent me by Lord Lilford, and are here given almost verbatim, omitting of course the names of localities:—

" In Andalucia is decidedly common in the Sierra Nevada, the Alpujarras, and all the region between Granada and Jaen. In a day's ride five or six may be seen flying over the hill-sides or gliding along the face of a cliff or down some ravine.

" In certain districts of the Sierra Nevada, where the Griffon does not intrude, the *Quebrantahuésos* is especially numerous, and the goatherds and shepherds, who look upon these birds as perfectly harmless as far as live kids and lambs are concerned, seldom molest them. They are therefore far from shy, and may generally be seen hunting round the outskirts of some village or farm, on the look-out for bones, offal, ordure, both of man and beast, or for soft materials to line their nests.

" In the Ronda mountains they are fairly numerous, becoming scarcer towards Gibraltar and Tarifa.

" On the 4th of February, 1876, I found my first nest of the Bearded Vulture in a low cliff in the Sierra Nevada. We had for several days previously seen one or two of the birds flying over the steep hill-side above the village, and, suspecting that they had a nest, watched them carefully and explored many cliffs and rocks without effect. However, on the morning of the 4th, as I was sitting, with an old cazador named Juan, on the edge of a low and broken cliff, not more than sixty feet high, a Bearded Vulture came gliding along below us and suddenly disappeared. Climbing down, we walked along the base of the rocks and finally stood below a narrow horizontal slit in the cliff, not more than fifteen feet above us, and Juan now asserted that the *Quebrantahuésos* had entered this hole. We shouted and threw in stones for some time without result, but at last a larger stone than usual brought out the Vulture. The entrance to the cave being very narrow, the bird, unable to spread her wings at once, fell almost on to our heads as we stood below; then, gathering way, she glided down a steep slope below us, and finally fell dead to a charge of small shot from Juan's rustly old single barrel. The bird proved to be a very large and magnificently-coloured female, measuring 3 feet 8½ inches in length and from wing to wing 8 feet 7 inches. Irides pale straw-colour, sclerotic membrane blood-red; bill bluish-horn; feet lead-colour.

"We then proceeded, with the aid of a rope, to inspect the nest, and found that the hole from which the bird issued led into a small cave, on the floor of which was a good-sized heap of heather-stalks, bits of esparto-rope, sheep's-skin breeches, and an old sandal (*alpargata*); a slight hollow lined with sheep's wool contained two richly orange-coloured eggs: one of these was on the point of hatching, the other addled. Some men were blasting the rocks for lead-ore about two hundred yards off, and goats were being constantly driven along the slope beneath the nest apparently without disturbing the sitting bird. The goatherd assured me that the *Quebrantahuésos* never injured his goats or kids, but was an innocent bird ('pajaro inocénte'), and not like an Eagle.

"On the 17th of January, 1884, I returned to this place and saw a pair of Bearded Vultures sailing along the rocks a few hundred yards from the nesting-place of 1876. On my return to the village my servant told me that he had been watching the *Quebrantahuésos* and had seen a *Cuervo* (Raven) fly out of the rock and drive them off. In the evening the old cazador, Juan, came in and said that there were many *Quebrantahuésos* still about, and that four years ago the Prince of Germany, *i. e.* Crown Prince of Austria, had visited the spot, and he (Juan) had taken the Prince to two nests, from which he shot a pair of old birds and took two young from each nest. The nest of 1876 was examined but found empty.

NEST OF BEARDED VULTURE.

NEST OF BEARDED VULTURE, NEAR VIEW.

"The next morning, January 18th, as we were passing along a mule-track over a pass, we noticed first one and then a second Bearded Vulture fly into a small cave only thirty feet up a cliff facing the road, which is much frequented by muleteers and labourers going to the olive-plantations. From the path below I could distinctly see both birds—one sitting on the nest arranging the lining, the other (the male) standing on the floor of the cave. Later on I saw one of the birds carry a large piece of wool into the nest, holding it, not as an Eagle would do, in its claws, but in its bill. For some time I watched both Vultures beating to and fro over the mountain-slopes. They fly with their beaks and eyes turned towards the ground, after the manner of Terns. The male, when on the wing, is conspicuously smaller than his mate.

"On the 19th I sent Francisco, a professional hunter of wild bees' nests and a splendid rock-climber, into the nest; he reported that it was lined with clean sheep's-wool, but had as yet no eggs. While Francisco was in the nest, the female bird watched him from an adjacent crag, but no sooner had he reached the valley below than she returned and stayed in the nest for a few minutes. On the 20th we went to look at some Bearded Vultures' nests of last year: one was only six feet below the brow of a cliff, and was, as usual, built in a small cave, being a small flattened mass of dead sticks lined with pieces of esparto-rope, and contained, as in the nest of 1876, an alpargata in the lining. Not far off was a nest of the Golden Eagle (*Aquila chrysaëtus*), a vast pile of sticks on an open ledge of the cliff.

"On the 21st we went to look at a nest about a league off, which turned out to be occupied by Golden Eagles; but Juan assured me that, although a pair of Eagles had nested in it in 1880, the year of the Prince's visit, *Quebrantahuésos* had bred in it the year before. Francisco went into the nest and found it empty; he had just come up, and we were talking to a goatherd, whose flock of goats, sheep, kids, and lambs were feeding about the rocks below, when suddenly a large bird appeared round a corner of the cliff, followed closely by two others. '*Quebranta-huésos!*' called out Juan; but I saw at once that they were Golden Eagles, and so did the goatherd, who shouted, with an oath, 'Son aquilas negras!' and ran down to his flocks, making all the noise he could to scare the Eagles away, who passed us within easy shot, going down the ravine, and then doubled back as if intent on a kid or a lamb. Two of these Eagles were fully adult, the other had white on the base of the tail, probably the young of the preceding year. I was struck with their laboured flapping flight, compared with the easy gliding, and apparently effortless, motions of the Bearded Vulture.

"On the 30th we went to inspect the nest of the 18th, and from the valley below the rocks I could, with my glasses, see the tail and ends of wings of the old bird as she sat on the nest, but could not see her head, which was directed to the back of the cave. We then inspected two old nests—one was in a hole in detached stacks of sandstone rock, the other, in a round hole in a low cleft very easy of access, was one of the nests harried by 'El Principe.'

"On the 31st Francisco arrived with ropes, and while Juan and he were laying down the rope I seated myself on a projecting rock level with the cave and about thirty yards from it. From this I could look into the hole and see part of the nest and the bill of the sitting bird. On a steep slope of débris fallen from the cliff above, and which reached to within ten yards from the cave, a large flock of goats, attended by a boy, were pasturing. The noise made by the goats or the cries of the goatherd attracted the attention of the Vulture, who occasionally stretched her head out of the cave to see what was going on below, but she did not appear to be the least alarmed; presently some stones, displaced by the rope above, came whistling down, and the bird, looking out again, caught sight of me for the first time. She hesitated for a moment, then launched heavily out of the nest, and, after one or two heavy flaps, sailed steadily away round an angle of the cliff;

as she passed close by me I could see every feather and the hairs in her beard. In a few seconds she reappeared, and as long as we remained continued sailing overhead watching our movements. Francisco now found his way into the nest from above, and called out that there were two eggs; these he lowered to me in a bag, and they proved perfectly fresh and of a uniform dull yellow-ochre colour, the colouring looking as if it had been carelessly laid on with a brush. This season 1884 was, on the sierra, very mild, the snow-line fully 1000 feet higher up than in 1876, a severe spring, when the Bearded Vultures were about to hatch their eggs on the 4th of February, so that the weather apparently does not influence their time of laying. These nests were at an estimated altitude of 4500 feet.

"In the lower ranges of the Sierra de Rónda, towards Gibraltar and Tarifa, the Bearded Vulture is not very common; the Griffon being, on the contrary, abundant in that district. The majority of the Bearded Vultures seen here have been birds in dark plumage, not fully adult.

"I have never seen the Bearded Vulture attempt to catch any living creature. Juan, the cazador, told me that they sometimes took rabbits and partridges; but the goatherds, whom I questioned on the subject, asserted that they only feed on carrion and dung, and I have watched them walking about among the female goats, apparently picking up the placentæ and droppings of goats, but never molesting either the mother or the kids.

"In food, nest, and nesting-place the Lämmergeyer is simply a big Neophron."

Description. See Plate (frontispiece).

FALCONIDÆ.

179. **Circus æruginosus** (Linnæus). **The Marsh-Harrier.**
Moorish. Hedia (*Favier*). *Spanish.* Aguilucho, Rapiña.
"The most common of the Harriers in Morocco, this bird is

both resident and migratory in the vicinity of Tangier. Those which migrate, pass to Europe in February and March, returning in September and October. They commence to breed late in March. Their eggs differ very much in shape, being sometimes round, sometimes elongated."—*Favier*.

In Andalucia, as in Morocco, over all low wet ground, the Marsh-Harrier is to be seen in vast numbers, particularly in winter. Great quantities remain to breed, sometimes as many as twenty nests being within three hundred yards of one another. The latter, loosely constructed with dead sedges, vary much in size and depth, and are usually placed amidst rushes in swamps, but sometimes on the ground among brambles and low brushwood, always near water, though occasionally far from marshes. They begin to lay about the end of March, and at that season fly up to a great height, playing about, and continually uttering their wailing cry. The eggs are bluish white, and usually four or five in number; they certainly vary in size and shape, and are often much stained. Like the eggs of all the Harriers that I am acquainted with, and many others of the Accipitres, when blown and held up to the light they show a bluish tinge. On the same day I found a nest containing only one egg, nearly ready to hatch, and another with six eggs (three quite fresh and the other three hard sat-on). I believe that, if the first set of eggs be taken they lay again in a fresh nest, as we found sets of fresh eggs as late as the 2nd of May.

Verner says: "Many nests are built on old Coots' and Purple Herons' nests among reeds eight or ten feet high, and in three feet of water. Irregular in time of laying, I found in 1875, on May 7, nest with two fresh eggs; on May 10, nest with three hard-set eggs; in 1879, on May 7, five fresh eggs, and another nest close by with four young whose quill-feathers were shooting out."

The Marsh-Harrier is a perfect pest to the sportsman, as, slowly hunting along in front, they put up every snipe and duck that lie in their course, making them unsettled and wild. I have repeatedly seen them flush Little Bustards; but these merely flew fifty yards to the right or left out of the Harriers' line of flight, and settled down again.

Cowardly and ignoble, they are the terror of all the poultry which are in their districts, continually carrying off chickens, and, like other Harriers, are most terribly destructive to the eggs and young of all birds.

On account of these propensities, I never let off a Marsh-Harrier unless it spoiled sport to fire at one. Sometimes, when at Casas Viejas and the snipe were scarce, to pass away the time, we used to lie up in the line of the Harriers' flight to their roosting-places; for they always take the same course, and come evening after evening within five minutes of the same time. Upon one occasion a friend and myself killed eleven, and during that visit accounted for over twenty. We also upon every possible opportunity destroyed the nest and shot the old ones; but it was the labour of Sisyphus, for others immediately appeared. However, there was a visible diminution of their numbers about Casas Viejas. We never found rats in their nests or crops, and believe they have not the courage to kill them: small snakes, frogs, wounded birds, eggs, and nestlings form the main part of their prey. I have seen the Marsh-Harrier hawking over the sea about two hundred yards from the shore, where there was shallow water, but could not discover what they were taking.

I do not know whether it is always the case with the Harriers, but, as far as my observation goes with regard to the Marsh-Harrier, it seems that the males do not sit, as I have shot, and seen shot, many from the nest, but never saw a male killed flying off the eggs, and have noticed that the males only leave the nesting-places to hunt for prey. I have also observed the same fact with Montagu's Harrier.

The very old males have the wings and tail ash-grey; when flying in the sun, these parts appear almost white.

Outer web of fifth primary notched; tail uniform above.

Adult male. Head creamy white, streaked with blackish brown; wing-coverts, secondaries, tertials, and tail ash-grey.

Female. Head buffish or creamy white, streaked with blackish brown; creamy-white margin on shoulders of wings. General colour dark brown; below chocolate-brown; tail brown.

Young of the year. Dark brown; head chocolate-brown. In the next plumage the head, chin, and throat vary from rufous to creamy white, more or less streaked with blackish brown; but in first plumage some are said occasionally to have the head creamy white; irides blackish. Length 21-23 inches.

180. Circus cyaneus (Linnæus). The Hen-Harrier.

Moorish. Bou hasân (Father of beauty). *Spanish.* Cenizo, Ave de San Martin.

According to Favier this "is the least common of the Harriers near Tangier, being seldom met with."

On the Spanish side of the Straits, though a resident bird, the Hen-Harrier is most frequently seen in winter; but their numbers fluctuate greatly. We observed more in the winter of 1871-72 than at any other time, particularly about Casas Viejas, seldom, however, coming across an old male.

Outer web of fifth primary notched.

Adult male. Pale slate-grey above; throat and *chest bluish ash*; upper tail-coverts and underparts below centre of breast white.

Female. Above brown; hind neck streaked with whitish; below whitish brown; breast streaked with dark brown; tail brown, with five bands of darker brown.

Young. Like female, but marked with rufous on back; and the bars on the tail are rufous. Length 21½ inches.

181. Circus swainsoni, Smith. The Pale-chested Harrier.

Favier states that this species occurs on passage in the environs of Tangier in April. In the Norwich Museum there is a specimen labelled "Tangier."

On the Spanish side it is not uncommon in spring, and doubtless breeds near Seville, where Lord Lilford was the first to obtain it in 1872.

Outer web of fifth primary notched; upper tail-coverts white, banded or spotted with ashy grey.

Adult male. Above pale slate-grey; *chest white.*

Female. Much as female of Montagu's Harrier, except the grey spots on upper tail-coverts. Length 17-20 inches.

182. Circus cineraceus (Montagu). Montagu's Harrier.

Spanish. Cenizo.

"This Harrier passes to Europe in March and April; but some remain to breed near Tangier, where they are nearly as common as the Marsh-Harrier, being seen during passage on all sides in pairs. They nest on the ground, laying five eggs, which vary much in shape, the colour being bluish white, marked with spots of clear blue, which, after the egg is blown, turn yellowish."—*Favier.*

Near Lixus, in Morocco, at the end of April, we found a regular colony: there must have been fifteen or twenty pair on a marsh across the river. We had no time to go round and examine the ground, and could not cross the river at that place; but we could see with my telescope the hen birds sitting dotted about the marsh. The males took a particular line across our side of the river; so I shot three for identification.

In the vicinity of Gibraltar this migratory Harrier is not often met with, except on passage; I did not observe them in winter. Near Seville they are very common, and dark specimens, some of them complete melanisms, are frequently procured.

Like other Harriers, they are terrible egg-destroyers, but otherwise harmless. They can be easily recognized by their smaller size, lighter and more Owl-like flight, their wings being longer in proportion than other European Harriers.

Outer web of *fifth* primary entire. Notch on inner web of the first and outer web of the second primary an inch beyond the tip of the primary-coverts.

Adult male. Above bluish grey; throat and chest ashy grey. Axillaries, flanks, belly, and thighs white, with rufous streaks. One *black band* across secondaries visible when wings are closed.

Female. Above brown; below buffy white, striped with russet.
Young. General colour dark chocolate-brown, lightest below. Length 18-19 inches.

183. Melierax polyzonus (Rüppell). The Many-banded Hawk.

Obtained by Mr. Drake at Mogador ('Ibis,' 1869, p. 153). The Zoological Gardens also had one living a short time back, which came direct from Morocco, and Lord Lilford received one from Mogador.

Above slaty blue. Cere and legs vermilion. Upper tail-coverts white, barred with slaty grey. Length 21 inches.

184. Buteo vulgaris, Leach. The Common Buzzard.

Moorish. Kesir Eknah (*Favier*). *Spanish.* Arpélla.

According to Favier, the Common Buzzard is seen in flights on passage in March and April, like the Black Kite. I have seen them myself crossing the Straits on the 11th, 15th, and 24th of March.

On the Spanish side they are very abundant from November to the end of February. We never detected any remaining to breed near Gibraltar; but from a nest in a pine-tree, containing two eggs, I shot one on the 29th of April near Seville.

In the Cork-wood of Almoraima there are certain high trees which are the favourite resting-places of Buzzards. These trees are always chosen to command a good look-out, and are used winter after winter in succession; if one bird is shot, another takes its place. They are too lazy to annoy the sportsman; so, except now and then killing one for identification's sake, I never molested them. I once observed a Buzzard feeding on the carcass of a donkey, in company with some Griffon Vultures.

This species is one of the most useful of birds, destroying vast numbers of rats, mice, voles, and moles; occasionally they take small rabbits; they seize their prey on the ground, watching for it from a tree or rock. In one locality in England they almost entirely subsist on earthworms. Yet this valuable vermin-killing bird has been in the British Isles nearly extirpated by foolish and ignorant game-preservers.

Varies so much in plumage as to defy description. Legs and toes short, and bare of feathers; legs about 3 inches long.

Very old birds are sometimes very dark bluish black above, and only slightly marked with light markings on breast.

Adults. Tail brown, barred with twelve or thirteen bands of darker brown.

Young. Upper breast white, with only a few spots; throat brown, with narrow white streaks; tail ashy brown, crossed with ten bars of darker brown. Length 20-23 inches.

185. Buteo desertorum (Daudin). Rufous Buzzard.

Moorish. Khabbas (great hunter, mighty sportsman).

"Resident near Tangier, and found in considerable numbers on all sides. Their food consists of rats, mice, snakes, frogs, large insects, leverets, rabbits, and chickens. They nest on rocks, laying two eggs (in March and April) of a white or greenish-white colour, spotted with yellowish or reddish brown; sometimes these spots completely cover the thick end of the egg. The males sit in their turn. The irides are yellow; the third and fourth quill-feathers, equal in length, are the longest in the wing. Twenty-four eggs of this Buzzard have passed through my hands."—*Favier.*

This red-coloured Buzzard is, as above stated, common in Morocco. On the 26th of April, 1871, we found a nest on the top of a very tall olive-tree in a santo or burial-ground in Garbia, shooting both the old birds, one off the nest, which was like a Kite's and lined with fresh olive-twigs and rags. It contained two eggs on the point of hatching; they were of a white colour, thinly marked all over with very small, short, reddish-black lines, and were more rounded than average eggs of either of the Kites, though I have seen eggs of both Red and Black Kite very like them.

In this santo, perhaps two acres in extent, were some of the tallest wild olive-trees I have ever seen, on which were, besides the Buzzard's nest, one of the Common Kite, with young, two of the Black Kite; and in a bramble-brake at the edge was a nest of Marsh-Harriers, with young. The day before, we took Black-Kite's eggs quite fresh, which shows the relative time of nesting of the above-named species.

We always saw this Buzzard in wooded districts, like our Common Buzzard, generally sitting on the bough of some dead tree; and this makes me wonder that Favier did not mention them as nesting on trees as well as rocks.

On the Spanish side of the Straits I never met with any; nor have I seen a specimen which could be referred to this species, but Arévalo mentions an adult female which was killed near Málaga on the 5th of February, 1873. Slightly smaller in size, the adults might be recognized within a hundred yards or so by their reddish colour; but the immature birds, dead or alive, could not be distinguished, except possibly by size, from those of the Common Buzzard.

Adults. Breast, thighs, upper tail-coverts, and tail rufous.
Young. Not to be distinguished from those of *B. vulgaris.* Length 20–21 inches.

186. Aquila chrysaëtus (Linnæus). The Golden Eagle.

Moorish. Ogab. *Spanish.* Aguila negra.

"Is found on passage near Tangier, passing north in January and February, returning in July and August. Some remain to nest on rocks in March and April."—*Favier.*

We found in April a nest of an Eagle, apparently of this species, on a very high cliff near Jebel Musa, opposite Gibraltar; but being unable to obtain the bird, we left the nest untouched.

On the Andalucian side, the Golden Eagle is found in the sierras, but is not common near Gibraltar, and fast decreasing; one pair used to nest at San Bartolomé. They no doubt take

GOLDEN EAGLE.

kids and lambs, and probably this crime is erroneously attributed to the Lämmergeyer. Towards Granada and Alora these Eagles are much more common, and we saw them close to Lanjaron, in April 1877.

Legs feathered in front to the toes, the last joints of which only are covered by *three large scales (Aquila)*. General colour dark brown; nape and hind neck light brown; thighs uniform dark brown; tail with one greyish bar on under surface. Length 32–36 inches.

Young. Basal half of tail *white*; base of body-feathers white. See Plate.

187. Aquila adalberti, R. Brehm. White-shouldered Eagle.

Spanish. Aguila réal.

The White-shouldered Eagle is stated by Favier to be rare near Tangier. He calls it *Aquila imperialis*, and gives a local name ("Larnaj") describing an adult bird. I have examined Moorish specimens in immature plumage, and seen what I considered to be this Eagle on the wing.

In wooded districts in the west of Andalucia this Eagle is universally distributed, being most abundant in the Cotos towards Seville and about Cordova, not unfrequently occurring near Gibraltar. A tree-nesting Eagle; the old bird sits very close, but not more so than some other Raptores. Three eggs is the usual complement; and these are generally laid during the first fortnight in March, being usually white; they are sometimes much spotted with reddish brown, and vary much in shape and size. One nest was lined with horse-dung as well as green twigs. In the winter they mostly roost close to their nesting-places. Since I first met with this Eagle in 1869, I find now, in 1894, that their numbers are much reduced, chiefly by or owing to collectors.

In a nest built in a pine-tree near Vejer, Mr. Stark informed me that he found seven rabbits, three partridges, and a stilt, all fresh. The two young birds in nest were both dead, apparently killed by a swarm of ants which inhabited a dead bough of the tree on which the nest was placed.

NEST OF WHITE-SHOULDERED EAGLE (March 28th, 1894).

Mr. Stark, in 1876, found that they breed in immature plumage; but this is not unknown with other Raptores.

Verner writes that "this Eagle was not uncommon in the Cork-woods about twenty years ago, but they have now, from persecution, retired to the more unfrequented parts of the country, and are to be found where there are any cork-trees big enough for their nests, which usually are lined with fresh green boughs of the ilex; but nests found in 1875 and 1877 were lined with goat's-hair and lamb's-wool, which I take to be exceptional cases. The White-shouldered Eagle nests with great regularity, laying three eggs by about the 8th of March, and this number seems to be the regular complement.

"It is interesting to notice that the habit of nearly all rock-nesting Eagles having two situations for their nests, never far

WHITE-SHOULDERED EAGLE.

apart, and which they occupy usually every alternate year, is also regularly followed by this tree-nesting species. In every instance in which I have found a nest there has been a second in a tree within a few hundred yards of the first one. The Snake-Eagle has the same habit, so much so that on finding an unoccupied nest, one has only to search the vicinity for a second one, and usually with success."

When sitting on trees or rocks, the white shoulders of this Eagle are very conspicuous.

The old birds are easily recognized on the wing from their very dark appearance. The immature are less easy to distinguish; for a long time some of them were thought to be specimens of *A. rapax*; and I remember being considered a heretic in ornithological matters for saying they were young White-shouldered Eagles.

The adults are very dark brown on the body and wings, except for the white patches on the latter, whence its name. The immature birds are at first of a uniform reddish brown, which becomes gradually lighter. They take, in captivity, three years to show any white in the wing.

Adult. See Plate.

Immature. General colour light brown; breast *uniform*. Length 31-33 inches.

188. Aquila nævia (J. F. Gmelin). The Spotted Eagle*.

The Spotted Eagle does not appear to have been obtained by Favier in Morocco. The only two specimens which I have seen from Andalucia were both from near Seville—one in spotted plumage (the same mentioned by Lord Lilford and Mr. Saunders in 'The Ibis'), and an adult male, killed on the 12th of November, 1870, and now in Lord Lilford's collection.

General colour dark reddish brown. Tail nearly uniform brown above.

Young. Wing-coverts and scapulars with large oval tips of white or brownish white. Length 26 inches.

---

* This term "spotted" is misleading, as only the immature birds are so marked.

189. Aquila rapax, Temminck. **Tawny Eagle.**

This Eagle is included in Favier's list. I never saw but one Spanish specimen, which, obtained near Málaga in winter of 1877, is in Lord Lilford's collection, and was of the light stone-coloured plumage (young?) figured as *Falco belisarius*, Levaillant, jun., Exp. Sci. Algér., Oiseaux, pl. 2 (1850).

Little seems to be known of the plumage of this African Eagle, which is much smaller than *A. adalberti*, the immature birds of which species were long supposed to be Tawny Eagles.

The adult tawny birds are known to pair with the light-coloured ones.

General colour from rich reddish brown to light stone-colour. Length 26-30 inches.

190. Haliaëtus albicilla (Linnæus). **The White-tailed or Sea-Eagle.**

Recorded as having been obtained near Cadiz, and Lord Lilford says it was apparently known to the country-people on the Lower Guadalquivir.

Lower half of leg bare of feathers; that and the toes covered in front with large scales.

Adult. Bill and iris light yellow; head and neck much lighter than back; tail *white.*

Young. Bill blackish; iris brown; tail whitish, much mottled with greyish brown. Length 28-34 inches.

191. Nisaëtus fasciatus (Vieillot). **Bonelli's Eagle.**

Moorish. Teir Thum (*Favier*). *Spanish.* Aguila perdicéra, Aguila de las rocas.

"This, the most common Eagle near Tangier, is resident there, though some migrate north in February, and return in July. They are seen alone or in pairs hunting over a wide extent, feeding chiefly on hares and rabbits; they nest on rocks and high trees, laying in March one or two eggs, never more, of a rather round shape, rough and white in colour, with sometimes

DESCENT TO NEST OF BONELLI'S EAGLE.

green and bluish stains. On the 29th April, 1867, I took a nest containing one young female, which was able to fly on the 1st of July and was very savage.

"They are so voracious and plucky that I have known two instances in which they allowed themselves to be caught rather than give up their prey: one was taken by a Moor throwing his burnouse over the Eagle, which had struck down a tame pigeon; the other driving a fowl into some brambles, was caught before it would quit its prey."—*Favier*.

Bonelli's Eagle is found generally distributed as a resident in all of the mountain-ranges of Andalucia. I know of the sites of many nests, but, not wishing to make them public for the benefit of dealers, refrain from mentioning the exact localities, merely observing that only one couple appears ever to breed in the same range of cliffs, each pair holding its own district. A pair nest annually at Gibraltar, at the "back of the Rock," to the south of the signal-station; there are never more than a pair, though there are four situations where there are nests, one of which has not been used for several years. The nests are built of sticks, and placed on small ledges of the steep rock, with one exception well open to observation from the signal-station, where I used to spend many an hour watching the old birds and their habits. For some years they used two of the nests alternately year about; and this is said to be a common habit of both this bird and the Golden Eagle. The sergeant in charge of the signal-station, and the signalmen, one of whom had been there eight years, all agreed that they never knew two nests in one season, or saw more than one pair of old birds. Lord Lilford asked me to try and obtain the eggs for him; so in 1870 I made arrangements, by aid of the "almighty dollar," with some men who had been goatherds at Catalan Bay, to endeavour to secure the prize. They laid ropes down from the top to a bush-covered ledge, which was about two hundred feet above the nest; thence one man lowered himself; but unfortunately the nest was so overhung that, though he could nearly touch the eggs, he could not take them, so was obliged to reascend unsuccessful. The next day we arranged with improved gear to renew the attempt; but a very officious official kindly reported me to the authorities as disobeying an ancient garrison order which prohibits animals and birds on the Rock from being destroyed; so I had to eat "humble pie" and give the affair up as a bad business. The

LAJA DE LA ZARGA, NESTING-PLACE OF BONELLI'S EAGLE AND GRIFFONS.

following notes as to the time of nesting may be interesting. Sergeant Munro, of the Royal Artillery, in charge of the signal-station, assisted me with two or three of the dates during my absence from the Rock.

In 1869 the Eagles nested on the lower site, about 300 feet from the base of the Rock, which here ends on the steep sand slope south of the village of Catalan Bay.

In 1870 they used the upper nest, and two eggs were laid;

INTERIOR OF CAVERN WITH NEST OF BONELLI'S EAGLE

the birds were sitting on the 20th of February; only one was hatched.

In 1871 the nest of 1869 was repaired, the birds beginning to renew it about Christmas 1870; two eggs were laid by the 6th of February, both of which proved fertile.

In 1872 the upper nest, that of 1870, was the favoured one: the repairs began on the 20th of December, 1871; the first of the two eggs laid was deposited on the 5th of February. On the 16th of March both were hatched, making forty days occupied in incubation. Both birds sometimes sat at the same time; but usually they relieved one another. They continually turned the eggs over with their bills; and sometimes, when taken, the eggs bear marks of this in the shape of scratches. The upper part of these nests was always entirely rebuilt with fresh green olive-boughs, lined with smaller twigs of the same. Some of the boughs accidentally dropped were afterwards picked up at the foot of the Rock, gnawed through as if by rats. It must have cost the Eagles some time and trouble to procure them, as olive is very hard and tough.

In 1873 I was not at Gibraltar; but on my return in 1874, on the 24th of February, it appeared that they had built in a fresh situation near the other sites, and that two unspotted bluish-white eggs, rather smaller than the usual type, had been taken the day previously by the aid of the same men whom I had employed in 1870. This nest was hid from view of the signal-station by a projection of the rock, and was easily obtained, the cliff there being less than half the height of that where the nest of 1870 is placed. In company with the officers who obtained these eggs, we took another nest of Bonelli's Eagle at some distance from Gibraltar. It was on some rocks where the previous spring they had had the good fortune to take two eggs. We found the nest built in a different situation, easily obtained by the aid of a rope, and very neatly built and lined with twigs and leaves of the cork-tree; it contained two splendid eggs, beautifully marked with red streaks and spots, similar to those taken in 1873, and doubtless laid by the same bird. I was informed that the latter nest was lined with leaves of the asphodel, and that the spoilers literally walked into the nest. I saw the situation myself; and it was certainly the easiest to reach that I know of, as they usually build on the face of steep cliffs.

A nest found in 1874 contained only one egg, which was addled; but curiously enough the bird was sitting hard on this rotten egg, and I succeeded in shooting the female. This nest was in a hole, and only about 50 feet from the base of the steep cliff in which it was placed, and was lined with twigs and leaves of butcher's broom (*Ruscus hypophyllum*). Not having enough rope to lower to the bottom of the rock, we had much trouble in getting the egg; however, we sent for more rope and lowered it down from above, tying a sack full of stones to the end to prevent it lodging in the rock; but after securing the object of our labours from below, we discovered that the rope, of which there was over 400 feet, had become fixed in the rock about halfway up, and no power would move it. The idiotic Spaniard whom we had left at the top, when he found that he could not pull it up, flung it down without tying a stone to the end; so it caught in several places; and by way of finishing he came down to where we were sitting, and, after pulling violently at the lower end, suddenly let go, when of course the rope flew up and lodged in the rock out of reach; so we had to leave it dangling about the cliff as a memorial or, rather, as a Spaniard remarked, " *un señal de los locos Ingleses.*"

The usual number of eggs of Bonelli's Eagle is two, and but rarely one; the colour is generally white, and I have only seen a few marked with red and buff spots and streaks.

At Gibraltar, Bonelli's Eagle may be often seen suspended, as it were, in the air, head to wind, apparently immovable, like an artificial kite, for sometimes nearly two minutes. At this time, when watched through a glass, no movement of the wings can be noticed beyond an almost imperceptible quivering; but the legs and feet are continually shifted as if used to balance the bird. When not breeding, they hunt together, one high above the other, suddenly stooping down on some luckless rabbit or else gliding off to take up a fresh aerial station whence to watch for their prey, which seems to be always taken on the ground. They feed chiefly on rabbits, but have taken poultry away from the signal-station; and Sergeant Munro informs me that one of the Eagles once struck at and seized his cat, but let it go after cutting its back open and drawing blood.

At Gibraltar, in February, I watched two Ravens for a long time bullying one of these Eagles, which now and then made a futile dash at his tormentors, but at last turned tail, leaving the Ravens masters of the situation. On another occasion, in the same month, I saw a Bonelli's Eagle flying about not far from the Osprey's nest, when down swooped an Osprey, like a stone, striking the Eagle on the back and knocking out a lot of feathers. Shrieking out, they were bound together for a few seconds, and then separated, neither apparently the worse for the encounter, and each flying off towards their respective eyries. They were so close as to be within easy shot when they "collided." A young bird about a month old was bought from a Moor at Tangier, and sent to me on the 18th of April; but it was so wild and savage that I thought it would kill itself, and all that I have since seen alive have been equally so.

The fully adult birds have a white patch on the back between the wings; and when viewed from above this mark is very apparent and will at once identify the species; when below them the white appearance of the underparts and their very powerful gliding flight distinguish them. To a novice they mostly resemble the Osprey when on the wing; but the latter has a more flapping flight and shows its whitish head.

The tarsus, feathered to the feet, is very long for the size of the bird, the thigh being still longer in proportion.

Adult. Above brown; feathers of mantle showing a whitish patch, owing to only the tips of the feathers being coloured; below white, streaked with black; irides golden yellow.

Immature. Fulvous brown.

Length 26–29 inches, tarsus 4½. From tip to tip of extended wings a female measured exactly 5 feet.

192. Nisaëtus pennatus (Gmelin). The Booted Eagle.

Moorish. Ta-ferma (*Favier*).

"This Eagle is migratory, crossing to Europe in March and April, returning in September; some remain to breed in the vicinity of Tangier to go south for the winter with the return migration, and they are abundant when on passage. They nest on high trees in April and May, laying from one to three white eggs, often much stained and with a rough surface."—*Favier.*

On the Spanish side this, the smallest of the European Eagles, is, about Gibraltar, entirely migratory. Many were noticed crossing on the 24th of March. They frequent wooded districts, and the most plentiful of the birds of prey in the Cork-wood during the summer, when their wailing cry may be heard all day long. The nests there were, without exception, on oak-trees, sometimes completely hidden in ivy. In the Cotos near Seville they generally built in pine-trees. The same nest is used year after year; if the old birds be shot, next season another pair take possession to repair and reline it with fresh green twigs of the oak. Two is the usual number of eggs; I have known three, but frequently only one; their general colour is pale bluish white, sometimes stained or spotted with faint buff marks. The earliest taken was on the 12th of April; but about ten days later is the best time to get them. This Eagle when put off the nest, instead of flying straight away, stoops down till it nearly touches the ground, and then flies away gradually rising.

Verner writes:—"This Eagle varies somewhat in its time of

nesting. On May 25, 1877, I took an egg from a nest, replacing it with a hen's egg; the next day a second egg was laid.

"On June 27th, 1879, I found a nest with a young bird about three days old, and an addled egg; on visiting this nest on 17th July the eaglet was only just shooting its quill-feathers. On July 1st I found another nest with two fully-fledged young, and on the 14th another with one fully-grown young. Most eggs that I have seen were stained with blood; indeed, it is unusual to get a clean specimen. On the 17th, when climbing to take the young Eagle from the nest, an old bird dashed off the nest and sat on a bough within thirty feet, screaming while I was securing the young. This is the only instance in which a bird of prey has ventured close to me when at their nests.

"I brought up several of the young: at first they were bold and fearless, but when full-grown became sulky and savage, and would not take food from me. I broke them by starving, and then putting food down near them, would read a book for an hour perhaps, or more, when at last hunger got the better of their temper, and they would suddenly dash at the meat, and, turning their backs raise their wings and make a screen round their food, within shelter of which they tore it to pieces. By degrees they grew tamer and could be carried, coming regularly to the lure. I flew two on Europa Flats, but was never certain of them. I kept these, as well as other Eagles and Kites, on blocks with jesses and a swivel and leash."

Their principal food, judging from the examination of nests and the crops of specimens, appears to be young rabbits. These Eagles are easily recognized by their small size when on the wing and by the light colour of the underparts. A local name which I have heard for them is "Bacallao," from the fancied but far-fetched resemblance in colour and shape which they are supposed to have when flying overhead to that staple article of Spanish diet, a split dried salt codfish; but I may as well mention that I cannot help thinking this name was fabricated for my special benefit.

The young birds generally are of a uniform dark reddish-brown colour, but this is not always the case.

Description. See Plate. Length 23–24 inches.

193. Circaëtus gallicus (Gmelin). The Snake-Eagle.

Moorish. Tair el hesân. *Spanish.* Culebréra (the snake-eater), Aguila parda, Melión.

"Migratory. Some remain to nest near Tangier, building on very tall trees or rocks, laying in April or May one egg, very round in shape, though slightly smaller at one end, of a white colour, sometimes marked with rusty spots. The males sit in their turn; the young do not fly till September. Those which pass over to Europe cross in March and April to return in October. Although not uncommon in the vicinity of Tangier, it is more so than Bonelli's Eagle. They will sometimes allow themselves to be killed on the nest rather than desert their young. Sixteen eggs have passed through my hands."—*Favier.*

"The Short-toed"—best named the Snake-Eagle—is very common both in Morocco and Andalucia, frequenting wooded districts and the valleys of the sierras, being by far the most abundant Eagle near Gibraltar, except the Booted Eagle in some localities. As far as could be observed, they are migratory, as I never saw one in the winter months—but Rafael Mena got one near Málaga on the 10th of January, 1882, a bird apparently of the second year, and the only specimen but one obtained by him there up to that date,—the absence of their chief food (snakes and lizards) at that season being quite sufficient to account for their departure, as the temperature at that season, even in sunny Andalucia, is quite low enough to cause these reptiles to hibernate.

This Eagle breeds about the middle of April; all nests I have seen were in cork, oak, or pine trees, and consisted of a mass of sticks, generally lined with fresh leaves and twigs of the cork-

NEST OF SNAKE-EAGLE IN CORK-TREE.

ANOTHER NEST OF SNAKE-EAGLE IN CORK-TREE.

tree. I found one exception to this among the ruins of the ancient city of Lixus near el Arish, or Larache, in Morocco, the nest being built in a thick mastick or lentiscus bush, the base of the nest actually touching the ground on the hill-side. In this instance there was no want of trees in the neighbourhood to account for the nest being placed in such an unusual situation.

On the 24th of April I shot the hen bird as she flew out of the bush. Had she remained quiet, probably the nest would not have been found; it contained the usual single large rough white egg, slightly incubated.

I never knew the Short-toed Eagle to nest in rocks, as Favier states, though have often seen them perched on crags and large stones; but it is now well known that no absolute rule can be laid down as to the breeding of many species of the Diurnal Raptores exclusively on rocks or trees; they simply accommodate themselves to the country, even nesting on the ground if trees, rocks, or ruins are not available.

Verner remarks that "all the nests I have seen of the Snake-Eagle were, with one exception out of about forty, on horizontal boughs of cork-trees, between ten and twenty feet from the ground. These Eagles take no pains to conceal their nest, but, owing to the similarity of the cork-trees and enormous extent of country covered by them, manage to escape detection more often than might be expected. The nest is abnormally small for so large a bird, some not being larger round than a hand-basin, and are an almost flat platform of sticks with a slight hollow in the middle.

"The earliest dates of eggs were: 26th of March, 1894; 16th of April, 1878, one fresh egg; 21st of April, 1878, and 25th of April, 1879, incubated eggs.

"On 25th March, 1877, I saw great numbers passing north at Gibraltar; and on 7th April, 1876, one with a broken wing was picked up close to Europa Lighthouse."

This bird appears to almost entirely live on reptiles, and is therefore very useful and to be encouraged. However, I have known of a dead Turtle-Dove in their nest, which the Eagle could hardly have caught uninjured.

The long tarsus, bare of feathers, will alone serve to distinguish it from any other bird of prey of its size to be met with near Gibraltar.

Adult. Above dark brown. Breast pure white, streaked with black. Primaries banded below. Cere, legs, and feet pale greyish yellow on a bluish ground-colour; iris yellow; inside of mouth pale blue. Length 26–30 inches.

194. Astur palumbarius (Linnæus). The Goshawk.

Moorish. El boz (*Favier*). *Spanish.* Azór, Gavilán.

"This Hawk is resident near Tangier, and is frequently seen during passage; but they are rarely met with in winter. They pass northwards in April; those which breed nest in May. The eggs are pure bluish white, often much stained with yellow. The young are so fierce that sometimes those in the same nest will kill and eat one another."—*Favier.*

The Goshawk, well known in the wooded districts in Andalucia under the same name as the Sparrowhawk, is considered "muy valiente," being said to carry off partridges when they fall to the gun: this I know from my own experience. I can but consider them rare, having only met with the nest once, on the 15th of May, 1871, when I shot the female bird as she flew off the nest, which was a mass of sticks on an alder tree, about fifteen feet from the ground or, rather, mud, in the thickest part of the Soto Gordo, in the Cork-wood. The nest was evidently not a new one, and seemed to be an old nest of some eagle repaired by the Goshawks. It contained three eggs on the point of hatching, stained yellow all over with dirt, so as to resemble the eggs of a Grebe which had been sat on some time. On washing one of these eggs, however, the bluish ground-colour appeared.

I saw at Tangier several eggs, stained in the same manner, marked as Goshawk's; and until I took their fac-similes did not believe them to be genuine.

Lord Lilford took a nest of the Goshawk, with three eggs (which appears to be the usual number), in the Coto Doñana, in April or early in May.

Above ashy brown; *thin white line* above ear-coverts; below white, thickly *barred* with ashy brown; tail ashy brown, with four broad bars of darker brown; iris yellow.

Young. Above brown; below and under wing-coverts light buff, *streaked* with blackish brown; tail brown, with five bands of darker brown; iris pearly white.

Length: male 19, female 23–24 inches.

195. Accipiter nisus (Linnæus). The Sparrowhawk.

Moorish. Bou-umeira takouk (Cuckoo-Kestrel). *Spanish.* Gavilán, Miláno jaspeádo (Marbled Kite).

"Is resident in the vicinity of Tangier, and common during passage in small flights, which pass to Europe during February, March, and April, returning in August and September."—*Favier.*

The Sparrowhawk is resident in wooded districts near Gibraltar, though not in any great abundance, being most frequent in winter and during migration. Noticed passing the Straits on the 28th of March, and I have dates of nests obtained on the 13th of May, 10th of May, and 17th of May in different years, the first two nests containing fresh eggs; all were in tall trees, in the Corkwood, near the Mill. Verner took a nest near Second Venta, with four eggs, on 8th May, 1878.

Toes rather slender; the middle toe very much longer than the others.

Adult male. Above slate-blue; nape mottled with white; cheeks and ear-coverts bright rufous; below white, barred with bright rufous; iris orange. Length 12 inches.

Female. When very old rarely assumes the same plumage; the adult females usually have the breast barred with greyish brown, with a *reddish patch* of downy feathers on the flanks. *Much larger* than males. Length 15 inches.

Young. Above brown; nape mottled with white; feathers of back edged with rufous brown; below white, barred with rufous brown; iris pale yellow.

196. **Milvus ictinus**, Savigny. **The Red Kite.**

Moorish. Siwâna. *Spanish.* Miláno real.

"Found in the vicinity of Tangier in much smaller numbers than the next species, being seen on passage only in pairs; the birds which remain to nest appear to be those which are the first to go south; the remainder cross to Europe in March, returning in October; a few, however, stay throughout the winter. The eggs, two or three in number, are very similar to those of the Black Kite, but always larger."—*Favier.*

The Red Kite is resident and to be seen almost everywhere on the Spanish side of the Straits—though in the immediate vicinity of Gibraltar they seldom occur except on passage; but Verner found between 1875-79 two pairs nesting about the first week in April, in some pine-woods not very far from the Rock, using Ravens' old nests. They are as common in winter as at any other season, and they particularly affect districts where there are many pine-trees, on which, in company with the Black Kite, they nest, but from a month to at least a fortnight earlier, and never in such numbers as that bird. The Red Kite is easily distinguished from the next species, when on the wing, by the light colour and much more forked tail; when flying overhead by the wings, which, underneath, are *light coloured*, with one dark patch on each; in the Black Kite the underparts of the wing are dark.

General colour rufous. Tail rufous and much forked; legs short; iris yellow. Length 24 inches.

197. **Milvus migrans** (Boddaert). **The Black Kite.**

Moorish. Siwâna. *Spanish.* Miláno négro.

"Seen near Tangier in immense flights, which pass over to Europe in February and March, to return in August and September. Many remain to breed, awaiting the return migration from Europe, when they all disappear for the winter."—*Favier.*

Though a Spanish name is given above, very few Spaniards

distinguish the difference between the Common and the Black Kite; "black," however, is a misnomer, as the primaries are the only part of the plumage which is of that colour. The name *migrans*, by which this Kite is generally known, is most appropriate, as they are entirely migratory—the earliest day on which I observed them crossing the Straits being the 5th of March, then in great numbers, other days on which large flights passed being the 26th, 27th, and 28th of that month, some on the 23rd, one on the 29th of April, and six or seven on the 5th of May. The latest date of the return migration was the 9th of October. Verner's dates of large flights passing are 25th, 31st, and 28th of March, in 1877, '8, '9. Meade-Waldo at Tangier noticed on 22nd March, 1892, quantities passing over to Spain at the same time as Cranes and Storks. More abundant in the vicinity of Seville and where there are pine-woods; very few remain to breed near to Gibraltar, but we noticed a pair about the western slopes of the Sierra Bartolomé on the 5th and 6th April, 1894. Both in Morocco and in Andalucia they nest, often in colonies, about the end of April; and on the 24th of that month we took two nests near Larache, each containing the usual number of two eggs, both lots quite fresh. The nests, built of sticks and placed in tall trees like those of the Common Kite, are lined with rags, paper, bits of rope, and such-like rubbish.

Verner remarks that these Kites have a very peculiar habit of collecting on the open patches of baked mud in the marisma, and crouching down like Pratincoles; he saw as many as twenty-two on 26th May, 1879, in this position, and although the ground was like iron, and all herbage burnt up by the sun, they appeared to be eating something at times.

The eggs are subject to great variation both in shape and colour; sometimes they are almost white, without any spots; others are richly marked all over with reddish brown; some only so marked at the ends, generally at the large one, though now and then at the smaller end.

Above dark brown, below rufous brown; bill black. Head and throat whitish, with black stripes. Tail brown, not much forked. Length 22 inches.

198. **Pernis apivorus** (Linnæus). **The Honey-Buzzard.**

Moorish. Khabbas el graïn (*Favier*). *Spanish.* Aguila de Móros.

"Only observed near Tangier during passage, migrating north during April and May, returning in August and September. The autumnal migration is not in such great flights as the vernal one, the greatest number seen in autumn being from twelve to fourteen, usually six or eight, while in spring flights of many more than a hundred may be seen crossing the Straits in a body. Their plumage is so variable, it is almost impossible to find two exactly alike."—*Favier*.

The Honey-Buzzard, as above stated, is to be seen in swarms during the spring migration, which extends over some twenty days, being at its climax about the 8th of May, but many hundreds passed on the 12th of May between Gibraltar and Málaga. The latest flight noticed was on the 15th of that month. When they have once passed the water the passage is usually made in a gyrating flight of eccentric circles, sometimes very high and as often within shot of the ground. They seem, when thus circling onwards, as if about to alight; but I never saw them do so, nor ever saw them except at the period of migration. Lord Lilford observed large flocks passing south in September.

We found the Honey-Buzzard nesting in the province of Liebana near Santander, in 1876; it would be interesting to know their most southern breeding-range.

Lores or spaces between eyes and bill *covered with feathers*; legs finely reticulated all round. (*Pernis.*)

Adult male. Head ash-grey; above brown; below white, the chest barred and spotted with brown.

Adult female. Like male, but has not the grey head.

Young. Head whitish; upper parts brown, marked with white; below white, streaked with brown.

A dark or melanistic form also occurs, in which the underparts are uniform brown, the young birds being striated with blackish brown.

Length 22-25 inches.

199. Elanus cæruleus (Desfontaines). Black-shouldered Hawk.

Moorish. Aisha hemika (*Favier*).

"Scarce in the vicinity of Tangier, being seldom seen—and then in very limited numbers, in February and March and again during September and October. They are more common near Larache, where some are found breeding in April. They live on birds and small mammals, and are very voracious. Their cry is a sort of whistle."—*Favier.*

On the African side of the Straits we found the Black-winged Hawk common near Tetuan in April, as well as about Cape Negro; near Tangier at that time we only saw two. They nest on trees, and (as in other countries in which I have seen them) keep to slightly wooded places, not frequenting open ground.

Meade-Waldo says they fly when it is nearly quite dark.

On the Spanish side this Hawk is very rare. I never obtained one; but Lord Lilford records a specimen ('Ibis,' 1865, p. 177) as occurring near Seville. Easily recognized on the wing by its greyish-white colour; it has a peculiar habit of hovering at about thirty yards from the ground, with the wings forming a sort of V or acute angle with the body, never bringing them level with one another until it flies off to take up a fresh position. They are rather wary when thus engaged in hunting for their prey.

Lores feathered.

General colour above ash-grey. Below and axillaries white; black patch on shoulders; iris crimson. Length 13 inches.

200. Falco peregrinus, Tunstall. The Peregrine Falcon.

Moorish. Teir el hor. *Spanish.* Alcón.

"Is not uncommon near Tangier, where some remain to breed;

$\frac{1}{3}$

the remainder are migratory, going to Europe in February and March, returning in November and December. They nest from March to May on rocks and on trees, laying four eggs, eleven of which have passed through my hands for sale."—*Favier.*

The Peregrine Falcon is common in Andalucia in winter; those Falcons which are resident belong to the subspecies or small race called *F. punicus,* as no doubt do those which Favier mentioned as nesting on the African side of the Straits.

Adult. Above bluish grey, paler on rump, barred with a darker tint. Crown, cheeks, ear-coverts, and short moustachial band blackish; below white, with a buffy tinge on the breast, spotted on the throat and upper breast, and *barred* on the lower breast with blackish; cere, eyelids, and legs yellow.

Young. Above brown, with buff margins to feathers; below whitish, with dark brown *streaks*; tail irregularly barred, tipped with whitish buff; cere, eyelids, and legs blue.

Length 15-20 inches.

201. Falco punicus, Levaillant, jun. The Mediterranean Falcon.

This small race of the Peregrine is resident about the Straits; one pair nest on the Rock near O'Hara's Tower, occasionally coming into the town and carrying off tame pigeons. A pair used to breed close to Cape Spartel, in the middle of a colony of Rock-Doves; but I did not observe that they molested their neighbours.

Lord Lilford kindly writes to me as follows:—"There is no specific difference between *F. punicus* and *F. peregrinus*; but the former is generally, if not always, the smaller bird, and never in my experience gets the *white* breast and *black* bars of the adults of the typical European race — especially noticed in winter-killed specimens from Egypt, Italy, Algeria, and Spain. As a rule, the adult *F. punicus* has the breast more or less tawny, and the barring closer than in *F. peregrinus*, but this is not invariable. *F. punicus,* in my opinion, is a good local race, like *F. anatum* and *F. melanogenys* of America and Australia."

In the 'Ibis' for 1887, p. 275, plate viii., Lord Lilford treats of this Falcon, and considers that without doubt it is "the Barbary Falcon" of our old English authors on Falconry.

In the 'Ibis,' 1882, pp. 305-321, the late Mr. J. H. Gurney gave an exhaustive account of the measurements and plumage of *F. barbarus*, *F. punicus*, and *F. minor*. It seems to me that there is no difference in the immature plumage of the three birds.

Description. See Plate.

202. Falco barbarus, Linnæus. The Barbary or Rufous-naped Falcon.

The true Barbary Falcon occurs near Tangier, as a specimen in the Norwich Museum came from there, and I obtained another from Olcese.

This bird is, without doubt, identical with *F. babylonicus*, which shows how little measurements can be relied on. *Falco barbarus* is figured, Ibis, 1859, pl. vi., *F. babylonicus*, Ibis, 1861, pl. vii.

Adult. Above as in adult Peregrine, but nape rufous; lower parts with rufous tinge; moustachial stripe large. Length 14-20 inches.

203. Falco lanarius, Schlegel. The Lanner.

Favier has, in his MS., under the head of *Falco barbarus*, evidently described the Lanner, as his measurements are larger than those of *F. peregrinus*, instead of smaller; and all the specimens of the Lanner which I have seen from Tangier, with one or two exceptions, were labelled "*barbarus*." Favier adds:—"This species, which the Moors confound with the Peregrine, is resident and as common as that species around Tangier."

This bird seems to be the most common Falcon in Morocco.

On the 1st of May, 1872, I obtained a female Lanner and three eggs. The nest was on some rocks near the above town. Two of the eggs were slightly sat on; the third, much lighter in colour, was addled, which is often the case with eggs faintly marked or differing from the usual colouring.

On the Spanish side of the Straits I did not succeed in obtaining this Falcon near Gibraltar, but have seen them on the wing, as has Verner in the Sierra Enmedio. They were found nesting on pine-trees in the Coto del Rey, near Seville. In one instance, an old nest was used, from which three years previously I had shot a Buzzard (*Buteo vulgaris*) and taken two eggs. The last nest found contained eggs at the end of March.

Adults. Forehead whitish; crown and nape pale rufous, with very narrow black frontal line; moustachial stripe very small and narrow.
Young. Crown and nape lighter. Length 16–18 inches.

204. Falco eleonoræ, Gené. The Eleonora Falcon.

I never met with this species on either side of the Straits; and there is no authentic record of a specimen having been obtained in Andalucia. Gilbert White's brother, the Rev. John White, writing from Gibraltar about 1776, mentions the Hobby as nesting at the "back of the Rock." If a Hobby did nest there, it could not well have been any species but the Eleonora Falcon, as the true Hobby (*Falco subbuteo*) is a tree-nesting bird. The Eleonora Falcon, however, occurs at Mogador, and used to breed there.

Adult. Entirely blackish brown. Wings as in next, very long.
Immature. Marked below somewhat as Hobby, but lower parts more rufous; black moustache. Tail much banded with rufous and black. Length 15½ inches.

205. Falco subbuteo, Linnæus. The Hobby.

Spanish. Alcotán.

According to Favier this little Falcon is seen near Tangier in pairs on passage only, "crossing to Europe in May, returning in autumn to winter further south."

Near Gibraltar the Hobby appears in the same manner; the

earliest dates on which I noticed them were the 8th of April, 13th of April, and 20th of April, in three different years, and we saw them near Seville very early in May. They have bred near Coria del Rio, and Arévalo mentions them also near Granada.

The Hobby takes its prey, birds and insects, on the wing, and no authentic record is known of its taking anything on the ground.

Adult. Above bluish black, with black moustachial stripe; throat and breast white, occasionally tinged with buff, the breast striped with black; thighs and vent rusty red.

Young. Buff edgings to feathers of back; thighs and vent only very slightly rufous. Length 12–14 inches.

206. Falco æsalon, Tunstall. The Merlin.

Spanish. Esmerejón.

"Occurs during winter near Tangier, coming from Europe in September, returning north in March."—*Favier.*

The Merlin is not uncommon in open ground in Andalucia in December and January. The earliest noticed was on the 24th of November, the latest on the 7th of March. About Casas Viejas they were very plentiful, and often to be seen chasing Calandra Larks; they were, for the most part, adult blue-backed birds [*].

Adult male. Above slaty blue, with black shaft to each feather; nape rufous; throat white; underparts rufous, streaked with blackish brown; tail blue-grey, the end broadly banded with black and tipped with white. Length 10 inches.

Female. Extremely rarely acquires the same plumage as the adult male; but usually resembles *young male*, being above dark reddish brown, margined with light brown; nape whitish, spotted with buff; underparts white, broadly streaked with brown; tail brown, crossed with narrow bands of lighter brown and tipped with white. Length 12 inches.

---

[*] My friend Colonel Delmé-Radcliffe, with his vast knowledge of practical falconry, considers the Merlin to be one of the most cowardly of the tribe. This is rather against the theory of book or table naturalists, that it is one of the most courageous of the Falconidæ, and there is little doubt that deeds commonly attributed to the Merlin are those of the Tiercel or male Peregrine.

207. Falco vespertinus, Linnæus. **The Western Red-footed Hobby.**

Favier confounded this insectivorous Falcon with the Hobby, calling it a variety; he, however, gives a description which identifies this species, and says "This variety is found near Tangier in April." They are certainly not common there, and said only to appear when there are locusts, which they follow from the east. In 1874, on the 27th of April, I saw two near Tangier; shortly afterwards some were obtained by Olcese; and just at that time flights of locusts arrived. Curiously enough, in 1874, on the very same day in April I saw one close to Tangier, and the next morning saw quantities of locusts as we were crossing over to Gibraltar.

On the Spanish side of the Straits one is recorded as having occurred near Seville; but they are in Andalucia only accidental visitors.

Claws yellowish white.

Adult male. Uniform lead-grey, except reddish-chestnut thighs, vent, and under tail-coverts; legs and feet red.

Female. Above ash-grey, barred with bluish black; head and nape rufous; below uniform dull chestnut.

Young. Like female, but head, nape, and underparts streaked with brown; outside tail-feather with both webs barred. Length 11–12 inches.

208. Falco tinnunculus, Linnæus. **The Common Kestrel.**

Moorish. Bou-umeira. *Spanish.* Cernicalo.

"Is both resident and migratory in Morocco. Those which migrate cross to Europe in February and March, returning in August and September. They nest by preference on old ruins and walls."—*Favier.*

It is needless to say much about this Kestrel, so well known in England. They are resident both in Morocco and Andalucia, and are very common, more so in autumn and spring, nesting in April on trees, rocks, and buildings.

Adult male. Head, neck, lower back, rump, and tail blue-grey, the latter tipped with white on a broad black band; back pale chestnut, with small black spots.

Female and young. Above entirely rufous, banded with black; tail rufous, with black bands and tipped with a broad black band. Old females occasionally partially assume male plumage, being marked with blue on rump and tail. Length 13-15 inches.

209. Falco cenchris, Naumann. The Lesser Kestrel.

Moorish. Souif (*Favier*). *Spanish.* Primilla.

"Is nearly as abundant near Tangier as the Common Kestrel, passing to Europe in February and March, returning during August and September."—*Favier.*

The Lesser Kestrel is almost entirely migratory, though a few remain at Gibraltar during winter. Vast numbers nest there, chiefly on the steep face of rock on the North Front. These birds arrive about the 15th of February; but I saw a great flight passing as late as the 4th of April. Probably these were birds which would breed much further north. They nest on rocks and ruins, particularly on the old Moorish buildings and towers, of which there are so many in Andalucia. In some, as for instance at Las Alcantarillas, near Seville, they swarm like bees at a hive, as also at Seville; while, curiously enough, at Cadiz they were absent.

So far as I am aware, the Lesser Kestrel never nests on trees like the common species. At the Coto del Rey, on the 26th of April, I took a nest with four eggs out of a hole in a wall which was within reach of the ground. In the Crimea, I remember, they nested in holes of river-banks. On the 12th of May, near Marchena, we obtained sixty eggs out of an old tower, and might have taken as many more. Some of these eggs were hard sat-on; and the old birds were caught on the nest, to be released after examination. The eggs varied very much, a few being almost colourless, others half white, half red, piebald in appearance.

Adult male. Much resembles Common Kestrel, but is smaller, and has the back uniform pale chestnut *without any spots.*

Female. Much as female of last.

Length 12½ inches. *Claws white.*

210. **Pandion haliaëtus** (Linnæus). **The Osprey.**

Moorish. Bou haut (Father of fish). *Spanish.* Aguila pescadór.

"This bird is not uncommon near Tangier, living among the rocks on the coast, where they nest in March, laying two or three eggs; the young do not fly until July. The migrating birds arrive in October and November, returning north in March."—*Favier*.

The Osprey is most abundant in the Straits in winter. We saw a pair catching fish near Cape Negro, at Lake Esmir, in April; and a pair nest on the rocks westward of Tangier and at Cape Negro: they also nest in nearly every favourable situation on the coasts. Another pair regularly breed at Gibraltar, on the rocks a little to the north of "Monkeys' Cave." The Rev. John White noticed the nesting of the Osprey at Gibraltar about 1776; probably this is the same situation, and has been used ever since. I first knew of the eyry in May 1869, when there were young in the nest; these did not fly till the middle of July. In 1871 the nest was taken in the middle of March, and then contained three eggs; the old birds did not leave the vicinity, and bred again the next season, but in a different situation close to the old one. The first site of the nest was only to be seen from the Europa Advance Battery, where I spent many an hour watching the old birds with a telescope. They, in 1894, were still at the old site.

Being positive that only one pair of Ospreys breed at Gibraltar, and knowing the date of laying of that pair, it is difficult to account for the fact of seeing, on the 23rd of April, one take up from the surface of the sea and carry off a stick or splinter some three feet long; and on the 30th of March I also saw another carrying a stick. Could this be done in play? On the 17th of February I saw one of these Ospreys give a Gannet, which had ventured too near the nest, a great buffeting, knocking him about and chasing him for half a mile. The Isla de Palomas, a small patch of rock near the celebrated and dangerous Pearl Rock, is a favourite resting-place of these birds; and one is usually to be seen there at all seasons, perched on a small pinnacle.

A brother officer of mine killed an Osprey on the wing at Europa Mess-house with a pea-rifle. The bird was flying high up over the sea; but the very strong westerly wind blowing at the time caught and landed it among the men's huts.

Adult. Above brown; below white, except brown on breast.
Young. Pale margins to feathers above; tail distinctly barred.
Cere blue. Legs and feet blue, very finely reticulated (or covered with minute scales) and prickly underneath; legs very short, about 2½ inches long; outer toe reversible; claws long, much curved, and very sharp. Length 23 inches.

Order **STEGANOPODES.**

Family **PELECANIDÆ.** Feet entirely webbed or all four toes connected by webs.

211. Phalacrocorax carbo (Linnæus). The Cormorant.

Moorish. Gharrak. *Spanish.* Cuérvo marino.

"The Cormorant is found near Tangier from December to February, and frequents the coasts, lakes, and rivers, where it is not uncommon."—*Favier.*

The above remarks equally apply to this bird on the Andalucian side. I never saw it in summer.

Tail of *fourteen* feathers.
Adult. General colour above *purplish black.* In spring slender white plumes on head and neck and white patch on thighs. These white marks are lost after breeding-season is over. Length 36 inches.
Young. Brown above, whitish below.

212. Phalacrocorax graculus (Linnæus). The Shag or Green Cormorant.

Favier includes this species in his list as *P. desmaresti*, stating that it "is rare near Tangier, but found during the whole year.

The Shag is very common and resident about the Straits. They nest at the island of Peregil, under Apes' Hill on the African coast, and occasionally, as in 1883, at the back of the "Rock."

Tail of *twelve* feathers.
Adult. General colour shiny blackish green *without any white*. In early spring a crest curled forwards on front of head. Length 27 inches.
Young. Brown above, whitish below.

213. Sula bassana (Linnæus). The Gannet or Solan Goose.

Spanish. Alcatráz; but this name is often applied to any large Gull.

Favier merely remarks of this bird that it "arrives in October and leaves during March, not being very numerous." There are always, however, during the winter season, great numbers of Gannets in the Straits, particularly close to Gibraltar, where, according to the wind, they may be noticed fishing on the leeward side of the Rock and watched darting down from a considerable height on their prey, often disappearing quite under the water. On the wing, to an inexperienced observer, they appear like a large Gull. The immature birds in their dull spotted dress, perhaps through not attracting so much notice, seem to be less in number than the more conspicuous white adults with their black primaries. The earliest dates on which this species was observed near Gibraltar were on the 11th of November, 1870, and the 12th of October, 1871, the latest being on the 28th of March, 1870, and the 22nd of March, 1871, and the 28th of March, 1872. Many on the 28th of March, 1876 (*Verner*), one near Valencia, 17th March, 1882, and several seen near Cape St. Vincent on the 30th of April, 1877.

Adult. Head and neck buffish white; the rest white, except the black primaries and primary-coverts; tail long and wedge-shaped.
Young. Head, neck, and upper plumage blackish brown, spotted with white; below white, very thickly covered with blackish-brown spots, but vary much. Length 30 inches.

Order **HERODIONES**. Family **ARDEIDÆ**.

214. Ardea cinerea, Linnæus. **The Common Heron.**

Moorish. Aishûsh, Bou-onk (perhaps "ouk," neck, more likely from cry). *Spanish.* Garza, Garza ceniza.

"This species is, in the vicinity of Tangier, both resident and migratory. Those which migrate pass over to Europe during February and March, returning in November and December, being at all seasons plentiful."—*Favier.*

The Common Heron visits the neighbourhood of Gibraltar in great numbers during the winter season; and they particularly frequent the district "between the rivers" near Palmones. Mostly departing by March, some few pairs are resident about Casas Viejas. I never found them breeding, but some of the numerous nests supposed to belong to the Purple Heron possibly had the present species for their rightful owner.

Male. General colour ashy grey; crown white; crest and nape black; hind neck pale grey; sides of breast black.

Female. Crest less developed and plumage duller.

Young. Crown ashy; sides of breast striped with black; no plumes on back. Length 36 inches.

215. Ardea purpurea, Linnæus. **The Purple Heron.**

Moorish. Siad el mraj (the hunter of the marsh). *Spanish.* Garza.

"This Heron is, in Morocco, a summer visitant, and nearly as numerous as the Common Heron. They pass north in April, returning in September, many remaining in the country to breed, frequenting reed-beds and rushes on the edges of lakes and rivers."—*Favier.*

The Purple Heron, in Andalucia, only remains for the nesting-season; and I never knew an instance of its occurrence in winter.

My earliest dates of arrival observed near Gibraltar were the 4th of April 1870, 7th of April 1871, 25th of March 1872, 7th of March 1874, 25th of March 1894. They are extremely abundant and generally easy to get a shot at, being seldom found in the open, but almost always among rushes or swampy jungle, and are very rarely seen to perch on trees. There was, about five miles from Gibraltar, beyond the First River (Guadarranque), on the right of the road to Los Barrios, a leech-preserve, grandly called the "laguna," perhaps two acres in extent and surrounded by poplar trees. This swamp was a dense mass of tall rushes (*Juncus*) springing up through masses of dead ones, the growth of years past, all so matted and tangled together as to make it very difficult to pass through them, more especially as the water was in places up to one's armpits. This delightful spot was a very favourite breeding-place of the Purple Heron; where there generally used to be three pairs nesting, also two nests of Marsh-Harriers.

These Herons commence to lay about the 13th of April, as a rule depositing three eggs (rarely four), as the following few instances of nests taken and seen will show:—on the 21st of April two nests—one with four, one with three eggs, all fresh; on the 18th of April two nests—one with one, the other with three fresh eggs; on the 6th May two nests—one with three fresh eggs, the other with three eggs hard sat-on. The nests, varying much in size and consisting merely of a few dried rushes collected together so as to form a sort of platform just clear of the water, are generally twenty or thirty yards apart. The eggs are light bluish green, similar to those of *Ardea cinerea*.

It is rather remarkable that Purple Herons should generally choose their building-places near to Marsh-Harriers, as the latter repeatedly rob them of their eggs. Many a nest have I seen with nothing but empty shells, the work of the egg-sucking Harrier.

Adult. Crown and crest black, with purple sheen; back, wings, and tail dark slate-grey; plumes on back *pale chestnut*; under wing-coverts chestnut; thighs rufous buff; breast rich *maroon-red*.

Young. General colour above rusty red; below brownish white. Length 30–32 inches.

216. Ardea alba, Linnæus. The Great White Heron.

We saw one at the lakes of Ras el Doura, on the 26th of April, but were unable to shoot it. I know the bird well, having shot them both in the Crimea and in India. Mr. James J. Walker, R.N., in 'Transactions of Entomological Society,' 1890, p. 364, mentions having seen this Heron at Esmir once or twice.

On the Spanish side I never saw one, or heard of a specimen being obtained; but Verner saw one at Laguna de la Janda, May 18, 1875, and Mr. L. P. Irby, 60th Rifles, saw another there in February, 1894; whilst they are reported by Arévalo to occasionally occur in winter at the Albufera, which is, however, rather beyond the district of "the Straits."

Entirely white; bill and iris yellow; legs and feet black.

In summer. Has bill black and many very long filamented plumes on back. Length 36–42 inches.

217. Ardea garzetta, Linnæus. The Little Egret.

Moorish. Bou-fala, Bou-bliga, Bou-bilira (*Favier*). *Spanish.* Garza blanca.

"This bird is not uncommon near Tangier in small flights when on migration. They pass north in April, returning during November and December; but some remain to breed in the country."—*Favier.*

The Little Egret is the least common of the small Herons in Andalucia, and, as Favier observes, some remain very late, as I have seen and obtained them on the 17th of November. The greater number arrive about the middle of April, first date observed 13th April, 1894, at Laguna de la Janda, and linger here and there on their route, gradually passing on to their breeding-places on the borders of the marisma and elsewhere.

They nest on trees, in some seasons, near Rocio, but are so molested that they change their ground frequently. When on the wing, and within a short distance, the black legs and bill are very apparent.

Entirely white; bill and legs black; iris yellow; bill yellow in winter.
In summer. Has long filamentous plumes on back, and two or three long feathers pendent from crown. Length 20 inches.

218. Ardea bubulcus, Audouin. Buff-backed or Cattle-Heron.

Moorish. Tair el bukkar (the Cow-bird). *Spanish.* Garrapatósa, Purgabueyes.

"This is the most common of the Herons around Tangier, and keeps in small flocks, always following herds of cattle, often sitting on their backs, and chiefly feeding on insects. A small proportion remain during the breeding-season; but the majority pass northwards in February, March, and April, returning late in the year."—*Favier.*

The Buff-backed Heron is very common in low-lying districts in Andalucia, and some are resident, breeding in the marisma; but they are very irregular in their movements, and chiefly noticed, while passing, during March and April, as they always attend cattle when in wet marshy ground. The Spanish herdsmen naturally object to have them molested, especially as there was at Casas Viejas a legend of a sporting Briton from Gibraltar having shot one as it sat on a cow's back—a story which unhappily was founded on fact, and only shows what the Englishman is capable of.

The local names of this Heron all originate from its habit of attending cattle and freeing them from parasites—*Garrapatósa,* from *garrapata,* a tick or louse; *Purgabueyes,* cattle-cleaner or purifier.

A male bird, which had been kept alive for about four years in the patio of the Fonda de Europa, at Seville, during the first week in April (his fifth spring, as far as could be ascertained) began to change the colour of the legs and the basal half of both mandibles to a pinkish red; the irides also changed to beautiful rich pink colour, with a very slight golden ring round the black pupil. This change was quite completed before the bird had fully assumed the buff-coloured back, which is the mark of the breeding-dress.

A female, in confinement with the above-mentioned, laid many eggs of a very pale bluish-white colour, showing a greenish tint inside when held to the light.

These captive Herons were quite masters of the various Kites and Buzzards confined in the same patio, and ceaselessly wandered around, hunting flies, which they caught when settled on the walls or ground, never attempting to take them on the wing; but, poising the head two or three times, as a man would a dart before throwing it, they never missed their aim.

In summer. Crown, nape, feathers hanging from lower neck, and plumes on back reddish buff; these feathers are elongated and hair-like, especially on the back; rest of plumage white; bill reddish at base, yellow at tip; iris rich pink, with golden ring round pupil.

In winter. Entirely *white*, except a patch of reddish buff on the crown; bill and iris yellow. Length 18 inches.

219. Ardea ralloides, Scopoli. The Squacco Heron.

Moorish. Aishûs (*Favier*; but he applies this name to all the Herons). *Spanish.* Garza canária (from colour).

"This species is nearly as common around Tangier as the last, occurring in small flocks during migration. Some remain in the country to breed, nesting on the ground among sedges, laying in May and June five eggs, which are more oval in shape than those of the Purple Heron, but of the same colour."—*Favier.*

I found this bird in great numbers about the swamps of Ras el Doura towards the end of April, where they were by far the most common of the Herons.

On the Spanish side the Squacco Heron is entirely migratory, arriving during the month of April. They are common in the marisma of the Guadalquivir; but I never observed any near Gibraltar, nor did I ever see them following cattle, like the preceding species. They nest late in the season; but I regret to be unable to give any personal information as to their breeding-habits.

This species (beautiful as all the family are) is, to my mind, by far the most handsome and elegant of all the European Herons.

Head light buff, with crest of from eight to ten elongated, narrow, pointed white feathers, bordered at the sides with black; plumes on back dark reddish brown to light buff, long and hair-like; wings, rump, tail, and lower parts, except the buff feathers pendent from neck, white; bill leaden blue at base, black at tip. Length 18 inches.

220. Nycticorax griseus (Linnæus). The Night-Heron.

Spanish. Garza de noche, Garza gris, Martinéte.

Favier says:—"This species is common near Tangier when on migration, passing in small lots, which frequent wooded spots close to lakes and rivers." We saw the Night-Heron near Larache in April, and near Tetuan at the end of March.

In Andalucia they are entirely migratory, chiefly arriving in April; but I have no date of their autumnal departure, and never observed any very near to Gibraltar. About the district of Seville they are common, nesting in companies on trees on the Rocina near Rocio and on the banks of rivers—like the other smaller Herons, breeding about the middle of May.

The Night-Heron, as its name implies, is a nocturnal-feeding bird, frequenting trees by day, and if disturbed usually flying from one tree to another; but I have scarcely ever seen them on the move by day, unless frightened up.

The immature birds, in their brownish spotted plumage, are, but for their arboreal habits, at a little distance very liable to be mistaken for the Bittern.

Crown, nape, and back brownish black, with green gloss; wings and tail ash-grey. Crest usually of three, but rarely of as many as six long, narrow, white feathers pendent from nape ; legs yellow ; bill black ; iris red. Females less brightly coloured.

Young. Without crest ; above dark brown, spotted with white ; below dull white, striped with dark brown. Length 21–24 inches.

221. Ardetta minuta (Linnæus). The Little Bittern.

"This species is, near Tangier, the most scarce of the *Ardeidæ*, being not often met with, and then always either alone or in company with the Squacco Heron. They arrive and pass on north in April, and return during August to winter further south."—*Favier.*

The Little Bittern is, in Andalucia, entirely migratory, arriving late in April. Considerable numbers nest among rushes and sedges. They are late-breeders, nesting early in June, and laying as many as six white eggs. I have no exact date of the autumnal migration ; but they are all gone by October.

Male. Crown, nape, back, tail, wing-quills, and upper surface of bill black, with greenish gloss ; underparts buff ; lower neck-feathers elongated ; feathers of upper breast blackish brown, margined with buff ; iris yellow.

Female. Crown blackish ; above chestnut-brown, margined with buff ; primaries dark brown.

Legs greenish yellow ; tail of ten feathers. Length 12 inches.

222. Botaurus stellaris (Linnæus). The Common Bittern.

Moorish. Sebnâ el Mraj (Lion of the marsh). *Spanish.* Pajaro tóro (Bull-bird), Guia de las Gallinetas (Guide of the Woodcocks).

The Bittern, according to Favier, "winters in Morocco, and is seen in abundance on passage, arriving during August and September, and leaving in February. They are found in pairs and in small lots, frequenting rushes and reed-beds." This bird, however, breeds as far south as the neighbourhood of Rabat, whence I have seen the eggs.

On the north side of the Straits they used to breed at Casas Viejas, at the Laguna de la Janda, and in the Soto Torero near Vejer, and still do so in the marshes of Rocio, near the Coto

Doñana. Nesting about the middle of May, they lay four or five pale brown-coloured eggs, placed in the midst of thick rushes. I was unable personally to find a nest, but had several eggs brought to me, and have often heard them calling in the daytime —a peculiar, booming unmistakable cry, whence, in almost all countries, their local name is derived.

They are more abundant in the winter months, arriving in the end of October, and in some places are at times quite numerous wherever there are rushes and sedges; and I have occasionally shot them in the sotos of the Cork-wood. Dull and sluggish in habit, it is not until nearly trodden on that they will rise; but on one occasion I remember finding several in some rather open marsh, and they flew up one by one far out of shot, seeking refuge in the nearest thick reed-bed. Though often flushed among sallows and bushes in the Soto Malabrigo, near Casas Viejas, I never saw the Bittern perch on bushes or trees there or in any other country.

Crown and nape black; general colour buff; a large ruff on front of neck; the back irregularly marked with black; primaries chestnut, *barred with blackish*; tail of ten feathers. Length 28-29 inches.

CICONIIDÆ.

223. Ciconia alba, Bechstein. **The White Stork.**

Moorish. Belareech, as pronounced correctly "Blarij." *Spanish.* Cigüeña.

"This Stork is seen on migration in vast numbers around Tangier, passing to Europe during January and February, some of the birds terminating their journey by remaining to breed in Morocco. These are the first to depart south, returning again year after year to the same places, and apparently by the same route as that taken in their gradual departure.

"Some large flights pass on without stopping; those which

migrate in August rest awhile on their way south; so during the autumnal migration (which lasts, like the spring, for about a month, the latter half of August and the first part of September) this species is extremely numerous and seen around the environs of Tangier in all directions; they are very tame, and often follow close behind the plough.

"The superstition which shelters this bird from molestation by the natives has been mentioned in my notes on the Swallow; but it may be added that some of the Arabs believe that the Storks originate from a wicked Kadi and his family, who, as a punishment for their great cruelty, were all changed into these birds, and that these *misérables* humble themselves to appease Allah, and, in the hope of some day regaining their original human form, pray without ceasing day and night, and whenever they rest, prostrate themselves and clack their bills."—*Favier*.

The White Stork, owing to the protection it everywhere receives, is much more abundant in Morocco than in Andalucia, although plentiful in some level districts in the latter country, being most common in the marismas and in the vicinity of Seville, nesting on some of the churches in that city. On the African side of the Straits, in many situations they breed on trees, generally in colonies, as well as on houses, but usually near villages; and almost every Moorish hovel has a Stork's nest on the top, a pile of sticks lined with grass and palmetto-fibre. It usually contains four white eggs, which are very rarely marked with pink blotches; these are sometimes laid as early as the 25th of March, and are very good eating, either hot or cold. When boiled hard, they have the white clear, as with Peewit's or "Plover's" eggs, the yolk being of very rich reddish yellow.

The White Stork is rather irregular as to the time of nesting, for we found in Morocco, on the same day (the 25th of April), young birds, eggs, and unfinished nests; and, to show how varied is the time of migration, saw on that day a flight of about a hundred, flying northward at an immense height. As they passed over the "Storkery," which was in a large grove of high trees, they lowered themselves to within a hundred yards or so of the nests, and after wheeling round a few minutes, as if to see how affairs were going on, they worked up in a gyrating flight to their original elevation, and continued their northerly journey, doubtless to the great delight of the resident Storks, who were in a great state of perturbation and disturbance at the appearance of their brethren. I may here remark that Storks usually migrate in large flocks at a great height, with a gyrating flight. The earliest date of their arrival that I noticed near Gibraltar was on the 11th of January; and they nearly all leave by the end of September. Feeding on insects of all kinds, mice, snakes, and other reptiles, they are most useful birds, and certainly deserve the protection and encouragement which they receive in Morocco, where they are in consequence excessively tame. Their grotesque actions when nesting, and their habit of continually clacking their bills together, making a noise like a rattle, render them very amusing to watch. I was informed by a Frenchman who had passed two years in the city of Morocco, that there, as well as at Fez and some other large towns in the Moorish Empire, there is a regular Storks' hospital, and that should one be in any way injured, or fall from the nest, it is sent to this institution, or, rather, enclosure, which is kept up by subscription from wealthy Moors, who consider the Stork a sacred bird. I merely mention this story to draw attention to the subject in case of any future ornithologists visiting these cities; and were not my informant worthy of credence, should have omitted noticing it.

White, except primaries, secondaries, scapulars, large wing-coverts, and bare space round eye, which are black. Bill and legs red. Length 42 inches.

224. Ciconia nigra (Linnæus). **The Black Stork.**

Moorish. Geringa (*Favier* and *D. Hay*). *Spanish.* Cigüéña negra.

"This species is much less common in the vicinity of Tangier than the White Stork (*C. alba*). They are seen crossing the Straits during the months of February, March, April, and May, returning in November to pass further south. During their passage, they keep in pairs and in small lots, frequenting much the same ground as the Crane (*Grus cinerea*)."—*Favier.*

From their shy and wild, and, as far as my observations go, solitary habits, the Black Stork on both sides of the Straits appears to be much less common than perhaps is really the case. I saw one near Tangier in October 1869, and another on the 26th of April, 1871, and have seen several specimens obtained in the neighbourhood. Verner reports seeing five daily near Tetuan between the 8th and 12th of January, 1890. Near Gibraltar I saw one on the 22nd of February, another on the 11th of January, 1872, near Seville, and obtained a specimen from there on the 18th of November, 1870. These were the only instances when I personally noticed them.

Head, neck, and upper parts blackish with metallic gloss; only breast and underparts white. Bill, legs, and bare space round eye red; irides reddish brown.

Young. Dark parts brownish black without gloss; bill and legs olive-green; feathers of head and neck tipped with buffy white. Length 39–40 inches.

PLATALEIDÆ.

225. Platalea leucorodia, Linnæus. **The White Spoonbill.**

Moorish. Bou-kar-kaba (*Favier*) (Father of the cymbals, "kar-kaba" being large wooden cymbals used by negroes). *Spanish.* Espátula, Paletón, Paléta, Patéra, Piláto, Cucharéta.

"This species occurs near Tangier when on passage. They

migrate north in March, April, and May, returning during October, and are never observed in winter."—*Favier.*

We saw many Spoonbills in April at the lake of Meshree el Haddar, near Larache; and they then appeared to be on migration.

The earliest occurrence of this species in spring near Gibraltar that I know of was one shot on the 9th of April, at the First River; and the latest seen was a single bird wading about the river Barbate, near Casas Viejas, on the 20th of November. They were common in the marisma in flocks in May; in some wet seasons they nest there, and also in the Soto Toréro, near Vejer, where, sad to relate, a Spaniard, in 1873, took upwards of seventy eggs early in May. He brought most of these eggs into Gibraltar, to some collectors who were there at that time; and next year he described to me the nests as merely made of a few sedges, and placed close (*junto*) together, each containing four eggs. The season of 1874 was very dry, and no Spoonbills appeared there; indeed, had it been wet, probably after being so robbed, the birds would not have nested again in that spot; but in 1875 Major Verner reports them again nesting there and also breeding during the following season in the Soto Malabrigo. He further reports seeing at La Janda a flock of about a dozen on the 20th of February, 1876.

White; lower neck and the short bushy crest tinged with yellow; bill black at base, yellow and broadly flattened at the end; chin bare and yellow; iris dull red. Length 32–36 inches.

Young. Without crest or yellow skin; bill blackish; iris black.

IBIDIDÆ.

226. **Ibis comatus**, Ehrenberg. The Red-cheeked Ibis.

Favier included in his MS., without any description, another species of Ibis as having once been obtained by him near Tangier. He called it "*Ibis calva*"; but it could hardly have been that

South-African species, and was doubtless this rock-frequenting and migratory bird, which has occurred at Mogador, and is said to have nested among the rocks on the island there.

<small>General colour iridescent green, with feathers of neck elongated and pointed. Bill, head, bare throat, and legs red. Length 24 inches.</small>

227. Plegadis falcinellus (Linnæus). The Glossy Ibis.

Moorish. Maiza (*Favier*), Maiza el Wad (*D. Hay*) (river goat). *Spanish.* Morito.

"This bird occurs near Tangier on passage, returning to pass the winter further south. Some must remain to nest in the country; for they are frequently met with during May, June, and July."—*Favier.*

We saw great flocks of the Glossy Ibis at the lakes of Ras el Doura towards the end of April; but they were very wary, as they are in Andalucia, whereas I remember in India we used to walk up to within thirty yards of them.

When flying they much resemble the Spoonbill in their manner of flight. They nest in Morocco, as I have seen eggs obtained in the country; and in wet seasons they breed in the Soto Toréro, near Vejer, and also in the marisma of the Guadalquivir; but I have no personal knowledge of their nesting-habits. The eggs are of a uniform pale bluish-green colour. Near Gibraltar I have only noticed this Ibis when passing late in April and in May. A female shot at the First River, on the 31st of May, had the gizzard full of minute shrimps; four eggs in the ovary were slightly enlarged, which tends to confirm what I have heard, that they are late breeders.

<small>Bill long, curved down (as in Curlew); face bare; general colour chestnut-brown; the back much glossed with green and purple; legs greenish grey. Length 22 inches.</small>

Order **ODONTOGLOSSÆ**.

Family **PHŒNICOPTERIDÆ**.

228. Phœnicopterus roseus, Pallas. **The Flamingo.**

Moorish. Nihof. *Spanish*. Flaménco.

Favier says:—"The Flamingo, near Tangier, passes northwards in April, May, and June, returning in August up to as late as December. The females are the first to arrive during the autumn migration. The males rejoin their mates in November, accompanied by the young of the previous year; the young of the year are never seen here. They are met with in large flocks on the lakes, always staying in the water, though they never swim about, and are very wary and difficult to approach. The only month in which they are entirely absent is July. Their temporary absence during other months is regulated by the quantity of water in the lakes; and as one month is not sufficient time for them to lay and hatch their eggs, they ought to nest not far from Tangier: indeed an old chasseur, worthy of belief, informed me that he had shot one which, when it fell, dropped an egg in the water."

The movements of the Flamingo are certainly very irregular and perplexing, and, no doubt, influenced by the amount of water in the brackish lagoons which they frequent. Most of these lagoons, being formed by rain-water, are brackish from the salt contained in the earth, and in very dry seasons hold hardly any water.

In very wet seasons these birds breed in the marismas of the Guadalquivir, and used to nest at Fuente Piedra between Cordova and Málaga.

Flights of Flamingoes are frequently seen passing near Gibraltar as early as the 4th of February, and as late as the 1st of May; and they again appear in August and September, when immature birds are met with. I have seen flocks of thousands in the marisma near the Isla Menor, and, by the aid of a stalking-horse, managed to shoot five at a shot. Usually they are extremely wild and shy, except during actual passage, when they alight to rest at the mouths of rivers.

Their note is not unlike that of the Grey-lag Goose, and more than once at night I have mistaken the sound for that of these Geese.

Verner sends the following extract from his journal for the year 1879:—"On the 27th of May, whilst in the marismas of the Guadalquivir, I made an expedition with Crown Prince Rudolf to obtain some Flamingoes' eggs, of which he wanted some Spanish specimens. After a long and tedious ride across the waste we finally left hard ground and traversed the mud-flats; these were either sun-baked or sticky, and for the last two miles or so were mostly covered with shallow water. The mud, where not dry, was very slippery, and two of our party (including myself) took a mud-bath, owing to our horses slipping and falling.

"After what seemed an endless journey under the broiling sun, we sighted an enormous flock of some thousands of Flamingoes, at where, the Spaniards said, was their usual nesting-station. When at a good distance from them they took wing, except a few which remained dotted about, and apparently crouching down on the mud. The day was extremely hot, and the usual mirage was intensified by the steamy exhalations from the fast-drying mud. Through this shimmering atmosphere the great flock of Flamingoes on the wing presented an extraordinary sight, resembling a drifting cloud, which seemed to change colour from a rosy pink to snowy white as the mass of birds wheeled and turned in their flight. On reaching the spot where the birds had remained behind when the main flock flew off, we found a few eggs (of which I myself took two) lying on small mud-hillocks raised above the water and slush; these eggs were fresh, white, tapered at both ends, and with the chalky surface of a Cormorant's egg.

"Unluckily, I was prevented from visiting the main colony of the Flamingoes, for the Crown Prince, having got the eggs he wanted, decided to return at once to where we had seen *Larus gelastes* in the morning, which bird, according to Dr. Brehm, who accompanied us, was not known then to breed in Spain.

"Two wild-looking men, frequenters of the marisma, who the Guardias contemptuously termed Indians, because of their savage appearance, and who had conducted us to the Flamingoes' nesting-place, assured me that if I would go on for a *media legua* they would show hundreds of nests placed together (*junto*). They described the nests as all small mud-hillocks, raised a few inches above the surface of the water when first built, but subsequently left high and dry as the water receded both from evaporation and natural drainage. These men were, of course, well acquainted with the camels, whose presence in the marisma they seemed to think the most natural thing in the world, since they had alike been born and bred in this extraordinary wilderness."

Mr. Abel Chapman appears to have visited this identical situation on 11th May, 1883, and gives an interesting account ('Ibis,' 1884, p. 66, pl. iv.) of the Flamingoes' nests, but which on that date did not contain eggs.

Head, neck, and throat black; *front* and *sides* of head and *upper* throat white; black mark between eye and bill. Length 25 inches.

Young in first plumage. Basal half of upper bill blackish; general colour greyish white, each feather above striated with dark brown; no pink in the plumage; legs and feet blackish.

Order **ANSERES.**   Family **ANATIDÆ.**

Subfamily CYGNINÆ.

229. Cygnus musicus, Bechstein. **The Whooper Swan.**

Spanish. Cisne.

This is the only species of Swan which I was able to identify in Andalucia, having examined one specimen shot on the Guadalquivir below Seville, where in some winters they occasionally occur.

Adults. White; bill, basal part to *below* nostrils yellow, the rest black.
Young. Greyish brown; bill flesh-colour. Length 60 inches.

[Cygnus olor, J. F. Gmelin. The Mute Swan.

Favier says:—"This Swan is tolerably numerous, and seen flying over near Tangier in small flights, rarely remaining in the vicinity; but they did stay in 1845 and 1849. They pass south in December, returning in April."

Most probably the above refers to the Whooper, which Favier does not mention; as it is unlikely that the Mute Swan would occur, I have omitted to number the species in my list.

Adults. White; bill yellow, with black tubercle above nostrils.
Young. Greyish brown; bill lead-coloured. Length 60 inches.]

Subfamily ANSERINÆ.

230. Anser cinereus, Meyer. The Grey-lag Goose.

Moorish. Wiz. *Spanish.* Ganso, Ánser.

The above names equally apply to *A. segetum.*

Favier's notes are the same for both this and the following species, viz.:—"This Goose, which the Arabs confound with *Anser segetum*, is as numerous as that bird near Tangier, arriving during November and December. They retire north in March, seldom making any stay near Tangier; they pass on to the large lakes and rivers."

On the Spanish side of the Straits the Grey-lag Goose is found in some winters at the Laguna de la Janda and in the various lagoons of the marisma of the Guadalquivir in enormous numbers. They generally arrive at the former place about the 20th of November, the earliest that I noticed in two consecutive years being on the 8th of November and the 25th of October. Commencing their departure about the 14th of February, they are all gone by the first week in March; Major Verner saw

THE FIRST RISE OF THE GREY-LAGS, LAGUNA DE LA JANDA.

many on the 9th in 1889, and they seem for the most part to migrate by day. Although, like Ducks, they "flight" at night—as a rule, rather later in the evening and later in the morning—they affect particular favourite spots and pools without any apparent reason for their likes and dislikes, some places never being frequented by them.

They can always be easily distinguished at some distance on the wing by the ash-grey of the shoulders, which colour, when they are on the wing, is very apparent, and they always can be known by their note or cry. They also, when flying, make a creaking noise, caused by the stiff primaries, somewhat resembling the rattling together of dry reeds, which can be heard only when they pass very close; and a very joyous sound it is for the gunner to hear.

Rump and wing-coverts *ashy grey*; bill flesh-colour; nail *white*; legs and feet *flesh-coloured*.
Adult. White round base of bill; breast with a few black marks. Length 35 inches.

231. Anser albifrons, Scopoli. The White-fronted Goose.

One of this species was obtained near Tapatanilla on the 8th of January, 1876, by Major Kelham, 74th Highlanders, and another was got near Seville by Ruiz. Lord Lilford further informed me that he recognized the cry of this Goose in the marisma.

Much smaller than preceding; bill orange-yellow; nail *white*; legs and feet *orange-yellow*.
Adults. White round base of bill; much marked with black on breast, most so in male.
Young. Without black on breast, and in first plumage without white round bill; bill and feet paler than in adult, and nail of bill brownish black, pale at the tip. Length 27 inches.

232. Anser erythropus, Linnæus. Lesser White-fronted Goose.

A male of this small race was obtained near Seville in February

1878, and I clearly made out two among a lot of other Geese near the Isla Menor in March 1882.

Resembles the last, but is very much smaller, and the markings of adults more defined.

233. Anser segetum (J. F. Gmelin). The Bean-Goose.

On the Spanish side of the Straits this species is much less numerous than the Grey-lag Goose; and it was some time before I could succeed in obtaining a specimen for identification. As far as my experience goes, I should say the present species occurs in the proportion of one to every two hundred of the Grey-lag; but as Favier considers both kinds equally common in Morocco, perhaps in some seasons the present species may be more abundant than in others.

Major Verner informs me (1894) that out of some hundreds of Geese that he has seen killed at La Janda during the last twenty years he only once saw any Bean-Geese, when, on February the 13th, 1890, he shot two out of a lot of seven.

No black on breast; bill blackish brown, nail *black*; legs and feet *orange-yellow*. Length 34 inches.

The Pink-footed Goose (*Anser brachyrhynchus*, Baillon), which does not appear to have yet been met with in the vicinity of the Straits, is much as last, but smaller; nail of bill *black*; legs and feet *flesh-colour*. Length 28 inches.

234. Bernicla leucopsis, Bechstein. The Bernicle Goose.

A single specimen of this coast-frequenting Goose, obtained near Seville several years ago, was in the possession of the landlord of the Fonda de Europa, possibly an escaped bird from San Lucar, and is the only instance yet known of its occurrence in Andalucia.

Head, neck, and throat black; *front* and *sides* of head and *upper* throat white; black mark between eye and bill. Length 25 inches.

Subfamily TADORNINÆ.

235. Tadorna cornuta (S. G. Gmelin). The Sheld-duck.

Moorish. Bou-he-baïda (*Favier*). *Spanish.* Páto tárro, Anseráta.

"This species is not regular in its appearance near Tangier, and occurs between November and February."—*Favier.*

Not observed in vicinity of Gibraltar, this coast-frequenting Sheld-duck is found near the mouth of the Guadalquivir, where they breed.

Male. Head and neck green, below that a white collar, with a broad rich chestnut band, covering the breast; wing-coverts white; wing-spot or speculum, formed by colours of the outer webs of the secondaries, green; fleshy knob on base of upper mandible; bill red; legs and feet pink.

Female. Smaller than male; less bright markings, and no knob on bill. Length 25-26 inches.

236. Tadorna casarca (Linnæus). The Ruddy Sheld-duck.

Moorish. Bou-he (*Favier*). *Spanish.* Páto tárro, Páto canélo, Labánco.

"This species is resident at no great distance from Tangier; and others are migratory, crossing to Europe during April and May, returning in September and October. In the immediate vicinity of Tangier it is scarce and only observed in small lots on the lakes and large rivers. Often they entirely, though irregularly, disappear for months at a time, probably going to marshes not very far off. The months during which they are usually absent are February, March, and June."—*Favier.*

They were repeatedly to be seen exposed for sale in Tangier market, with their throats slit in Mahometan fashion, but are very poor food, not worth cooking, as was the case in India, where the Ruddy Sheld-duck is best known to Anglo-Indians as the Brahminy Duck.

They are quite inland birds, though occasionally frequenting salt lagoons, and are much more frequent on the African than on the Spanish side of the Straits, where I never met with any, though have seen a few in Seville market in spring and the end of autumn. They breed near the mouth of the Guadalquivir, and used to do so at Fuente Piedra; also no doubt elsewhere north of the Straits. They nest in holes in cliffs and rocks; and an account is given of one nest by Mr. Salvin, in 'The Ibis' for 1859 (p. 362). In Morocco they are very wary; and I recollect, in company with a brother officer, trying in vain to approach three which we saw near Vincent's Farm, Sharf el Akab, in October: but at last they luckily pitched close to a horse feeding in the marsh; so we stalked up behind the animal to within twenty-five yards of the birds, bagging all three.

General colour rufous buff; crown light buff; wing-coverts white; wing-spot green; bill, legs, and feet blackish.

Sexes alike, except that the male has a blackish ring round neck. Length 25 inches.

Subfamily ANATINÆ.

237. Anas boscas, Linnæus. **The Wild Duck** (Mallard, male).

Moorish. Zerak el ras (Blue head). *Spanish.* Páto reál.

"The Wild Duck frequents the vicinity of Tangier throughout the year. Those which are not resident cross to Europe during March and April, returning in November and December. Those which remain to nest begin to lay during the month of February; and eggs may be occasionally found as late as the beginning of June. Tame Ducks are called *Bourk* by the Arabs."—*Favier*.

The Moorish name given above is not appropriate, the head of the Mallard being green.

In Andalucia the present species is abundant in winter; and a considerable number remain for the breeding-season, hatching by about the 25th of April; but are so molested by egging that it is a wonder that any young are brought up.

Wing-spot *purple*; tail of sixteen feathers; bill rather longer than head.
Male. Head and neck green; four central tail-coverts black, lengthened and curled upwards.
Female. General colour brown.
Male in summer. Resembles female. Length 21 inches.

238. Anas strepera, Linnæus. The Gadwall.

"This species is as scarce near Tangier as *Fuligula rufina*, the Red-crested Pochard; and their appearance, which takes place between February and March, is irregular and uncertain."—*Favier*.

The Gadwall, on the Spanish side of the Straits, cannot be termed a common bird. I only met with them on a few occasions: one shot at flight on the 26th of November, 1869, another shot at flight on the 22nd of December, 1871, at Tapatanilla, and three others killed there in February 1874, are my only personal experiences; but I have seen them in Seville market in February and March.

Lord Lilford informed me that he saw ten or twelve Gadwall at the lakes of Santa Olaya, in the Coto de Doñana, in the early part of May, and considered that they were breeding, although he was unable to discover a nest then; afterwards they were found breeding there. He also informed me that the local name there was "Frisa"—a word which signifies coarse cloth or frieze, probably from grey colour. The Portuguese name given by Arévalo for this Duck is "Frisada."

The note of the Gadwall, in winter, is a hoarse croak, by which they can be distinguished at "flight."

Wing-spot *white*; bill shorter than head, and narrowing slightly towards tip. General colour grey.
Male. Chestnut on shoulder of wing.
Female. Brown and grey. Length 20 inches.

239. Spatula clypeata (Linnæus). The Shoveler.

Moorish. Bou-zlafa (father of the bowl). *Spanish.* Paletón, Sardinéro, Páto eucharéta.

"This Duck is, in some winters, common near Tangier, arriving during September and October, leaving for the north in February and March."—*Favier.*

The Shoveler is met with in considerable numbers on the Spanish side of the Straits, and chiefly frequents shallow waters, as they do in every country in which I have seen them. They mostly arrive around Casas Viejas and on the Laguna de Janda in October; and I have known of their occurrence there in August, but have no certain knowledge of their nesting in the neighbourhood; indeed I never saw any later than the end of April, but Lord Lilford informs me he has fairly good evidence of their breeding in the marisma of the Guadalquivir.

The only species of the genus found in Europe; owing to the shape of the bill, they cannot be well mistaken for any other Duck.

Bill *broadly dilated* at the end, being twice as broad near the tip as at the base; wing-spot *green.*
Male. Head and neck green; shoulders pale blue; iris yellow.
Female. Dark brown.
Male in summer. Resembles the female. Length 20 inches.

240. Dafila acuta (Linnæus). The Pintail.

Moorish. Bou-sbula (*Favier*) ("sbula" is "ear of corn"; "seboula," a "two-edged dagger"). *Spanish.* Páto rabúdo, Páto caréto.

"This Duck is, during the winter season, nearly as plentiful in the vicinity of Tangier as the Wild Duck (*Anas boschas*). They arrive during September and October, and leave in April and May."—*Favier.*

On the Spanish side I never found the Pintail before the month of November; it is exceedingly abundant in some winters on the Laguna de la Janda and other large open pieces of water, and is in consequence very difficult to shoot by day without the aid of a stalking-horse. These Ducks mostly depart during March, some lingering on later into the month of April, the latest that I myself observed being on the 5th of that month.

Tail graduated, of sixteen feathers, two centre feathers much elongated in male, slightly so in female; wing-spot *dark green*, glossed with *copper*; bill as long as head.

Male. Head, cheeks, chin, sides of neck, and upper neck in front rich dark brown; two centre tail-feathers black.

Female. Brown above, greyish white below. Length 24–28 inches.

241. Marmaronetta angustirostris (Ménétriés). The Marbled Duck.

Moorish. Ashab (grey), Bourk el biad (white duck) (*D. Hay*).
Andalucian. Ruhilla, Pardilla.

This Duck, on both sides of the Straits, appears in spring, to remain only for the breeding-season, and is exceedingly abundant in Morocco, where, at the lakes of Ras el Doura in April 1871, we saw flocks numbering many hundreds; and they are frequently seen exposed for sale in Tangier market.

Favier states that they arrive during March and April, departing in October, and that after the Common Teal they rank as the most common Duck in the country.

On the Spanish side I heard of three being seen at the end of February, and saw six or seven myself on the 23rd of March; but the majority do not appear until late in April, though I have noticed them passing near Gibraltar early in that month. As a rule, they mostly leave by the end of September; but of course stragglers remain later.

The Marbled Duck breeds during the last week in May, nesting in patches of rushes. The nest is like that of a Teal, containing a good deal of the down from the breast of the female; and eleven eggs appear to be the usual complement. The latter much resemble those of the Common Teal, being of a yellowish-white colour. Favier states that they also nest in rushes during

May and June, and that incubation lasts from twenty-five to twenty-seven days.

I was unable to find this Duck near Casas Viejas or about the Laguna de la Janda; but in the marisma of the Guadalquivir, especially near the Coto del Rey, they are very numerous.

In flight, the Marbled Duck somewhat resembles the female Pintail; but it is more of a Teal, as Lord Lilford observes. We found them in Morocco wary and difficult to approach; but in the dusk they "flight" very low, and by watching the direction taken by them for one night you may on the next evening be tolerably certain of shooting a good many; and they are excellent eating.

Sexes alike. Bill narrow.
Entire plumage light brown and grey. Secondaries creamy brown. Bill, legs, and feet black. Length 14½ inches.

242. Querquedula crecca (Linnæus). The Teal.

Moorish. Frifar (*Favier*). *Spanish.* Sarcéta.

"This species is abundant near Tangier during winter, passing north in February and March, returning in September and October."—*Favier.*

The Teal is very numerous on the Spanish side, and, from their habit of haunting small streams and marshes, more easily shot than any other of the Ducks. Their numbers vary considerably, as in some seasons they are much more abundant than in others. They chiefly arrive during October, leaving for the north in March, and have been known, though very rarely, to breed near Casas Viejas. Lord Lilford observed a single bird at Santa Oláya in May 1872, and has fairly good evidence of their nesting in the district since that date.

Wing-spot black and *green*; tail of sixteen feathers.
Male. Head and neck chestnut, with broad green stripe from eye down sides of neck, margined on sides of head with buff.
Female. Above dark brown, feathers edged with grey; below whitish. Length 13-15 inches.

243. **Querquedula circia** (Linnæus). **The Garganey** or **Summer Teal.**

Spanish. Capitán.

"This Teal appears irregularly near Tangier, only on migration, and does not occur every year. They arrive during February and March, passing on to the north, and are seen returning south in September."—*Favier.*

The Garganey seems to be equally irregular in its appearance in Andalucia, as I only saw one in Seville market in March 1869, and did not again meet with any till March 1874, when they were for a few days not uncommon about Casas Viejas and near Seville. Lord Lilford informs me that he saw a pair at Santa Oláya, near Rocio, in May 1872, and that since then they have been found nesting there.

Male. Wing-spot *green*, between two bars of white; wing-coverts or shoulders *bluish grey*; neck and breast dark brown, with pale brown crescent-shaped bands.

Female. Much as female of *Q. crecca*, but *without* green metallic speculum; shoulders with very slight grey tinge. Length 15–16 inches.

244. **Mareca penelope** (Linnæus). **The Wigeon.**

Moorish. Bou-khe-siwa. *Spanish.* Silbón (Whistler), Páto franciscáno.

"This species is the most abundant Duck near Tangier, being found in large flocks throughout the winter months. They commence to arrive in August and September, and leave during March and April."—*Favier.*

Exactly the same may be said of the Wigeon on the Spanish side of the Straits, except that I never saw any so early as Favier mentions. They begin to arrive early in October; but the greater number do not appear until November; and they are then by far the most common Duck, in some winters swarming in thousands on the Laguna de la Janda. Their departure for the north begins about the end of March; but a few linger on throughout the whole of April.

Tail of fourteen feathers; bill shorter than head.

Male. Forehead and crown buffish white; wing-coverts white; back white, finely vermiculated with black; wing-spot *green*.

Female. Above brown and greyish brown; head and neck mottled with light brown and blackish brown; shoulders of wings greyish white; wing-spot *greyish*.

Males in summer lose the whitish crown, and to a certain extent resemble the females. Length 20 inches.

Subfamily FULIGULINÆ.

245. Fuligula rufila (Pallas). **The Red-crested Pochard.**

"This Duck is accidentally met with around Tangier, but is a very rare species. I only obtained two—one in 1835, the other in 1849."—*Favier.*

I never met with this Pochard on either side of the Straits, and have seen but one specimen said to be Andalucian. A more eastern species (frequenting still, deep waters, and seen rarely on rivers), they are of more common occurrence in the south-east of Spain; and Lord Lilford mentions them as common on the Albufera near Valencia, where they used to breed.

Wing-spot white; tail of fourteen feathers, as in next four species.

Male. Head and upper neck *reddish chestnut*; feathers on crown forming an *erectile crest*; back yellowish brown; lower neck, breast, and belly black; bill and legs vermilion; iris red.

Female. Crown dark brown without crest; cheeks, neck, and sides of throat *light grey*; bill and legs reddish brown. Length 21 inches.

246. Fuligula ferina (Linnæus). **The Common Pochard.**

Spanish. Cabezón, Cenizo.

"This species arrives during October to remain in Morocco for the winter, departing for the north in April and May."—*Favier.*

We found the Pochard common about the lakes near Tetuan, and shot one there as late as the 30th of March. On the Spanish side of the Straits I have rarely seen this Duck near Gibraltar, and then only in winter; but at times a good many are to be seen at the Laguna de la Janda. In the marisma below Seville they are much more abundant, and Lord Lilford informs me "that in August 1892 a female Pochard and a quantity of eggs were brought to him from the marisma; and the man who brought them declared that in the previous spring and summer, Pochards, which were almost unknown there, were only slightly less abundant than Marbled Ducks, which latter were in most extraordinary profusion owing to the abundance of water."

In the spring of that year, 1892, I never saw the country around Gibraltar so flooded, the Laguna de la Janda resembling an inland sea.

Wing-spot *grey*; bill black, longer than head, broad band of blue across the middle.

Male. Head and neck chestnut-red; breast and upper back black; back and scapulars white, finely vermiculated with black; iris red.

Female. Markings as in male, but with dull brown head and neck; dark brown breast and upper back. Length 17–19 inches.

247. Fuligula nyroca (Güldenstädt). The White-eyed Pochard or Ferruginous Duck.

Moorish. Ziriguil (*Favier*). *Andalucian.* Negréte, Pardóte.

The White-eyed Pochard may be considered, like the Marbled Duck, a summer resident on both sides of the Straits, and is most abundant in Morocco.

I saw many hundreds at the lakes of Ras el Doura towards the end of April, being even then in large flocks. We shot them at flight in the evening at the same time as some Marbled Ducks; but the two species did not fly together. There were also a few of the White-eyed Pochards about the lake of Esmir at the end of March. Favier writes of the present species, that it is "abundant near Tangier, arriving from the south during May and departing in November and December, totally disappearing for a time in winter [*]. They are most abundant at Ras el Doura, breeding in June and July, the incubation lasting thirty days."

On the Spanish side this Duck is common during the breeding-season in some parts of the marismas, and commences to nest about the end of April. Lord Lilford obtained a nest in May 1872, in the Coto de Doñana, composed of dead dry water-plants, flags, &c., lined with thick brownish-white down and a few white feathers. It was placed at a short distance from the water, in high rushes, and contained nine eggs. Although they generally pass south early in autumn, some are found occasionally in the winter months, I once saw and shot a single bird as late as the 6th of December, which, albeit in fair condition, from its excessive tameness, was probably from some cause incapable of migration.

I have always found this Duck, like its allies, *F. rufina* and *F. ferina*, frequenting deep, still, weedy water rather than shallow open places; and the flesh of the present species is not only, like theirs, excellent eating, but far surpasses either in that respect.

Wing-spot *white*; tail short, of fourteen feathers, much graduated; bill lead-coloured, longer than head.

Male. Head, neck, and general colour above chestnut-brown; underparts greyish white; iris *white*.

Female. Marked as male, but duller; iris dull white. Length 15–17 inches.

248. Fuligula cristata (Leach). The Tufted Duck.

"This species is in some years very abundant near Tangier, arriving here for the winter in November, and returning north during February. In some seasons they are not to be met with, but were common in the years 1845, 1846, 1849, 1850, 1858, and 1861."—*Favier.*

Kelham saw great numbers at Esmir in March 1881.

---

[*] It is remarkable that the instances recorded of this Duck's appearance in the British Islands should have been often in the winter months.

The Tufted Duck is sometimes plentiful in winter on the Laguna de la Janda, is well known in the marisma, and I have occasionally seen them in the Bay of Gibraltar.

Wing-spot white.

Male. Head and neck glossy purplish black, with an occipital crest or tuft; breast, belly, sides, flanks, and speculum white; the rest of plumage black; iris yellow.

Female. Crest smaller; brown where black in the male; underparts brownish white. Length 17 inches.

249. Fuligula marila (Linnæus). The Scaup Duck.

This Duck is a rare visitant in the Straits, but has occurred in the Bay of Gibraltar in December; marine and coast-frequenting, they are not liable to much notice and seldom likely to appear in the markets.

Wing-spot *white*; bill very broad, about as long as head.

Male. Head, neck, upper breast, rump, and under tail-coverts black, with green gloss; back and scapulars white, broadly vermiculated with black; belly white; iris straw-yellow.

Female and young male. White band round base of bill, broadest in female; head and neck dark brown, as are all the parts which are black in the male. Length 18 inches.

250. Clangula glaucion (Linnæus). The Golden-eye.

All to be stated regarding this northern species is that they rarely occur about the Straits in winter.

Bill much shorter than head; tail of sixteen feathers, as in next.

Male. Head and neck glossy green; feathers on crown slightly lengthened; *small white spot* at base of bill; scapulars white; wing-spot white.

Female and young male. Head and neck ash-brown; no white spot on head; wing-spot white, divided by a black line. Length 16–19 inches.

251. Œdemia nigra (Linnæus). The Common Scoter or Black Duck.

Moorish. Bourk-el-behar (Sea-Duck). *Spanish, Málaga.* Coquinero, Páto negro.

Favier states that the Scoter is "found in abundance near Tangier, arriving sometimes as early as August, retiring northwards in April."

I found this Duck in some seasons very common about the Straits, especially after rough weather in Gibraltar Bay; but they do not appear except in small lots. The earliest noticed was on the 12th of November; the latest on the 12th of March, 1872; and was very abundant off Málaga in March 1882.

Adult male. *Entirely black*; bill black, with centre of upper mandible yellow, and a knob at the base.

Female. Sooty brown; chin and throat whitish; side of head greyish white; bill without knob.

Young. Cheeks, chin, sides, and front of neck dull greyish white; belly speckled with brown and white. Length 21 inches.

[Œdemia fusca (Linnæus). The Velvet Scoter.

Is recorded from Valencia, by Vidal, but has not been observed within the district treated of in this work.

Adult male. Velvet-black, except the large wing-spot, eyelid, and patch below eye, which are white; iris yellowish white.

Female. Blackish brown, but with *white* wing-spot. Length 21 inches.]

Subfamily ERISMATURINÆ.

252. Erismatura leucocephala (Scopoli). **The Spiny-tailed or White-faced Duck.**

Spanish. Porrón.

"This species occurs near Tangier on passage, passing north during April and returning to winter further south in October. Some of the spring migrants remain in the country to breed in June, laying as many as ten pure white eggs, with a rough granulated surface. This Duck is not at all regular in its appearance, but in some seasons is quite common."—*Favier.*

In Andalucia the Spiny-tailed Duck occurs as above, chiefly

on the coast and on large lakes, but I never met with any near Gibraltar.

Bill longer than head, much swollen at the base.
Tail *long, pointed, and stiff*.
General colour chestnut to buff, vermiculated with blackish grey.
Male. Crown black; forehead, sides of head, chin, and nape white.
Female. Crown and nape dark brown. General colour more chestnut than in male, white streak below eye to nape, chin and upper throat white. Length 17½ inches.

Subfamily MERGINÆ.

The following—Mergansers, or "Saw-bills"—have the bill slender and straight, the edges with strong saw-like teeth pointing backwards.

253. Mergus merganser, Linnæus. The Goosander.

The Goosander is recorded by Favier as having been once obtained by him near Tangier in October 1862, and another was found dead on the shore near that town during the winter of 1869-70, the only instance in which I met with any. Arévalo records this species from Málaga.

The immature males of this and the next two species can be at once distinguished by the trachea, which in the males has more or less bony enlargement at the base, while in the females it is uniform in size throughout the entire length.

Male. Head and upper neck glossy metallic black, slightly crested; lower neck and underparts white; rump and tail *ashy grey*; bill blood-red, and, as in next, longer than head; iris red.
Female. Head and upper neck light chestnut, crested; above slate-grey; below white; wing-spot white.
Young. Like female, but without crest. Length 26 inches.

254. Mergus serrator, Linnæus. The Red-breasted Merganser.

Spanish. Páto de siérra (Saw-duck).

This species is not mentioned in Favier's MS., but is found in some winters in considerable numbers in the Bay of Gibraltar, generally during December and January.

Male. Head and neck glossy metallic black; crest of narrow elongated black feathers; white collar on neck, showing much when flying; rump *white*, with wavy black lines; tail uniform brown; bill vermilion; legs orange; iris red.

Female and young. Like those of preceding species, but much smaller, and head darker, black bar across wing-spot. Length 22-24 inches.

255. Mergus albellus, Linnæus. **The Smew.**

The Smew occurs in some winters about the Straits in immature plumage.

Bill shorter than head.

Male. Black, grey, and white. Head and neck white; black stripe through eye to nape; slightly crested; rump ash-grey.

Female. Head and nape chestnut, crested; above slate-grey; black patch from bill to eye; rump greyish black.

Young male. Like female, but has no black patch between eye and bill. Length 14–17 inches.

Order COLUMBÆ.   Family COLUMBIDÆ.

256. Columba palumbus, Linnæus. **The Ring-Dove** or **Wood-Pigeon.**

Moorish. Kamôr.   *Spanish.* Palóma torcáz.

"This Pigeon is found near Tangier throughout the year. Some are migratory, crossing to Europe in March and April."— Favier.

In some localities in Morocco the Wood-Pigeon positively swarms. In April, up a valley near the Fondak, to the south-west of that place, on the road between Tangier and Tetuan, it would have been easy to shoot a hundred in a day, they were in such numbers and so excessively tame. Two or three, which we shot to eat, had their crops full of the tuberous root of some weed which had been ploughed up and was lying in quantities about the fallow fields. During the same month, about three years previously, we noticed considerable numbers near Larache; but there they were much more wild, though not so shy as in England or Andalucia. In the latter country, about Gibraltar, a few pairs nest in the Cork-wood and other wooded districts; they are most abundant during the winter months, though I never saw any great quantity.

Adult. *White* on outer wing-coverts; white patch on each side of neck.
Young. Without white patch on neck. Length 16–17 inches.

257. Columba œnas, Linnæus. The Stock-Dove.

Moorish. Hamam el Berri (Wild Pigeon).

The Stock-Dove is neither mentioned by Favier nor Mr. Drake as occurring in Morocco. We found them near the Fondak between Tangier and Tetuan at the same time and place that the Ring-Doves were so abundant, and they are sufficiently common to be known to the Moors there by the above-mentioned name, which, by the way, is the same as that used for the next species, *C. livia.* They were in some numbers, and we shot one or two for identification, being further informed by the Moors that they nested in holes of trees. They evidently were breeding at that time; but we failed to discover a nest during the very short period that we remained there. We also noticed the Stock-Dove in April near Larache, and Meade-Waldo observed them in March 1894.

On the Spanish side of the Straits I only observed this species once near Gibraltar, but Arévalo mentions them as occurring near Málaga.

The absence of the white patches on the carpal joints of the wings will often serve to distinguish them, when flying, from the Ring-Dove, independently of their smaller size, while the absence of the white rump equally distinguishes them from the Rock-Dove—not that the latter species is usually met with in the same locality.

Adult. Sides of neck with metallic-green patch; axillaries grey.
Young. Without patch on neck. Length 13 inches.

258. Columba livia, J. F. Gmelin. **The Rock-Dove.**

Moorish. Hamam el Berri. *Spanish.* Zurita, Palóma bráva.

"This is the most common of the Pigeons about Tangier, living in rocks and even in the ramparts of the town, breeding both in a wild and in a domestic state all the year round."—*Favier.*

The Rock-Dove is plentiful on both sides of the Straits wherever there are rocks and caves, inland as well as on the coast. Many are resident at Gibraltar, on North Front and at the "back of the Rock"; and at one time some sport was to be obtained upon getting permission to shoot them; but a "young and inexperienced" arrival one day, instead of killing pigeons, shot one or more of the celebrated Gibraltar Apes, for which he, amongst suffering other indignities and punishments, was afterwards known as "Du Chaillu." In consequence of this exploit, all leave to shoot there was thenceforth withheld, and very rightly so.

Pied and white varieties are frequently seen; whether escaped tame Pigeons or real wild Rock-Doves, I cannot say, probably the former.

Lower back and *rump white*; two conspicuous black bands across the wings; axillaries white. Length 13 inches.

259. Turtur communis, Selby. **The Common Turtle-Dove.**

Moorish. Imam, Stitsia, Targal. *Spanish.* Tórtola.

"Is a summer resident near Tangier, vast numbers arriving to cross the Straits in flocks during April and May, returning in September and October, then to retire south for the winter. This species is without doubt the origin of the domestic Turtle-Dove [*], called *limama* or *dekrallah* (praise of God), some of which birds are pure white."—*Favier.*

[*] Favier's opinion is given, but it is not certain which species is the origin of the domestic Dove.

The Common Turtle-Dove is seen in extreme abundance in Andalucia, during its stay being a great object of pursuit to the Spanish *tirador*, who, in August, often makes a *puesto*, or hiding-place, near some favourite drinking-haunt of the doves, and shoots them much in the same way as the Partridge—that is, on the ground, three or four in a row; only with the Doves he has, of course, no *reclamo*, or call-bird.

The Turtle-Dove chiefly arrives during the first week in May, more coming in that week than during all the rest of their migration, which is about the time that the seed of the Greater Honeywort (*Cerinthe major*) is ripe, and on which they feed on arrival. I first saw one in 1870 on the 11th, and in 1872 on the 14th of April. They mostly disappear by the beginning of October. The latest I noticed was a single bird at Casas Viejas on the 31st of October. In my note-book I have one recorded as seen on the 9th of October, in the middle of the Bay of Biscay.

Head, nape, rump, and outer wing-coverts bluish ash; under tail-coverts white; collar-patch of four rows of black feathers tipped with white on each side of neck; tail graduated, two centre feathers brown, the rest slate-grey, the ends and outside web of outer pair white.

Young. Without neck-patch. Length 11½ inches.

260. Turtur senegalensis (Linnæus). The Egyptian Turtle-Dove.

This species is mentioned by Mr. Drake as found commonly in the southern part of Morocco, but does not appear to have been obtained by Favier, nor were any met with by us, in the north-west of that country.

The absence of spots on the back, and its smaller size, will distinguish it from any other species likely to be met with in Morocco.

Feathers of the fore neck bifurcated, black, with two rufous spots at end of each, forming collar; rump bluish lead-colour. Length 11 inches.

Order **PTEROCLETES**. Family **PTEROCLIDÆ**.

261. Pteroclurus alchata (Linnæus). The Pin-tailed Sand-Grouse.

Moorish. El Gäta. *Spanish.* Gánga.

Favier states this species to be "scarce near Tangier, but common about Dar el Baidar"; and says "they cross the Straits in spring, returning in August and July."

This beautifully marked bird is the most common Sand-Grouse on the Spanish side, although very local, being abundant about the edges of the marisma, where they nest late in May, as also near Granada. Some may be migratory; but I have seen them in January near Seville. I never saw any in the neighbourhood of Gibraltar.

The flight of both species of Sand-Grouse is very powerful; and sometimes they go to such a height that, although you can hear their croaking hoarse call, they are almost out of sight. Becoming excessively tame and familiar when kept in confinement, in a wild state they are very difficult to approach without a stalking-horse, and when obtained are, in my opinion, of no use to eat. They are very difficult birds to skin, the feathers coming out like those of a Pigeon.

Eggs of this Pin-tailed Sand-Grouse, taken near Seville, are of a reddish-buff colour, marked all over with spots of reddish brown and light grey.

The European and African form has been separated as a distinct species, *P. pyrenaicus*, because they are of richer colour than Asiatic birds (!).

Lower breast and belly white. Chest chestnut, with black line above and below. Two centre tail-feathers much elongated and pointed.

Male. Throat black.

Female. Throat white. Length 13½ inches, tail 5½ inches.

262. Pterocles arenarius (Pallas). **The Black-bellied Sand-Grouse.**

Moorish. El Koudri. *Spanish.* Cortéza.

Favier merely mentions that this Sand-Grouse "occurs in Dar el Baidar."

On the European side, this large species of Sand-Grouse, though extremely local, is resident in the marisma and near Utrera, nesting late in May, but does not appear near Gibraltar. I do not think there is any migration of this bird. The different species of Sand-Grouse lay three eggs only, of an *elliptical* form, placed on the bare ground without any nest; eggs of this species taken near Seville are of a pale cream-colour, marked all over with faint spots of very light brown.

Belly uniform black; centre tail-feathers not elongated.
Male. Throat chestnut.
Female. Throat yellowish white. Length 13 inches.

Future visitors to Morocco should look out for *Pterocles senegallus* (Linnæus), which most probably occurs in the southern part of the country, and has no pectoral zone. Chest and upper parts covered with round black spots. Length 13 inches.

Order **GALLINÆ.**   Family **PHASIANIDÆ.**

263. Caccabis rufa (Linnæus). **The Western Red-legged or French Partridge.**

Spanish. Perdíz.

This Partridge is, throughout Andalucia, plentiful and resident, frequenting the *monte* or scrub, not, as in some parts of England, being found in cultivated places. Never known to occur on the African side of the Straits, it is not even found on the Rock of Gibraltar, which would seem rather strange, as it is to be seen on the Queen of Spain's Chair, and occasionally on the plain below within a couple of miles of the neutral ground. Mr. Stark, in February 1876, found "large packs of this Partridge on the Sierra Nevada at an elevation of some 7000 feet."

Almost every Spanish sportsman, or *cazador*, keeps one or more of these birds as call-birds (*reclamos*), each wretched Partridge being confined in a cage which is so small that the unfortunate bird has scarcely room to turn round. To add to this cruelty, at certain seasons they are never given water, as it is supposed to be fatal to them; but in a wild state they drink a great deal, and during the scorching month of August, and the first half of September, one of the favourite Spanish methods of shooting them is to make a hiding-place (*puesto*) near their drinking-haunt, placing call-birds on each side of the water out of the line of fire—so that, when a covey comes to drink, as many as possible may be mowed down at once by the concealed "sportsman," who, throughout the whole year, regardless of the season, shoots them whenever he can, the acme of his diversion being to shoot a Partridge from the nest. However, it may as well be mentioned that these men shoot for profit, not for sport. In spite of this ceaseless persecution, Partridges do not decrease, which is truly wonderful. Since the above was written a close-season has been established, but not observed.

Light-coloured and white varieties of the Red-legged Partridge are of not unfrequent occurrence: for some years in succession there was a white covey near the Guadiarro on the road to Gaucin. They breed in May, and the eggs vary greatly in size, being subject to the same variations as those of *C. petrosa*, but usually larger than the eggs of that bird, although sometimes smaller.

Sexes alike, except that male has knobs or blunt spurs on legs. Black gorget or collar from bill through eyes, enclosing a white throat; dirty white below this collar, spotted and streaked with black; bill, eyelids, and legs red; tail chestnut, of fourteen feathers. Length 14 inches.

264. Caccabis petrosa (J. F. Gmelin). **The Barbary Partridge.**
Moorish. Hejel.

"The Barbary Partridge," says Favier, "is resident around Tangier, and very common, sometimes perching on trees."

This species is far more common in proportion in Morocco than *C. rufa* is in Spain, and chiefly frequents palmetto scrub; in some localities it is so numerous that it would be quite easy for one gun to bag fifty brace in the day. The flesh of this Partridge is not so good even as that of the Common Red-leg, which does not say much in its favour, but they submit to captivity very well, and may be kept alive in coops like fowls, to be used as required—and, after being fed on corn for a month or so, improve greatly in a culinary point of view.

As is well known to all ornithologists, the Barbary Partridge is the only species found on the Rock of Gibraltar, being in great numbers there. Sometimes they may be seen sitting on the stones within a few feet of the sea, and a pair or two used even to frequent the rocks below the "rope ladder" at Europa. Although protected from guns and carefully preserved from the attacks of human beings, they suffer considerably from the number of cats which abound, and are also preyed on by Genets and Eagles, whilst lizards and snakes destroy the eggs and young.

This bird, like other Partridges, is very noisy at dusk: in the nesting-season they have a peculiar long-drawn croaking cry, which puzzled me for a long time before I could make out from what bird it came; but whether the male only thus calls I do not know, though I suspect such to be the case.

They commence to lay about the 15th of April. The eggs are very similar to those of *C. rufa*, and vary much in the markings, some being quite free from the usual small freckles.

The Rev. John White mentions this Partridge as being plentiful at Gibraltar about 1770, and not being found on the mainland of Spain.

This species is at once distinguished by the *chestnut collar* round the neck, studded with small white spots, and is also a smaller bird than the Common Red-leg, besides having a metallic-blue tinge on the wing-coverts. The legs are not always red, sometimes being a pale buff colour. Length 12½ inches.

265. Francolinus bicalcaratus (Linnæus). Double-spurred Francolin.

This is no doubt the species mentioned by Mr. Drake, and occurs as far north in Morocco as Rabat, where I am informed the local name is "Ragh"; and of late years many have been sent alive from Mogador to England.

The male has two pairs of spurs. The sexes are alike in plumage.
Above brown vermiculated with black; chin and throat white. General colour below buff, each feather with a black racquet-shaped shaft-streak. Length 12½ inches.

266. Coturnix communis, Bonnaterre. The Common Quail.

Moorish. Summin. *Spanish.* Codorníz.

Favier states that the Quail is very abundant on passage on the Moorish side of the Straits, many remaining to breed, the majority crossing over to Europe during March and April, returning in October and November.

On the Spanish side of the Straits it appears to me that the chief vernal migration of the Common Quail is during the months of March and April, whilst the autumnal passage is almost entirely executed during the latter half of September, at that time their numbers being sometimes almost incredible.

The Andalucian cazadores profess to recognize two kinds of Quail—those which are migratory and called "*Criollas*," and those which are resident and so named "*Castellañas*." There is certainly much difference in the colour of the plumage and of the legs, the Criollas being lighter-coloured and slightly smaller birds than the Castellañas, which are very dark; otherwise, in habits, note, and eggs, there is no difference, although at a glance the resident and migratory races can be easily distinguished.

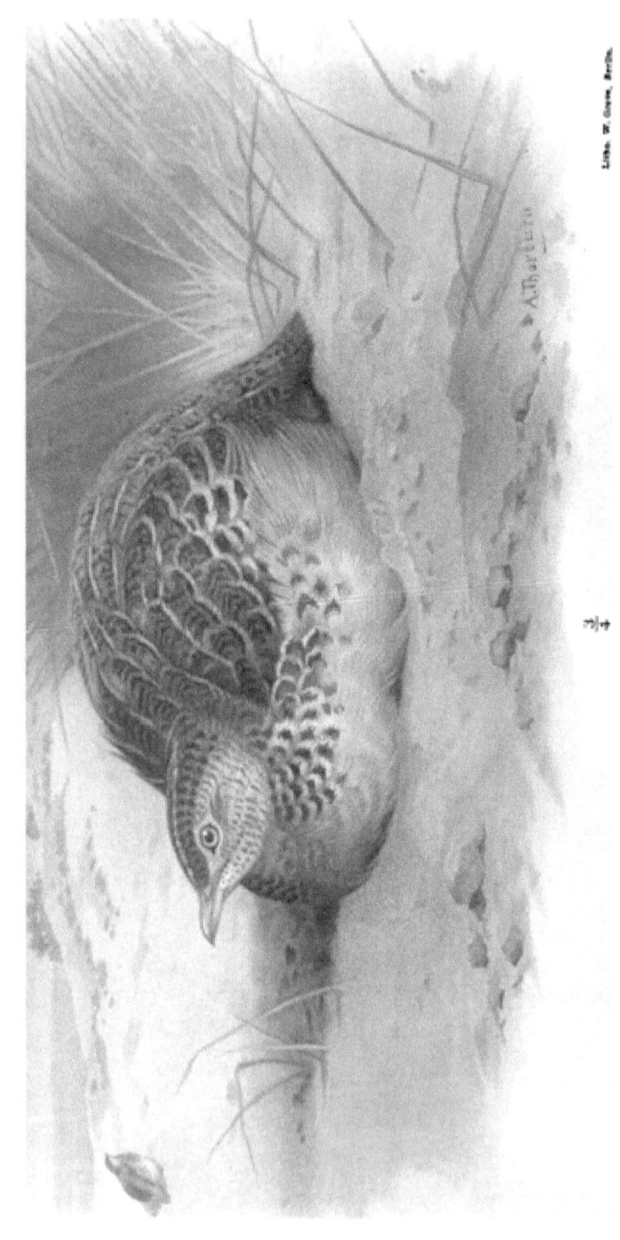

There are a great number of these resident Quails, which, throughout the winter, seem to collect together and haunt certain favourite spots, these places never being without them. You may kill three or four and hunt about unable to find more; but go to the same place in a few days' time, and you will find that some fresh ones have taken possession of the ground.

In summer Quail are universally distributed all over the cultivated country; in autumn the best place to shoot them is in the maize-fields or, rather, stubbles. Vast quantities are caught in the spring with small nets by the aid of the " Quail-call " (*pitillo*). The birds begin to call their love-note about the 9th of March; after that time their " *quit que-twit* " is to be heard on every side as long as the nesting-season lasts. They commence to lay in May; and I have known of a nest with eleven eggs taken as late as the 17th October.

General colour buff, marked much as Partridge above.
Male. Chin and throat blackish.
Female. Chin and throat buff; larger than male. Length 7 inches.

Order **HEMIPODII.** Family **TURNICIDÆ.**

267. **Turnix sylvatica** (Desfontaines). **The Andalucian Bush-Quail or Three-toed Quail.**

Moorish. Zerquil (*Favier*). *Spanish.* Torillo.

" This little Quail is both resident and migratory in the vicinity of Tangier, and is a much less common bird than the ordinary Quail; those which migrate pass northwards during May and June, and are seen on the return passage in September and October. They nest in July, depositing *four* eggs in any slight depression of the ground, often among corn. The young, from the moment of exclusion, are attended by both male and female— all remaining together in parties for some time, in the same manner as Quails. I kept a female bird in captivity for about thirteen months, feeding it on millet and water. This bird was very fond of eating flies, and also used to devour the ants which came into its cage to carry away the dead. Very gentle in its character, the call of this bird was very *triste*: it cooed day and night, much in the manner of a Turtle-Dove, only the note was more subdued and lengthened. I have reason to believe that these Quails would breed in captivity, although this individual bird did not lay."—*Favier*.

On the Spanish side I was unable to detect any migration of this bird, though it is said by Andalucian bird-catchers and cazadores to be migratory. The probability is that they are so, but yet am inclined to think the reverse, as they are found in the same localities in equal numbers at all seasons of the year.

Near Gibraltar it is very local and nowhere plentiful, apparently less so than is really the case, for they are difficult birds to flush, and if put up once will rarely rise a second time. Scattered here and there, they chiefly frequent palmetto (*Chamærops humilis*) scrub, and appear to be most common near the coast, being more abundant to the east of the Queen of Spain's Chair, especially about the Lomo del Rey and a place called Las Agusaderas. In their flight and habits, from what I could observe of them, they resemble the Indian Button-Quail (*Turnix dussumieri*).

I have often seen them among the rough grass and bents close to the sea-shore, but always near palmetto, and one bird in particular for a long time frequented a patch of thick herbage near the mouth of the "First River"; whenever I rode by, my dog used to flush it, till at last one day, wanting a specimen, I went purposely to shoot the bird; but, of course, upon this occasion my friend was not to be found, nor did I again see one there for some months.

They are scarce between Algeciraz and Tarifa, but occur towards Vejer, and are tolerably plentiful on the palmetto-covered high ground above Casas Viejas, called La Mesa; further than this I did not meet with them personally, nor could I obtain any near Seville.

The nest is, from the skulking habits of the birds, extremely difficult to obtain. I never had the good fortune to find one, but had one lot of eggs brought to me from near San Roque, on the 6th of July, 1869. The finder said the nest was under shelter of a palmetto bush, and merely consisted of a few bits of dried grass. These eggs, four in number, which is, without doubt, the regular complement laid by all the Three-toed Quails*, were very slightly incubated, and in appearance much resembled those of the Common Pratincole, *Glareola torquata*, only being, of course, much more diminutive. Later in July I received several eggs from Mogador, which exactly resembled the Spanish ones; but not having been blown and being hard sat-on, the shells were so tender and rotten as to be useless. My friend Captain S. Reid, of the Royal Engineers, informed me that he had the luck to find a nest, placed in grass near the shore on the eastern beach, on the 19th of May, 1873; this nest contained four incubated eggs, as did another from near Tangier obtained by Olcese. Verner tells me that on the 11th of August two eggs hard sat-on were brought him by a Spaniard, who had caught the old bird on the nest. There were four eggs, but he broke two whilst catching the old one.

The males of this species, and, I believe, of all the genus, are very much smaller than the females; this difference is so striking that the cazadores always declare there are two species. I have at different times kept these little birds alive, and sent them to England, and they are easily reconciled to captivity, becoming very tame and confiding pets; at times they coo in a moaning way, whence their trivial Spanish name of *torillo* or little bull. They also have another single note, much like that of the female Quail but less loud.

This bird was called by Latham in 1783 the Gibraltar Quail.

The Anglicized name of Hemipode is fallacious, as Nature

---

* Captain Loche, *fide* Canon Tristram, seems to have been singularly fortunate in finding a nest with seven eggs ('Ibis,' 1859, p. 80).

produces no half-footed animal, whilst the absence of the hind toe or hallux is not peculiar to the Turnicidæ. Bush-Quail, Three-toed Quail, or Button-Quail, as in India, would be more appropriate as English names.

Sexes alike. Centre of chest bright rusty. Length : male 6 inches ; female 7½ inches.

Order **FULICARIÆ**.   Family **RALLIDÆ**.

268. Crex pratensis, Bechstein.   The Landrail or Corn-Crake.

Moorish. Zelga (*Favier*).   *Spanish.* Rey de los Codornices (King of the Quails), Guia de los Codornices (Guide of the Quails), Polluéla rúbia.

"This Crake is found in Morocco on passage, crossing the Straits during the month of February, returning in August, September, and October, being occasionally obtained throughout the winter months."—*Favier*.

The Landrail does not seem to remain in Andalucia during the breeding-season, as I never heard its well-known cry ; but I have seen them as late as the 2nd of May. They are not obtained in any abundance, but, like other Rails, are, no doubt, more common than they appear to be, and occur most frequently in October and February, being sometimes found during the winter months.

General colour above brownish buff, each feather on back with a black centre ; axillaries *chestnut* ; bill shorter than head—as in the three following species. Length 10¼ inches.

269. Porzana maruetta (Leach).   **The Spotted Crake.**

Spanish. Polluéla (under which name the next four species are also included).

"This bird is met with near Tangier during passage, but not in any great number, and is the most common of the family, haunting thick beds of rushes in swamps and on the edges of lakes and rivers."—*Favier.*

The Spotted Crake is extremely abundant on the Spanish side, being more numerous than the Water-Rail, and is most frequent in spring and autumn. Many remain during the winter months; and they are found also in the breeding-season.

General colour above olive-brown; each feather on back with blackish centre, and spotted with white; axillaries barred with white; breast spotted. Length 8½ inches.

270. Porzana bailloni (Vieillot). Baillon's Crake.

Favier says of this bird:—"Very rare; I only met with one, in 1857." But I obtained two near Tangier in spring of 1877, and probably it is common.

Seldom seen, owing to its skulking propensities. We found this prettily marked Crake very common when snipe-shooting at Casas Viejas from October to February. We also obtained it at the Laguna de la Janda in May. Many are resident, breeding at the end of April, when they make a small nest of sedges and grass placed at the edges of swamps, laying from five to seven olive-brown eggs spotted with darker brown, very like Jay's eggs.

Above dark reddish brown, marked with black; cheeks, throat, and breast slaty blue; flanks *black*, barred with white; more white streaks and spots on back than in next species; under wing-coverts mottled with whitish.

Young. Chin and throat white; breast and belly buff. Length 7 inches.

271. Porzana parva (Scopoli). The Little Crake.

The Little Crake is not noticed by Favier as occurring in Morocco; and on the Spanish side of the Straits I never could succeed in meeting with any, though have seen specimens said to be Andalucian, and Arévalo records them from province of Málaga. Owing to the powers of concealment which these small Rails possess, it is very difficult to obtain them, and impossible to learn much of their habits. Without the aid of a good dog it is very hard to compel them to rise; and in consequence they appear to be much more rare than they really are. I recollect finding a nest of this or Baillon's Crake situated in a very small isolated patch of swamp; and instead of trying to snare the birds, I stupidly endeavoured to flush them with three good water-dogs; but it was quite useless; we could find no signs of them whatever; so the unidentified eggs were valueless, as the resemblance is so great between the eggs of this and Baillon's Crake, that unless the bird be obtained it is impossible to tell to which species they belong.

Much like last, but larger, and with flanks *slate-grey*; white spots only on centre of back; under wing-coverts uniform. Length 8 inches.

272. Rallus aquaticus, Linnæus. The Water-Rail.

Spanish. Rascón, Rascón de agua.

"This bird is found on passage near Tangier in about the same numbers as the Landrail, frequenting the edges of rivers and swamps, where they hide up in the sedges."—*Favier.*

The Water-Rail is very common in all suitable localities on the Spanish side; and their croaking frog-like call is always to be heard in the swampy jungle at Casas Viejas. Being to a great extent a migratory bird, they are most common in winter; but, owing to the cover being more thin, at that season all the Rails and Crakes are easier to obtain. They build in rushes or sedges, laying about the 20th of April. On the 13th of May we found two nests, from each of which Mr. Stark succeeded in snaring one of the old birds; these nests, built entirely of dry sedge and lined with a few bits of dry grass, were just raised above the water, and measured 6 inches in height, depth, and diameter; the hollow of the nest was $4\frac{1}{2}$ inches across by $2\frac{1}{2}$ deep. Each nest contained seven eggs hard sat-on—one lot being of the usual type, the other resembling more those of the Spotted Crake, or, rather, looking like miniature Waterhen's eggs with larger blotches than usual.

Bill reddish at base, longer than the head, and slender. Above brown, blotched with black; below slaty blue; axillaries, belly, and flanks black, barred with white; legs and feet brown. Length 10 inches.

273. Gallinula chloropus (Linnæus). **The Waterhen** or **Moorhen.**

Moorish. Zelga-kahla (*Favier*). *Spanish.* Pólla de agua.

The Moorhen, according to Favier, is "resident in the vicinity of Tangier, being met with in abundance; many, however, are migratory."

It is needless to say much about a bird so well known as our Common English Waterhen. They are not so common in Andalucia as the Spotted Crake; but I was unable to detect any migratory habits on the Spanish side of the Straits, where they are tolerably plentiful and generally distributed in all suitable localities, often being seen about the gardens at the edge of the small stream at Algeciraz and at Vejer, seeming, as in England, to be fond of living in the vicinity of houses and cultivation. They nest about the end of April.

General colour above olive-brown, below greyish black; scarlet frontal plate in adult, greenish brown in the young; legs and feet greenish. Length 13 inches.

274. Porphyrio cœruleus (Vandelli). **The Purple Waterhen.**

Moorish. Kazeid (*Reid*). *Spanish.* Mancón azúl, Calamón.

"This bird is chiefly migratory, and not common near Tangier, passing north during the months of February and March, and returning in December and October. They are occasionally to be seen during the month of January, but not every year. Those which remain for the breeding-season construct their nests in the midst of wet sedges or rushes, depositing, in April, from three to five eggs. When these birds are moulting they are very easy to obtain, as they lose all their quill-feathers at once, and so cannot fly."—*Favier.*

The Purple Waterhen (a large and very handsome bird) is, on the Spanish side of the Straits, very irregular in its appearance both as to time and locality. In some years, during January and February, they are to be seen near Gibraltar in situations where they do not occur at any other time, and are then, doubtless, on migration.

In wet seasons they nest near Casas Viejas in April, in the Soto Malabrigo, where I have shot them as late as the 27th of October. They are very difficult to flush without a dog; when they rise they make a flapping noise, and with a heavy flight merely take refuge in the nearest thick patch of rushes or wet sedgy jungle, whence, from being Crake-like in their habits, it is almost impossible to make them rise a second time. Some are to be found in a few places at the edge of the marisma of the Guadalquivir. The nest resembles that of the Common Coot; and the eggs, which are richly coloured, are laid towards the end of April.

The gizzards of those which I have examined contained nothing but vegetable matter (grass, seeds of rushes, &c.), with a good deal of coarse gravel.

Purplish blue, darkest on tail; tail-coverts white. Bill and frontal shield bright red; legs and feet red. Length 16-18 inches.

275. Fulica atra, Linnæus. The Common Coot.

Moorish. El Ghor (*Favier*). *Spanish.* Mancón, Gallaréta.

"This Coot is resident near Tangier, but is not very numerous, often consorting with *Fulica cristata*. Some are migratory, passing northwards during the months of January and February, and returning in August and September."—*Favier.*

We found the Common Coot abundant near Tetuan in March; and they are common on the Spanish side, particularly in winter, when very large flocks appear, and some are then to be seen on the inundation at the North Front. They breed about the middle of April in all large swamps, particularly at the Laguna de la Janda, where, though the nests are numerous, it is almost impossible to see the birds, owing to the density of the grass and rushes.

Front toes with rounded lobes.

General colour slaty black; secondaries tipped with white, forming a wing-bar; broad white shield on forehead; legs bluish grey; iris crimson. Length 16 inches.

276. Fulica cristata, Gmelin. The Red-lobed Coot.

Spanish. Gallaréta.

"This bird is both resident and migratory near Tangier. Those which migrate return from the north in September. The nest and eggs resemble those of *Fulica atra*, with which species they associate, but are much more numerous."—*Favier.*

This Coot breeds at Ras el Doura in numbers about the 20th of April; and, as above mentioned, the eggs are not to be distinguished from those of the Common Coot (*F. atra*); so unless the bird be snared on the nest, the eggs cannot be said to be identified.

In Andalucia they have been obtained about the Laguna de la Janda, but are much more common further east.

I prefer to call this bird Red-lobed, as it certainly is not crested, and resembles the Common Coot in all respects except having two red lobes or caruncles on the white frontal shield and not having a white wing-bar or white tips to the secondaries. Length 16 inches.

Order **ALECTORIDES.** Family **GRUIDÆ.**

277. Grus communis, Bechstein. The Common Crane.

Moorish. Gharnook (*Favier*). *Spanish.* Grúlla.

"This Crane, common in flocks, is found in Morocco only during the winter season, arriving in October and November; they leave for the north in February."—*Favier.*

On the Moorish side of the Straits the Common Crane does

not appear to remain to nest, as I looked in vain for them in the marshes there during the month of April.

On the Spanish side some thirty to forty pairs breed in the district (comprising many thousand acres) which extends from Tapatanilla along the Laguna de la Janda to Vejer, and thence eastward to Casas Viejas. These birds commence to lay about the last week in April (but Verner records a nest with two fresh eggs on the 4th of April, 1876), constructing their nests somewhat like those of the Swan, of sedges, grass, and rushes. The nests vary much in size, some being quite five feet across, others perhaps not much more than eighteen inches: some are deep, and stand high up; others are almost level with the water, in which they are always built. The nest is always placed among sedges or rushes sufficiently short for the bird, when standing up, to be able to see around, and is never built in tall reeds. They are very easy to find, as the old birds never fly direct to the nest, but alight some twenty or thirty yards away and, walking up to it, form regular tracks like a cattle-path; so by following one of these tracks you may be sure of finding the nest: nor do the old birds fly straight away from the nest, but walk off quietly to the end of one of these paths and then take wing. When approached while sitting on the nest, the bird slips off, crouches down, and runs away for some yards.

Mr. Stark watched a pair of Cranes for two or three days from a hill which directly overlooked a marsh where the process of building was being carried on; and he informed me that only one bird worked at a time, the other standing on guard. The nests are never in very close proximity to each other, and never contain more than two eggs, placed side by side so as almost to touch, both the small ends pointing in the same direction. Sometimes the second egg is not laid until two or three days after the first, and they differ much in size and shape in different nests; but the pair in a nest are always alike in size, shape, and colour, which varies from light buff to an olive-brown, sometimes marked all over with brown and reddish-brown spots, generally thickest at the larger end; but some eggs are almost spotless.

These noble-looking birds are very much harassed during the breeding-time; and being said, I believe correctly, not to lay a second time in the season after the nest has been robbed, they will, I am afraid, soon cease to breed near Casas Viejas, as they have almost done in the marisma of the Guadalquivir, owing to ceaseless persecution. According to what one hears, they used years ago to nest there in great numbers. However, it is the same story everywhere: all wild birds are in Europe certainly decreasing at their breeding-places, owing to egging, drainage, and what is termed civilization; and soon it will come to nothing but Dorking Fowls and domestic Pheasants.

These Andalucian-breeding Cranes are very largely reinforced by the autumn migration, which arrives early in October; and they then form immense bands of from two to three hundred in number, though generally they keep in smaller lots of from five to thirty or forty. Those which do not remain to nest, pass north in March. On the 11th of that month, in 1874, Mr. Stark and myself had the pleasure of seeing them on passage; and a grand and extraordinary sight it was, as flock after flock passed over at a height of about two hundred yards—some in single line, some in a V-shape, others in a Y-formation, all from time to time trumpeting loudly. We watched them for about an hour as they passed, during which time we calculated that at least four thousand must have flown by. This was early in the morning, and we were obliged to continue our journey; but when we lost sight of the vega of Casas Viejas, over which the Cranes were passing in a due northerly direction, there appeared to be no diminution in their number, and, as my friend remarked, "One would not have believed there were so many Cranes in all Europe." These birds must have crossed the Straits from Africa that morning, the place over which we saw them passing being not twenty miles in a direct line from Tarifa, and a line drawn in the direction from which the birds came would have fallen a little to the west of that town. At Adra on the 16th of March, 1882, we saw eleven Cranes passing north at a great height.

In the winter of 1870-71 I found that Cranes could be easily shot in the evening by waiting for them in the swamps where they resort to pass the night, as they "flight" earlier than Ducks; and although in the daytime no bird is so wide awake, they are quite stupid in the dusk, flying, if you keep perfectly still, within a few yards. It is, however, a barbarous shame to shoot such a fine and noble bird. Although the Spaniards gladly take them to eat, to my mind their flesh is coarse and worthless; but in India, where they feed much on grain and on rice-stubbles, they are, on the contrary, much sought after for the table. One or two shot in the evening near Casas Viejas had been eating beetles and insects, which in winter seems their chief food. They do a great deal of damage to beans when ripening and to newly sown grain of all descriptions.

General colour slate-grey; inner secondaries bluish black, forming elongated plumes.

Adults with a red warty patch on crown. In young this is absent, and the grey feathers on back are mixed with brown. Length 48 inches.

278. Grus virgo (Linnæus). The Demoiselle Crane.

Spanish. Grúlla morúna (Seville).

The only note which Favier has relative to this handsome Crane is that "it is scarce and seldom obtained near Tangier, passing northwards without making any stay, during March, April, and May."

Favier's successor at Tangier evidently considered this species a rare bird; for he asked fifteen dollars (over £3) for a specimen, and at that price it was likely to continue for some time on his hands. He stated that the local name was "Bou-gernan" (father of thistles); but if the bird be as rare as Favier implied, how could it bear a local name?

On the Spanish side I failed to meet with this Crane near Casas Viejas, but strongly suspect that in some seasons they nest there; indeed a pair of Cranes' eggs that were brought to me were so small that I could not refer them to the Common Crane, but could of course obtain no reliable information about them. Indeed, an egg unidentified is worse than useless to the ornithologist; and unless the collector takes and identifies specimens himself, he had better not keep them.

In the marisma of the Guadalquivir there is no doubt that in former years the present species used frequently to breed. Specimens are often to be obtained near Seville during March, April, and the early part of May, and again in August. Judging from this, they must nest somewhere a little further north.

General colour bluish grey, sides of the head, throat, neck, the lengthened pointed feathers on upper breast, and quill-feathers black; from each eye a tuft of lengthened white feathers extending backwards. Length 30 inches.

OTIDIDÆ. No hind toe.

270. Otis tarda, Linnæus. **The Great Bustard.**

Spanish. Abutarda.

Favier states that this Bustard "occasionally migrates to Morocco during winter from the European side of the Straits, but very rarely remains for the breeding-season."

I have seen one or two specimens obtained near Tangier, and Mr. Drake also mentions one; whilst Mr. Meade-Waldo kindly informs me that in the spring of 1892 he met with many, and saw one band of twenty-three. He found a male on a small plain which when fired at flew round and round, not seeming to like to pass over the hills; at last he got right up, and went away like a goose.

On the Spanish side of the Straits the Great Bustard is first to be met with near Gibraltar on the plain below Facinas, about ten or twelve miles from Tarifa; northwards from there they are to be seen in gradually increasing numbers all along the vega of the Laguna de la Janda up to Casas Viejas and along by Medina Sidonia to the plains which lie towards Jerez and the marisma of the Guadalquivir. They are found in abundance along the line of railway to near Utrera, being more plentiful in the open corn-growing country about Marchena, Coronil, and Carmona than in any other district that I have visited; thence to the north side of the Guadalquivir they are also common, particularly about Brenes and Alcala del Rio, sometimes appearing very near to Seville—in fact in all open country the Great Bustard may be expected to be seen in varying numbers. I never saw any very large flocks, but occasionally have observed as many as fifty together; from ten to twenty-five is the usual number seen at once. I did not detect any migration of the Great Bustard, which is singular, as in the Crimea some very large flights appeared on passage in autumn; however, doubtless they migrate, as they are occasionally seen, and in 1889 two were shot very near Gibraltar; certainly they shift their ground in Spain, as they are most numerous about the vega of La Janda during the breeding-season, which tends to the belief that they pass over to the African side of the Straits. In a wild state they feed chiefly on grass and vegetable substances; and when kept tame they will devour any amount of grasshoppers, insects, &c., the best food for them, however, being cabbage-leaves.

Bustards are very difficult to approach except by some such stratagem as driving a cart near them, when they seem to fear no danger; but the best way of obtaining them is by driving when the corn is sufficiently high to shelter the guns, which it usually is by the end of March. It is necessary to have for a Bustard-drive, with any chance of success, at least four guns; the more the better; and as the birds fly almost always well within shot of the ground, they are very easily killed if they pass over the spot where a gun is posted. Indeed, considering the size of the bird, it is wonderful how light a wound will bring one down.

BUSTARD-DRIVING.

I have seen an old male when winged and, as it were, brought to bay, turn round and charge his pursuer. This diversion of Bustard-driving is rather an expensive pastime, and often, like the Irishman's pig, they refuse to be driven in the required direction; so, beyond the novelty of the affair, and the sight of so many of these truly noble birds on the wing, there is nothing very exciting in the sport, if it may be so called; and, as in all "driving," there is no sporting-skill required on the part of the shooter. Nevertheless the thorough enjoyment of the bright and glorious climate, and the sense of freedom to go where you wish without being warned off as a trespasser, and last, but not least, the sociable nature of the "entertainment," render a few days' Bustard-driving very agreeable: they ought not to be shot after the third week in April, as they then begin to lay; but most of those killed, I am sorry to say, are destroyed during the breeding-season. There is, moreover, the lamentable fact that the game is not very much worth having, the flesh being dry and coarse; at least such has been the case with almost all that I have tasted.

One circumstance in favour of these excursions after Bustard is that they are easily managed from Seville by starting by the early morning train and returning late in the evening, and there is no trouble in having to search for uncomfortable country quarters for the night.

The man we always employed to drive was one Molino, of Algaba, a small village or pueblo on the Guadalquivir, above Seville, a wiry active little fellow, but with an enormous capacity for meat and wine. He never attempted to drive the birds with more than three men, including himself; but his skilful management, owing to his knowledge of the birds and the ground, and consequently of the route they would take, was something marvellous. Molino was always employed by some Sevillaños, who regularly several times in the spring go out dressed in green, like Free Foresters at the Crystal Palace: and a suitable dress it is; for the colour being that of the corn or grass in which the *tirador* lies hid, the Bustards are not nearly so likely to notice the ambuscade. The day these verdant gentlemen choose for their "funcion" of Bustards is invariably Sunday; and sometimes they succeed in killing a dozen birds in the day, usually about the vicinity of Las Alcantarillas. In August, near Casas Viejas, and, I am informed, also in other places, the Spaniards ride down Bustards with dogs, continually flushing them till they are exhausted; but probably young birds only are thus caught. They are also said to tire out the Red-legged Partridge in the same way. This is very likely, as I have seen these Partridges when driving in Norfolk, after being flushed two or three times, allow themselves to be caught quite uninjured.

The Great Bustard is easily noticed when on the ground where the cover is not too high to hide them; and at times their size appears gigantic as they fly with a slow, measured, laborious-looking flight; but their pace is much faster than it appears to be; and when put up they often fly a distance of at least two miles. They have great power of concealment; and I remember an instance of one which was unable to fly, from some injury he had received in one of his wings. We saw this bird in a corn-field of some forty acres, and forming line we tried to catch him; but he suddenly disappeared in the corn, which was not more than two feet high, and in many places not a foot high. We spent an hour in vain hunting for him with a dog; so, after beating the whole field over more than once, we sat down in view of the ground to eat luncheon. In about a quarter of an hour the Bustard appeared some three hundred yards off in the middle of the corn; so I went straight at him, running as hard as I could. He again disappeared; but going on I suddenly spied something white running, as it were, close to the ground, and rushing after it, up jumped the Bustard, running along and flapping his wings; unable to catch him (for he ran as fast as I could), I was compelled to shoot him, a magnificent *Barbon* of about thirty pounds weight. I could not have believed so large a bird could crouch so low and at the same time make such good running.

About Casas Viejas a few Bustards are to be found near the banks of the rivers Barbate and Celemin, where, from the nature of the ground, which is intersected by the windings and branches of these rivers, which are nearly dry in August, it is sometimes possible to stalk them under cover of the banks, and is very good ground to have them driven over; but the Spaniards then could not be made to understand such work.

The Great Bustard nests in corn or grass early in May, laying two olive-brown eggs marked with spots and blotches of dark brown. Verner says he has twice come across nests containing four eggs, but the Spaniards say two is the complement laid by each hen, and if more than that number are found in a nest then two hens have laid together. He found a nest as late as the 27th of June, 1879, containing three fresh eggs. They appear to be polygamous, whilst the Little Bustard undoubtedly pairs. The gular pouch, which always exists in the old males or *Barbones*, is sometimes very large and necked in the middle, somewhat like an hour-glass, the lower part being the largest; this shape is not constant and perhaps the result of age.

Male. Head bluish grey; general colour above reddish buff, with black bands on each feather; wings white or greyish, except the dark primaries; tuft of long bristly white feathers from base of bill; band of rich chestnut across breast, with grey band underneath, below this white.

Female and young male. Without bristles on throat or band on chest, and back more loaded with black. Length: male 45 inches, female 36. Greatest weight of a male 37 lb. (*Verner*), others have recorded to 36 lb.

280. Otis tetrax, Linnæus. The Little Bustard.

Moorish. Bou-zerat (Father of the armourer: Râd, "thunderer"), Sáf-sáf; Sirt, sirt (from call or note). *Andalucian.* Sisón, Francolino.

"The Little Bustard is abundant in the vicinity of Tangier in small flocks, which are very wild and wary. They migrate to the north during the months of April and May, returning in October and November. In addition to these migratory birds, great numbers are resident during the nesting-season. The males do not attain the full breeding-plumage until their third year, and by October regain the dress of the females."—*Favier*.

My experience of the breeding-plumage of the Little Bustard is rather different from the above; for, as far as I have been able to ascertain, the males lose the black markings of their nuptial dress by the end of August, if not before. I could not make out the exact period; but never saw a black-marked male which had been killed after the middle of August. The adult males never lose the minutely marked or vermiculated plumage on the back, which part in the females and young males is more spotted or blotched, like the feathers of the Great Bustard. I found the Little Bustard equally common in Morocco as in Andalucia on all open low cultivated ground. On the dead level, or vega, of the Barbate near Casas Viejas at times, in early autumn, they positively swarmed in flocks sometimes of as many or more than a hundred together, frequenting this flat ground till swamped by the rains. They then resorted to higher and undulating ground, and these large flocks gradually dispersed and broke up into lots of from five or six to twenty in number. They are, as Favier remarks, exceedingly wary, except during the breeding-season and in the month of August. At other times the only way to obtain them was by driving, very uncertain work, as, unlike the Great Bustard, they usually rose high up at once, and their power and rapidity of flight is astonishing for their size and weight.

They were often to be seen flying somewhat like Golden Plover, twirling and twisting about at a great elevation; and sometimes I watched them rise and go to such a height that it would have been difficult to tell what birds they were unless I had seen them fly up from the ground.

During August, when very hot, between eleven and four, they lie "like stones" in long grass, requiring a dog to flush them; but the heat is then so excessive that one is almost as likely to get a sunstroke as a Little Bustard, and I myself could never stand such work.

The nearest place to Gibraltar that these birds are seen is on the plain between Los Barrios and Palmones, where occasionally in autumn and winter a few appear; but they are too much bullied by Gibraltar sportsmen to remain there long. The Moorish names given above are significant of the rattling noise which the Little Bustard makes in rising; and when the flock is large this can be heard a very long way off. There is none of this sound of the wings in the rising of the slow-flying Great Bustard.

When on the wing, the Little Bustard, except when at a great height, may always be recognized by its white or, rather, pied appearance, caused by the greater part of the wings being white. When these are closed, and they are settled on the ground, this white does not show, and they are very difficult to make out or notice, particularly as they usually frequent ground which has some cover (in the shape of weeds, thistles, or grass). In the breeding-season they keep entirely among thick herbage, and at that time I never could get a sight of one on the ground.

In my opinion there is no bird better food than the Little Bustard, and they are equal to the Indian Florican in this respect, which is saying a great deal for them.

The male Little Bustard in the breeding-season has a most peculiar call, which can be easily imitated by pouting out and pressing the lips tight together and then blowing through them; the birds when thus calling seem to be close to you, but are often in reality half a mile off. They must possess powers of ventriloquism, as I have often imagined that they were quite close to me, and upon hunting the spot with a dog found no signs of them anywhere near; indeed, at that season it is sometimes as difficult to make them rise as a Landrail. They nest in the beginning of May, laying three shiny smooth olive-green eggs, more or less blotched with dark brown, which are placed among the corn or long grass.

Male in spring till August. General colour above sandy brown; throat and cheeks bluish black, with two white gorget-marks across.

Adult male. Back *vermiculated* with black, but otherwise in winter resembles the female.

Female. Back spotted or *blotched* with black on sandy-brown ground-colour; underparts white; iris golden yellow. Length 16–17 inches.

281. Eupodotis arabs (Linnæus). The North-African Bustard.

This large Bustard was obtained by Mr. Tyrwhitt-Drake in the north of Morocco; and towards the south, about Mogador, it is stated to be common.

Larger than the Great Bustard (*Otis tarda*), it has the entire back covered with those delicate vermiculated feathers, sandy brown crossed with fine lines of deep brown almost black, which are so valuable for artificial flies. Similarly marked feathers are found in the other species of *Eupodotis* in India, the Cape, and Australia.

282. Houbara undulata (Jacq.). The Western Houbara or Ruffed Bustard.

This Bustard is not mentioned by Favier; but I saw one specimen which had been obtained near Tangier in August; further south it is stated to be frequently met with.

In Andalucia is a rare straggler and has occurred near Málaga.

Above blotched, not vermiculated. Crest of white feathers; black and white ruff on sides of neck. Length 26–30 inches.

Order **LIMICOLÆ**.   Family **GLAREOLIDÆ**.

283. Glareola pratincola (Linnæus).   **The Pratincole.**

Moorish. Gharrak (*Favier*), Harrak-diad (*Drummond-Hay, P. Z. S.* 1840). *Spanish.* Canastéla.

Favier's notes on the Pratincole are confined to remarking "that it arrives from the south and passes to Europe during the month of April, being observed returning thence in September to join those which have remained near Tangier for the breeding-season. All disappear south for the winter months."

We found this bird in April, on the dried mud at the lakes of Meshree el Haddar, south of Larache, in countless thousands. They had not then begun to lay; so possibly some of these swarms would pass on northwards. We there witnessed a number of these birds mobbing a Marsh-Harrier which had intruded on their ground, buffeting and bullying him just as Peewits will do when a Hawk passes near their breeding-ground. At times at least a hundred Pratincoles were dashing at once about the Harrier, which soon made its best way out of their district. Pratincoles are very crepusculine in their habits, flitting up and down over the surface of a river or a pool much after the manner of the Indian Skimmer (*Rhynchops albicollis*) very late in the evening — as late, indeed, as they can be distinguished. They are then silent, but by day, especially when disturbed, their cry is ceaseless; and the Moorish name given by Favier is doubtless derived from, as it is suggestive of, their note. They are generally very tame and fearless, often allowing one to approach within a few yards, and are birds of very powerful flight, reminding one much of the Terns in this respect.

On the south side of the Straits the Pratincole is found in large numbers wherever there are lagoons, which, drying up in spring, leave a surface of sun-baked mud on which they deposit their complement of three eggs only, about the second week in May. The earliest egg I saw was taken on the 3rd of that month, and they mostly arrive about the 20th of April, the earliest date on which I saw one being the 4th and 10th of that month in two consecutive years. Verner noticed six at Palmones, near Gibraltar, on the 21st of April, 1878. They fly very high when on passage, and attract notice chiefly from their cry. The latest date of the return migration observed was the 14th of October, when a young bird was procured.

In some seasons they breed about the edges of the Laguna de la Janda, but the marisma of the Guadalquivir is their chief resort.

A friend of mine, who shot several on the autumnal passage, informed me that they were excellent eating; but in this respect I can give no personal information.

Axillaries *chestnut-red*; tail much forked.
Above dull brown; rump and tail-coverts white; throat buff, bordered by a black line meeting at the gape, forming a bridle or collar; wings very long, about 7¼ inches. Length 9–10 inches.

CHARADRIIDÆ. Hind toe absent in most species.

284. Œdicnemus scolopax (S. G. Gmelin). **The Stone-Curlew.**
Moorish. El Karunna. *Spanish.* Alcaraván.

The Stone-Curlew is found on both sides of the Straits as a resident in considerable numbers, nesting generally about the beginning of May, and depositing its complement of two eggs usually on stony dry ground.

These birds are far more common in the winter months, and most so during their migration, which is northwards during March and April, and southwards in October, November, and December. They pass in lots of from five or six to fifty in number, and are chiefly observed on ploughed fields, generally near the banks of rivers, where I have sometimes shot them as they flew by when waiting for ducks in the evening, and they are doubtless nocturnal feeding birds. Except in the breeding-season, when they are very noisy, I have found them rather wild.

Two obscure white bands across (extended) wings; breast streaked; chin and throat white; tail rather long and graduated; bill yellow, terminal half black; legs yellow; iris *very large* and yellow. Length 16 inches.

285. Cursorius gallicus (J. F. Gmelin). The Cream-coloured Courser.

Moorish. Gueta (*Favier*); but this name applies also to *Pterocles alchata*.

"This Courser appears annually during July in some numbers on the plains of Sharf el Akab, not far from Tangier. Their stay there and their numbers vary according to the abundance or scarcity of insects, and also with the temperature; for unless the latter is favourable, they are rarely met with, and none were seen during the year 1854. They leave these plains in August or the first part of September. Early in summer they ought to be found nesting near Sharf el Akab, as in May, 1847, a male was brought to me by a chasseur, who rescued it from a Falcon which had struck it down.

"Their food is entirely insects or larvæ, particularly *Pentatoma torquata* and different sorts of grasshoppers. They are met with in small lots, usually frequenting dry arid plains, where they spread out in all directions, running about after insects, and are very wary and difficult to get a shot at. Their cry of alarm is much like that of the Plover. They rest and sleep in a sitting position, with their legs doubled up under them. Should they not fly away when approached they run off with astonishing swiftness, manœuvring to get out of sight behind stones or clods of earth; then, kneeling down and stretching the body and head flat on the ground, they endeavour to make themselves invisible,—though all the time their eyes are fixed on the object which disturbs them, and they keep on the alert ready to rush off again if one continues to approach them.

"The age of the young birds can be well made out by the zigzag markings with which the plumage is speckled, which becomes clearer each moult till the end of the second year, when they assume the regular adult livery. There is no difference at any age in the plumage of the sexes.

"In 1849 they did not leave till the 11th of September, when a chasseur brought me one slightly wounded in the wing. I tried to keep this bird alive; but it died directly the weather became cold. It proved on dissection to be a female; and from the large size of the eggs in the ovary it appeared as if it would soon have nested, probably in October or November, when doubtless they retire to a much warmer climate.

"Towards the end of August, 1851, two others were brought to me, both slightly wounded—one an adult, the other an immature bird. To prevent the birds this time from dying of cold, I placed them by day in a room where there was always a fire kept up. At night I put them in a box, making a door at the side, lining the top and sides with cotton-wool, placing sand an inch deep on the bottom; this was warmed and dried by putting a charcoal brazier inside during the day. I fed the birds on grasshoppers till November, when these insects became very scarce, and, as each bird ate fifty daily, it was necessary to change their diet to the larvæ of coleoptera, which, after some reluctance, they began to take. This food suited them better than grasshoppers, the birds becoming fatter, at the same time eating less. They did well till January, when, the adult bird pining and refusing food, I tried to save it by cramming; but this was useless, as it died in February, and on dissection I found that death was caused by a very large tumour in the stomach. It proved to be a female; and from the ovaries it appeared the season for laying had passed.

"The surviving bird continued well till the end of January; then, appearing ill, I fed it by hand till April, when as the weather became warmer it grew more healthy. I then shut it up in a cage with a white Turtle-Dove. The Courser was the stronger bird, and did little else than play with the Dove; but they lived in perfect harmony. In May, sexual desire was shown in a very marked manner; but, unluckily, the Dove was also a female. During the exhibition of this passion the Courser used to make a noise which may be expressed thus, '*rererer*.'

"This continued till the middle of June, then entirely ceasing till the next year (1853), when it resulted in the Courser laying eight eggs—the first on the 15th, the second on the 16th, the third on the 30th of May, the fourth on the 1st, the fifth on the 11th, the sixth on the 14th, the seventh on the 23rd, and the last on the 25th of June. In 1854 she laid again, with the same irregularity, twelve eggs—the first on the 17th of May, the last on the 28th of July. Though in perfect health, treated and fed in the same way, she did not lay in 1855—but in 1856 laid two eggs, on the 6th and 7th of July. In 1857 she again, at irregular intervals, laid ten more eggs—the first in May, the last in July. In 1858 none were laid. In 1859 she produced four more eggs —the first two on the 6th and 7th of July, the others on the 9th and 10th of August.

"Shortly afterwards this bird, in perfect health, plumage, and vigour, was lost to ornithology, owing to the war between Spain and Morocco; for on the 25th of October I was ordered, with other French subjects, to embark in the French war-steamer 'Mouette,' and not knowing when I should return, and still less how to take care of my bird, I made up my mind to let it go; but it was so tame that it either would not or could not use its wings; so, in my dilemma, I gave it in charge of a Moor during my absence; but, unfortunately, on my return in April 1860 I found it had died.

"From my observations it seems that these birds could be

domesticated and bred so as to be perhaps used for the table; but their value would make them rather expensive luxuries, worthy of comparison with those splendid feasts given by the ancient Roman Emperors; for each bird would cost more than twelve dozen capons.

"Meanwhile, considering the eggs laid by the above-named female bird, the size of the testes of the males and ovaries of the females in August and September, one may conclude that they breed more than once a year, and that the complement of eggs is two. These are rather elliptical in shape, of a cream-colour, spotted or marbled with red, bluish ash, and brown."—*Favier*.

This Courser occasionally wanders across the Straits, having been obtained near Málaga, in 1877, and two which were shot at Coria, near Seville, in 1883, are in Lord Lilford's collection.

General colour sandy buff; primaries and primary-coverts black; axillaries *black*; bill as long as head, slightly curved; legs greyish white. Length 9½–10 inches.

286. Charadrius pluvialis, Linnæus. The Golden Plover.

Moorish. Tullit.   *Spanish*. Chorlito.

"This Plover is very abundant around Tangier in large flocks, which arrive during October and November, and which return to Europe in February and March."—*Favier*.

The Golden Plover occurs as above on the Andalucian side of the Straits; but at the same time their numbers fluctuate very much, in some winters the quantity seen being very great. Upon their first arrival they are generally tame; but being so much sought after by the *cazadores*, they soon learn their danger and become more wary. The earliest noticed near Gibraltar was on the 1st of November; the latest was on the 6th of March.

The best ground for Golden Plover is the vicinity of Tapatanilla. They always frequent the same places; and if put up from any spot are almost certain to return in less than an hour. I regret to say that occasionally the Spaniards catch them like eels, by laying night-lines or hooks baited with a worm in their feeding-places: this is a most cruel method of procuring them, as the unfortunate birds linger in agony for hours, often being left till they flutter themselves to death.

Male in spring. Above blackish, spotted with yellow; chin, throat, breast, and belly black.
Female. Less black below, being mottled with white feathers.
In winter. Below white, chest and flanks marked with brown. Axillaries *white.* Length 9 inches.

287. Charadrius fulvus, J. F. Gmelin. Asiatic Golden Plover.

A specimen of this Eastern Golden Plover was killed near Málaga in 1878, and is in Lord Lilford's collection.

Axillaries *smoky grey*; otherwise as last, but slightly smaller.

288. Squatarola helvetica (Linnæus). The Grey Plover.

Spanish. Redolin.

Favier only remarks that "this Plover is found near Tangier between the months of December and March."

The Grey Plover appears chiefly to arrive near Gibraltar during the middle of November, and, though frequently seen in autumn and spring, cannot be said to be at any time abundant. I have noticed them on the small plash of water which after heavy rains is formed on the western part of the Neutral ground.

On the 22nd of May, 1869, I killed a pair at one shot near the mouth of the Guadiaro, the male being in almost perfect summer plumage, the female not being so far advanced, and the eggs in her ovaries very slightly developed. It is very remarkable that this northern-breeding bird should linger so late in such a sunny southern country; and the day above mentioned was very hot for the time of the year. But the Grey Plover is not singular in thus remaining south so late; both the Knot and the Curlew Sandpiper loiter equally late into the spring.

The marks by which this species is to be distinguished from the Golden Plover are the presence of a very small hind toe and the black axillaries; it is, moreover, a larger bird, and shore-frequenting, very rarely being found inland like the Golden Plover.

Axillaries *black*; small *hind toe* present.

In spring. Above white, barred with black; underparts black, or black marked with white.

In winter marked much as Golden Plover, but the yellow spots of that species are replaced by white, young birds only being marked with a few yellow spots. Length 10-12 inches.

289. Eudromias morinellus (Linnæus). The Dotterel.

"This bird, which appears to travel in company with *Cursorius isabellinus*, is found near Tangier sparingly on its annual passage during August and September, frequenting in small flocks the same dry places that the Courser inhabits; and, like them, it seems to dread the cold."—*Favier.*

Could Favier occasionally have seen the Dotterel on mountain-tops in Scotland, he would not have supposed them to fear the cold; but curiously enough he omits to mention the date of their appearance in spring; and I have no record in my notes of observing them at that season on the Spanish side of the Straits: the few I have seen were in autumn, the latest being shot about the 9th of November. Probably they pass straight on, and thus appear rarer than is the case; but doubtless their line of migration must be further to the east.

Axillaries *greyish*. Crown nearly black with white lines below, all round above eyes to bill; chin and throat white; upper breast chestnut-red; belly black.

Females brighter than males. Length 9 inches.

290. Ægialitis hiaticula (Linnæus). The Ringed Plover.

Moorish. Kouba (*Drummond-Hay*) ("the hooded one," *vide* Crested Lark). *Spanish.* Andarios, Correrios, Frailecillo (the first two applied to all small Waders).

"This Ringed Plover is, near Tangier, found in small numbers in pairs and companies on the sea-shore. They arrive during the months of September, October, and November, returning north again in April and May."—*Favier*.

Though without absolute proof, I am nearly sure that this species occasionally remains to breed near Gibraltar, having shot them as late as the 28th of May, and having seen eggs obtained near Seville as early as on the 23rd of March; but this is the only instance I know of their nesting so far south. During autumn and until April the Ringed Plover is extremely plentiful along the coast, and most so in the month of March.

Above hair-brown; forehead white; fore crown black, reaching to and below eyes on each side, and to base of bill and ear-coverts; throat white, forming a complete ring, below this a broad black band round breast; both these collars narrowing to a line round nape; rest of underparts white; eyelids, legs, and feet orange; basal half of bill yellow, rest black.

Females have the collars less clearly defined.

Young brown where black in adults; bill black; legs brown. Length 7-7½ inches.

291. Ægialitis curonica (J. F. Gmelin). The Little Ringed Plover.

This small inland species is not mentioned by Favier in his MS., although included by Mr. Drake in his 'List of the Birds of Morocco.' We found them very common in that country on river-banks during the month of April. Equally abundant at that time on the Spanish side, the Little Ringed Plover is only seen during the breeding-season. They mostly arrive about the 14th of March, some passing on; others remain to nest, depositing, about the 14th of May, four eggs on the sand or shingle by the sides of rivers. The earliest eggs Major Verner found were on the 13th May, 1875. Many pairs nest on the river Barbate, near Casas Viejas. There is, of course, no approach to a nest; but the eggs, with the small ends inwards, are placed in a slight depression probably formed by the birds themselves in the sand or gravel.

Resembles last, but much smaller, is a more inland bird, and has shaft of first primary only *white*; eyelids golden yellow; legs and feet pale brown. Length 6¼ inches.

292. Ægialitis cantiana (Latham). **The Kentish Plover.**

Moorish. Bou-hejaira (father of stones, *Favier*). *Spanish.* Charrán, Andarios.

"This bird is very abundant near Tangier, and generally found at the mouths of rivers. Many are resident, those which are migratory arriving during September and October, leaving northwards in March and April."—*Favier.*

The Kentish Plover is by far the most plentiful of the seashore Waders on the Spanish side; and they are always very tame, being seldom molested by the Spaniards. The local name of *Charrán*, which I have heard for them near Gibraltar, signifies a low unmitigated blackguard, and the application of which to this harmless and charming bird is not easy to understand. This name is also applied near Málaga to some species of Terns.

This little Plover is found throughout the year, but is most abundant during the seasons of migration; they are very active, nimble little birds, running along the shore sometimes in front and within a yard of one's horse's feet; frequently running out on the wet sand as one wave recedes, to rush back again as another returns, like the Sanderling; but they are much too agile ever to be caught by the influx.

About the 20th of April they commence to lay their four stone-coloured eggs, marked with black spots and streaks. Some regularly breed on the dry sandy hillocks and banks near the mouth of the First River (Guadarranque); but, like the other species of *Ægialitis*, they frequently nest far away from the shore, as on the dried mud of the marisma. Verner took four fresh eggs on the 9th of May, 1879, near Gibraltar, and he remarks that the Kentish Plover in England nearly always lays only three eggs; that is to say, between 1885 and 1893, of many nests he saw only one contained four eggs, and the fishermen about Dungeness, who rob the nests for collectors, assert that three eggs and no more is the invariable number.

Bill and legs *black*.

Male. Above hair-brown; forehead white, black patch on fore crown; rest of crown and nape buff; black line through eye from bill to ear-coverts; a black patch on each side of breast, *not* forming a collar; rest of underparts white.

Female. No black on fore crown, but that and crown uniform with the back; the patch on each side of breast same colour as back. Length 6½ inches.

293. Vanellus vulgaris*, Bechstein. The Peewit, Lapwing, or Green Plover.

Moorish. Biliat, El Thudi (the Jew). *Spanish.* Ave fria (cold bird), Judia (Jewess).

"This Plover occurs near Tangier in abundant flocks throughout the winter months, arriving from the north during October and November, crossing back again to Europe in February and March.

"The superstitious Arabs believe that these birds are Jews changed into the shape of birds, and also believe that they still retain all their Israelitish characteristics, even wearing the black Hebrew skull-cap."—*Favier.* Hence the name "El Thudi."

We observed towards the end of April three or four pairs of Peewits, which were nesting at the northern end of the lakes of Ras el Doura. As we had not sufficient time to go further than the commencement of these lakes, possibly many others were to be found breeding still further south. The place where we saw them was some eighty miles at the least to the south of Tangier. On the Spanish side of the Straits very few, compared with their numbers in winter, remain to breed in the marismas of the Guadalquivir, where we found the nest with young on the 26th of April. Curiously, none remain to breed about the Laguna de la Janda, or, as far as could be ascertained, anywhere but in the marisma. The majority of the Peewits arrive near Gibraltar

---

* This is an instance of abolishing the long-used and distinctive synonym (*cristatus*) for a vague one, because of two years' priority.

about the middle of October, and take their departure north about the first week in March. During the winter they are to be found on every level piece of ground; and have occasionally been seen on the green glacis of the batteries near the Alameda at Gibraltar, and often noticed on the "North Front"; while at times they are found on hill-sides at a considerable elevation if there be any grassy and suitable open spot. They seem to be more scattered and dispersed about than is usual in England, although large flocks may sometimes be seen.

The Peewit used to be an unfailing source of diversion to the British subaltern, and also to the "sportsman" of the Rock, who, a marvel of leather straps, gaiters, bags—leather all over—used to sally out of Gibraltar for a Sunday's shooting, accompanied generally by a bob-tailed, mangy, lean, and hungry-looking species of pointer—by appearance warranted to devour immediately anything his master might kill; but the unfortunate animal probably seldom had the opportunity of having its appetite so gratified.

Hind toe present and well developed.

Above glossy green; crown, throat, and breast black; *crest* of long slender black feathers; upper and under tail-coverts *rufous*; legs flesh-coloured.

Young. Crest short; feathers above with buff edges; legs dark brown. Length 13 inches.

294. Vanellus gregarius (Pallas). The Black-bellied Lapwing.

Mr. Saunders mentions having seen one specimen of this Lapwing hanging up in Cadiz market, whilst Arévalo records some from near Málaga.

Is an eastern bird, having the gregarious habits of the Golden Plover. When on the wing the white secondaries show markedly.

Secondaries entirely white; shortest primaries black on the outer webs and white on the inner webs; hind toe present. Length 13 inches.

Adult. Crown black, bordered below by a broad white stripe above eye to nape; belly black, bordered below with chestnut to the vent.

Young. Crown dark brown; band from forehead to nape buffish white; breast white, marked with dark brown.

295. Hæmatopus ostralegus, Linnæus. The Oystercatcher.

Moorish. Aisha el behar (*Favier*) (the pied one of the sea) *Spanish.* Ostréro (*Arévalo*).

"This species is found near Tangier on passage, passing north during April and May, and returning in October."—*Favier.*

Favier also states that the Oystercatchers sometimes remain to nest. Very possibly this is the case; but the eggs which were marked as "Oystercatcher's" by him were to all appearance those of the Stone-Curlew.

On the Spanish side this bird is not at all numerous near Gibraltar, and appears irregularly from autumn to spring, the latest recorded was one observed by Lord Lilford on the 5th of May near the mouth of the Guadalquivir.

No hind toe; bill yellow, longer than head.
Plumage black and white; head, neck, scapulars, and terminal half of tail black; rump, upper tail-coverts, and axillaries white; legs pink; eyelids crimson. Length 16 inches.

296. Strepsilas interpres (Linnæus). The Turnstone.

Moorish. Shorno (*Favier*). *Spanish.* Revuelve-piedras (Málaga) (*Arévalo*).

"This bird is not numerous, being found near Tangier on the coast and sometimes on the edges of freshwater lakes. They are more abundant near Rabat. Arriving from the north in September, they return in February."—*Favier.*

The Turnstone is found on the Spanish coast in autumn and spring. I never saw them in any numbers, and chiefly observed them about the end of March, occasionally in company with the Ringed Plover.

Hind toe present; bill black, strong, straight, and pointed, shorter than head; chin and throat pure white.

In spring. Back and wings marked with chestnut and black; *lower back and rump white*, the latter crossed by a black band; legs and feet orange-red.

In winter, chestnut colour absent; legs pale red. Length 9½ inches.

SCOLOPACIDÆ.

297. Recurvirostra avocetta, Linnæus. The Avocet.

Moorish. Bou-am-hait. *Spanish.* Avocéta.

"This species is not common in the vicinity of Tangier, being only met with on passage, on the edges of rivers and lakes, in small flights, which pass northwards during March, April, and May and return south in November."—*Favier.*

I never met with the Avocet near Gibraltar. In some seasons many nest in some parts of the marismas during the month of May, and specimens of both eggs and birds are occasionally brought into Seville.

Bill black, curved upwards and pointed.

White, except crown to below eye, hind neck, primaries, and some of the inner secondaries and wing-coverts, which are black; legs and the partially webbed feet light blue; iris red.

Young. Crown and hind neck brown. Length 18 inches.

298. Himantopus candidus, Bonnaterre. The Black-winged Stilt.

Moorish. Bou-ksaiba (*Favier*) *. *Spanish.* Cigüeñéla.

"This bird is not found close to Tangier, but frequents fresh-water lakes further south, where many remain for the breeding-saason; others, arriving during the month of April, pass on northwards and return in November. They appear to migrate by night."—*Favier.*

* "Ksaiba" is diminutive of "Kasba," a reed, and probably applies to the thin legs of this Stilt, not to their aquatic habits.

This Stilt is, in spring, one of the most common of the marsh-birds on both sides of the Straits. At Meshree el Haddar, in Morocco, and in the marisma of the Guadalquivir their numbers were perfectly marvellous. In some seasons they have nested at the Laguna de la Janda. They frequent open shallow pools and lakes, and are very seldom seen where there is grass or rushes, being, as a rule, very tame and confiding; while their conspicuous black-and-white plumage and noisy habits render them certain to attract attention, either as they fly with their long pink legs stretched out, Heron-like, behind them, or as they wade about, usually up to their knees, in the shallow water, where they seek their food in the shape of aquatic insects, gnats, and flies.

The Black-winged Stilt is almost entirely migratory; but in some years a few undoubtedly remain in Spain throughout the winter, as I have seen small lots on the 26th and 27th of November in different years, many on the 22nd of December, and others on the 14th of January. The chief number appear towards the end of March and beginning of April; and they are then not unfrequently seen near Gibraltar at the mouths of various rivers, but soon pass on to their breeding-places, where they nest in colonies and deposit their four eggs on the half-dried mud. I have seen eggs as early as the 28th of April; but the majority lay about the 10th of May.

Bill black, twice as long as head, slender, straight, and jointed; hind toe absent; nape, upper hind neck, wings, and back black; underparts white; legs pale pink, about 4½ inches long.

Old males have pure white heads. Length 13 inches.

299. Phalaropus fulicarius (Linnæus). The Lobed-footed Stint or Grey Phalarope *.

Favier mentions only two specimens of this bird as having been

* "Phalarope," like "Hemipode," is an Anglicized compound name only understood by ornithologists. An English name, as used by Jerdon, is more intelligible to the world in general.

obtained by him near Tangier, in December, 1858. Mr. Drake also refers to this Phalarope as having been shot near Tangier during the month of January; and others have since occurred.

On the Spanish side one was killed on 29th of November, 1872, others on the 4th of December, 1875, and they occur irregularly, as in England, sometimes in numbers.

These birds never appear to go on the land except to nest, and are always seen swimming, often far at sea.

<small>Front toes as in next species lobed, like a Coot.
Bill short and *wide*; tail graduated.
In summer. Below chestnut.
In winter. Forehead and crown white; grey nape, white wing-bar; below white. Length 8 inches.</small>

300. Scolopax rusticula, Linnæus. The Woodcock.

Moorish. Hejel el himar (red partridge), Khadim el ajel (the servant of haste), Bou-monkar (Father of the bill), applied to all long-billed birds. *Andalucian.* Gallinéta. *Spanish.* Chócha.

The Woodcock, according to Favier, is "not abundant around Tangier, arriving during November and departing in March."

Uncertain, both in numbers and as to time of arrival near Gibraltar, in some seasons Woodcocks are tolerably plentiful, as in 1873; in others, as in the winter of 1871–72, they are very scarce. Five or six couple in the day for two guns is a very fair bag; but there was an instance of a Spanish cazador bagging twenty-one in a day near Algeciraz; those who wish for good Woodcock-shooting had better not try either Andalucia or Morocco, but go to the east of the Mediterranean.

My earliest note of the arrival of a Woodcock about Gibraltar was on the 17th of October, but very few arrive until the middle of November. The latest noticed was on the 8th of March; but I have seen them in Seville market on the 22nd of that month. I obtained near that city a fine white variety, which is now in the Norwich Museum.

Second-hand information is not always trustworthy, but the

postmaster at San Roque, the late Mr. Macrae, an official well known in those days to the garrison of Gibraltar, and upon whose veracity and knowledge of the bird I can depend, told me that once, and only once, he saw at break of day a regular flight, or what the Spaniards would call a "band" of Woodcocks passing south. He described them as being about twenty or thirty in number, but the light was so dim he could not see where they went to.

Feathers on breast barred; sixteen tail-feathers with silvery-white tips on underside; greyish tips above. Length 13 inches.

301. Gallinago major (J. F. Gmelin). The Great or Solitary Snipe.

Spanish. Agachadiza real.

Favier only mentions a single specimen of this Snipe as having been obtained by him near Tangier, in 1859. It is, however, included in Mr. Drake's list, 'Ibis,' 1869, p. 153, as twice noticed in March.

The Great Snipe is only met with near Gibraltar on passage, "here to-day, gone to-morrow." I saw two and shot one at Casas Viejas on the 24th of October, 1868; one was killed near Gibraltar on the 17th of October, 1871; and I know of another obtained in April. It is there a well-known bird, but, passing north late in April and early in May, and returning again in September and October, is not very liable to be noticed; and probably their chief line of migration lies more to the eastward.

This Snipe is usually very tame, and, lying closely, shows the external white feathers of the tail very much when rising; and generally alights again within a short distance, never uttering any sound.

Belly barred to the vent; sixteen tail-feathers, lower half of the four outside pairs *white* in adults, white with brown bar in young. Length 11½ inches.

302. Gallinago cœlestis (Frenzel). The Common Snipe.

Moorish. Bou monkar (Father of the bill). *Spanish.* Near Gibraltar, Agachadiza; further north, Agachóna; near Málaga, Agachadéra.

Favier remarks that on the African side " the Common Snipe is found very plentiful around Tangier from the month of October until February," which may be said of them likewise as regards the Spanish side of the Straits; and although better sport is to be had with this (in a sporting sense) king of birds on the Moorish side, the amusement is, as has been already stated, greatly reduced by the want of accommodation and utter absence of comfort; not that there is much of the latter in many places on the Andalucian side. At Casas Viejas, Snipe sometimes arrive as early as the beginning of September. I have heard of a straggler during August (one was shot by Verner in the Soto Malabrigo on the 21st of that month in 1879), but the greater quantity do not put in an appearance till the end of October and the first week in November. They commence their departure in March; and by the first week in April all have disappeared except a stray loiterer, perhaps a wounded bird. We noticed one as late as the 3rd of May, having observed it for several days previously in the same situation, and would not shoot it, wishing to see how long it would remain: this bird did not appear to have anything the matter with it. I never heard the drumming noise of the Snipe in Andulacia—though at home in England I have occasionally heard them drumming of an evening in the New Forest as early as the 20th of January, the weather then being unusually mild, and the place where they were heard being their regular nesting-ground.

I have often noticed that, in the marshes both in Morocco and Andalucia, the best ground for Snipe was a spot where sedges and rushes had been burnt during the summer; but the consequent absence of cover in these places rendered it useless to try and walk up to the birds, and the only way was to stand or sit

A DEEP PLACE IN THE MALABRIGO SOTO.

perfectly still in the most favourite spot and await their return. I have more than once taken a chair down and sat in it, waiting for their flight overhead, much to the astonishment of the native population, who could not understand such a proceeding.

Varieties or races of this species, varying in size and colour, have been named *russata*, *delamottii*, and *brehmi*; but it is difficult to perceive any distinction, as these varieties are not constant. "Sabine's Snipe" is merely a dark variety.

Axillaries white, barred with blackish grey; tail-feathers fourteen. Length 10½ inches.

303. Gallinago gallinula (Linnæus). The Jacksnipe.

Moorish. Saiga (*Favier*).

This bird is stated by Favier to be "nearly as common in the winter months around Tangier as the Common Snipe, arriving during November, and departing northwards in February."

On the Spanish side of the Straits the Jacksnipe is generally distributed throughout the winter, and is extremely numerous about some favourite black muddy spots at Casas Viejas and in the "ojos," or land-springs, at the edges of the marisma, but is by no means so plentiful as the Common Snipe. Towards the end of February, Jacksnipes assemble together very much; and this gathering of them is a sure prelude to the general departure of most of the Snipes for the north. The greatest number of the present species that I ever saw anywhere was in some of the "ojos" westward of Coria del Rio, near Seville; these circular spots, about ten yards in diameter, were very muddy and sparingly covered with short sedge. Many of them held fifteen or a dozen Jacksnipe; and the often-cited, and perhaps imaginary, individual who is said to have found a single Jacksnipe afford him sport for months until his friend unluckily killed it, would here, indeed, have been in happy hunting-grounds.

I could not ascertain any good local Andalucian name for this bird. I have heard some; but they were too absurd and varied to repeat. The Jacksnipe is said occasionally to arrive in Andalucia towards the end of September; but my two earliest notes of their arrival are the 24th and the 27th of October near Seville.

Purple gloss on back; axillaries white; tail-feathers twelve, centre pair longer than the rest. Length 7½ inches.

304. Calidris arenaria (Linnæus). The Sanderling.

Spanish. Churrilla de tres dedos (Málaga) (*Arévalo*).

"This bird is abundant during migration near Tangier in small flocks along the coast, crossing the Straits during March, April, and May; they are found returning south as late as December. I found numbers near Tetuan in February 1848 at the mouth of the river, where they are known to the Moors under the name of Medrouan."—*Favier.*

On the African side we saw large flights of Sanderlings early in April between Tetuan and Ceuta. On the Spanish side they are common from autumn to spring along the sea-shore; the latest noticed was during the first week in May.

Legs and bill black; bill as long as the head and straight; *no hind toe.*

In spring. Upper parts rufous and black; head, throat, and upper breast rufous, marked with black.

In winter. Grey above, white below; rump ashy grey; bill as long as the head. Length 8 inches.

305. Tringa subarquata, Güldenstädt. The Curlew Sandpiper.

All that Favier has in his MS. relative to this bird is that it "passes near Tangier during the month of April, returning south in September."

I never obtained the Curlew Sandpiper on the autumnal passage; but in some years vast numbers passed at Gibraltar towards the end of April, usually in lots of from ten to twenty in number; they were occasionally mixed up with Dunlins, and were chiefly to be seen at the mouths of rivers, particularly about Palmones, where one was shot with the first primary in each wing white. When flying they are easily distinguished by the white rump, which is then very conspicuous. They are in good red or breeding-plumage by the 26th of April; that is to say, the male birds are; but the females are slower in assuming this dress, and probably never become as bright as their mates. About Gibraltar this Sandpiper and others bear the trivial name "pitillo." Lord Lilford informs me that he met with the present species at the same place and time as the Knots, and in equal numbers. Curiously, during that spring, Curlew Sandpipers were unusually abundant near Gibraltar, but not a single Knot did I obtain or see. There is, however, not very much ground suitable for the various species of *Tringa* in the vicinity of the Rock.

Bill *curved* downwards; rump *white*.
In spring. General colour dark reddish chestnut, marked above with blackish.
In autumn. General colour grey above; below white. Length 7 inches.

306. Tringa canutus, Linnæus. The Knot.

Favier merely remarks of this species that they "pass near Tangier in June." If such be the case, it must be very early in that month. The Knot is somewhat irregular in appearance about the vicinity of Gibraltar; and I have rarely met with any, and the few seen have only occurred in April and May. Lord Lilford, however, found them in countless numbers about the 10th of May near the edge of the Coto de Doñana. They were at that time in their fine red or summer plumage, and doubtless *en route* to their breeding-grounds in the extreme north.

Bill black, quite straight, longer than head.
Plumage changes much as in last, but the red is not so dark; rump and upper tail-coverts whitish, barred with blackish; legs and feet black. Length 10 inches.
Young. Feathers on back bordered with dark bars, tipped with buffy white; below tinged with buff; legs and feet yellowish green.

307. Tringa alpina, Linnæus. The Dunlin.

Favier remarks that the Dunlin "passes to Europe from the

Moorish coast during the months of April, May, and June, returning to winter further south in October and November."

This well-known species, however, is to be seen throughout the winter near Gibraltar, sometimes in considerable numbers. Occasionally they wander far up the rivers some distance from the sea, especially in the spring.

The majority of these Dunlins arrive in flocks about April and May, when they have assumed their full summer dress with black breasts.

Mr. Chapman found a nest of the Dunlin in the marisma containing four eggs.

Bill very slightly bent down towards the tip and longer than head; bill, legs, and feet black.

Summer. Belly black; general colour above reddish brown, marked with black.

Winter. Belly white. General colour above ashy grey. Length 8 inches.

308. Tringa striata, Linnæus. The Purple Sandpiper.

This species, which might perhaps be well termed the Rock-Sandpiper, from the habit of frequenting rocky and stony coasts, is altogether omitted by Favier as a Moorish bird.

They are not common in autumn and spring.

Bill as in Dunlin, but base dull yellow.

Rump and upper tail-coverts nearly *black*, with a purplish tinge; seventh to ninth secondaries nearly white; legs rather short and dull yellow. Length 8 inches.

Young have feathers above with white margins.

309. Tringa minuta, Leisler. The Little Stint.

This small Sandpiper is not mentioned by Favier as occurring on the Moorish coast; but is found there from autumn to spring, and we fell in with vast flocks at Meshree el Haddar on the 26th of April in company with Dunlins and Ringed Plovers; they had then attained their full breeding-dress. Mr. Irby, 60th Rifles, obtained them at Tangier on the 18th of March, 1894.

On the Spanish side, the Little Stint occurs in like manner; but I never saw any large numbers near Gibraltar.

Plumage above much as in Dunlin both in summer and winter, but bill quite straight.
Outer tail-feathers *ashy brown*; legs and feet black. Length 6 inches.

310. Tringa temmincki, Leisler. Temminck's Stint.

This Stint is not referred to by Favier or recorded by Mr. Drake as occurring on the African side of the Straits, where, however, they are of course to be found as on the Spanish side, being common there during the winter and found in small parties of from six to a dozen or more in number. They keep much to the muddy banks of tidal rivers, especially frequenting the salinas, or salt-pits; a sure locality for them used to be the abandoned or unused salinas near Palmones, between Algeciraz and Gibraltar, and they are very seldom seen alone, being usually tame and easy to obtain. I failed to observe any later than the month of March; but no doubt they further prolong their stay in southern parts.

Bill straight; legs and feet greenish brown.
Outer tail-feathers pure *white*. Length 5¾ inches.

311. Machetes pugnax (Linnæus). The Ruff (male). The Reeve (female).

Moorish. Habeeb el tchibeeb (the friend of the Godwit).

"This species is only observed near Tangier when on migration, crossing to Europe during March, returning in July, August, and September. Those which return in the last days of July still exhibit traces of the breeding-plumage."—*Favier.*

The greater number of Ruffs pass northwards through Andalucia in April; but flocks occasionally occur during January, February, and March, some passing as late as the last week in May. The males, or "Ruffs," are then in their inconvenient-looking nuptial plumage, but they have not yet been detected nesting so far south.

Axillaries *white*, no white on primaries, secondaries, or central upper tail-coverts; outside tail-feathers mottled; bill straight, as long as head.

Male in spring. With a ruff of various shades from black to pure white and chestnut.

Female, and male in winter. Without ruff. Legs yellowish brown. Length: male 12¼ inches, female 10¼.

312. Totanus ochropus (Linnæus). The Green Sandpiper.

Spanish. Lavandéra.

"This species is not uncommon in winter around Tangier, frequenting the edges of lakes and the banks of rivers alone or in pairs. They depart northwards during February and March, reappearing by August and September."—*Favier.*

The Green Sandpiper, a bird in which I have from my boyish days in Norfolk always taken a special interest, is in Andalucia, as in England, extremely irregular and uncertain in its movements, changing its ground continually, and fluctuating greatly in numbers; days elapse without seeing a single bird, and suddenly several appear, but are seldom observed in any greater number than two or three together; generally they are solitary in their habits, and without exception frequent shores of freshwater lakes, ponds, and streams. The loud note of this Sandpiper and the white tail-coverts, which show markedly on the wing, can hardly fail to cause recognition. The curious fact of their nidification on trees in old nests of other birds has probably led to their nests in many countries being overlooked; and who can tell that they may not yet be found breeding in Andalucia?

The Green Sandpiper is most common in the winter months near Gibraltar; and the only month in which I have not seen any has been July; but then I had no opportunity of so doing. This Sandpiper always has a musky odour.

Bill straight, longer than head, as in the genus *Totanus*.

Above greenish brown, with minute white spots; below white; rump and outer tail-feathers on each side *white*; axillaries brownish black, with narrow white bars; legs dark green. Length 9½ inches.

313. Totanus glareola (J. F. Gmelin). **The Wood-Sandpiper.**

This bird is not noticed by Favier as occurring in Morocco; but there were plenty to be seen towards the end of April at the lakes of Ras el Doura and other swamps in that country; and near Gibraltar I have observed them frequently on passage from the 9th of March to the beginning of the month of May.

Being, as far as my observations go, entirely a freshwater Sandpiper, the species most resembles in habits the Marsh-Sandpiper (*T. stagnatilis*).

Above greenish brown, each feather margined with buffy-white spots; upper tail-coverts white; axillaries white, sometimes with a few dusky bars; legs pale olive, 1½ inches long. Length 7½ inches.

314. Totanus hypoleucus (Linnæus). **The Common Sandpiper.**

Spanish. Lavandéra chica.

"This is the most common of the Sandpipers around Tangier, passing north during April and May. They are seen returning in August, September, and October."—*Favier.*

The Common Sandpiper in Andalucia prefers the banks of running streams and salt or tidal marshes, being not much noticed in freshwater marshes or about stagnant pools. Near Gibraltar, particularly when on passage in spring, they greatly frequent the sea-coast wherever there is much seaweed thrown up by the tide; and I have repeatedly observed them on rocks, like the Purple Sandpiper.

The present species swarms about the Straits in March and April, passing in lots of four or five together. I have no record of any in November, but saw one on the 24th of October and one on the 7th of December; they are not abundant in spring until the month of March, their passage being at its height about the 15th of April. Though I never succeeded in finding a nest, am positive some remain to breed, as in the end of May, near the mouth of the Guadiaro, a pair, from their manner, were certainly nesting; but all my efforts to discover the situation were futile. Arévalo says they breed in Andalucia.

Above greenish brown; axillaries white; secondaries brown, with white bases and tips. Length 7¾ inches.

315. Totanus cinereus (Güldenstädt). The Terek Sandpiper.

This bird has been once obtained near Málaga. Is a freshwater Sandpiper, and an Eastern species, ranging to in winter as far south as S. Africa and Australia.

Bill slightly turned up, as in Greenshank; secondaries marked with white; axillaries white. Length 8½ inches.

316. Totanus stagnatilis, Bechstein. The Marsh-Sandpiper or Lesser Greenshank.

This eastern species has been obtained near Málaga and Valencia (*Arévalo*).

Is a freshwater Sandpiper, and a miniature Greenshank, having grey secondaries, but a straight bill. Length 10 inches.

317. Totanus canescens (J. F. Gmelin). The Greenshank.

All that Favier has to say of this bird is that it is met with on passage, "returning south during the month of October to winter probably in the interior of Africa"; and as the Greenshank is recorded by Andersson as common in Damara Land, Favier was not much out in his supposition. He does not, however, mention the date of its vernal migration, which takes place in March, April, and May, the birds being most frequently seen during the latter month, and the latest recorded by me was the 22nd of May. I have also noticed them in November and January, but never in any numbers; in all probability their chief line of migration lies further to the east.

The Greenshank is a very noisy bird, and sure to attract notice by its loud whistling cry, which, as is well known, consists of two notes.

Secondaries *uniform grey*; bill black, longer than head, and slightly turned upwards; legs olive-green.

In breeding-season has blackish marks on back and black spots on flanks, most developed in the female. Length 13-14 inches.

318. Totanus calidris (Linnæus). The Common **Redshank**.

Andalucian. Archibébe.

Favier states that "this Redshank is very abundant near Tangier, in small lots, which frequent the edges of rivers and lakes, and mostly pass northwards during March and April, returning to remain for the winter in September and October. Some, however, remain in the country for the breeding-season."

We found the Common Redshank in some numbers at the lakes of Ras el Doura towards the end of April; and they were then evidently beginning to nest, but were not in anything like the quantity which breed in some parts of the marisma of the Guadalquivir, where they breed a little later than the Peewit, which is there the earliest marsh-nesting bird. In Andalucia this Redshank is, though frequently seen in winter, and much too often for the sportsman, chiefly migratory, passing north in great abundance mostly towards the middle of April, when many are to be seen and heard shrieking out their three notes about the old salinas or abandoned salt-pits at Palmones, near Gibraltar; and a great many fall victims, to appear ultimately in the market; but they are quite unfit to eat.

Secondaries, axillaries, and upper tail-coverts *white*; legs and feet red in adults, yellowish in young. Length 10-11 inches.

319. Totanus fuscus (Linnæus). The **Dusky Redshank**.

Favier's notes relative to this species are as follows:—"Frequents the vicinity of salt marshes near Tangier during the months of September and October"; but the brevity of his remarks on most of the Waders and aquatic birds would lead one to suspect that Favier, like many other Frenchmen and all Spaniards, had a cat-like antipathy to water.

On the Spanish side of the Straits I never shot a specimen of the Dusky Redshank; but it occasionally occurs in spring and autumn. Their whistle is a single note.

Larger than last; secondaries white, *barred* with grey; upper tail-coverts white, *barred* with blackish brown; legs red. Length 12 inches.

320. Limosa lapponica (Linnæus). The Bar-tailed Godwit.

Moorish. Tchibeeb (*Favier*).

"This species is, during passage, nearly as numerous in the vicinity of Tangier as *L. ægocephala*. They arrive from the north during September, and, passing on further south, return and cross over to Europe during the months of February, March, and April. The chasseurs of Larache call this Godwit *Boumeraisa* indiscriminately with the other species."—*Favier.*

The Bar-tailed Godwit, chiefly from frequenting salt-marshes and estuaries of rivers, is not noticed near Gibraltar in such numbers as the larger Black-tailed Godwit, and is only observed on passage. The latest date I have of seeing them in spring was on the 10th of May; and the earliest date of their appearance recorded in autumn was the 21st of September; but no doubt they pass much sooner than this. I did not observe any during the winter months.

Bill as in next species very long.
Rump *nearly white*; axillaries barred with black and white; tail barred in spring and in young birds; adults in winter have tail ash-grey, marbled at the base, long tail-coverts barred.
Female Godwits much larger than males.
In summer. Below pale red, darker in male.
In winter. Below white, above greyish brown; feathers with dark shaft-streaks. Length 15-16 inches.

321. Limosa belgica (J. F. Gmelin). The Black-tailed Godwit.

Moorish. Tchibeeb (*Favier*). *Andalucian.* Abujéta, Sarscruélo.

"This Godwit is found on passage near Tangier in abundant flocks, migrating to the north during the months of February and

March; they are observed returning in August and September."
—*Favier.*

Favier also further asserts that this species occasionally remains to breed in Morocco—a statement which sounds improbable, and therefore to be received with reserve, though it would not perhaps be more surprising than the fact of the Crane, Peewit, and the Dunlin nesting so far south as they have been proved to do.

The Black-tailed Godwit appears in Andalucia during February, in bands of from four or five to as many as two or three hundred, frequenting the grassy marshes or rather inundated ground about Casas Viejas and the marisma. They are very restless, and continually on the move, uttering their loud cries. As they are usually rather wary and difficult to get a shot at, the best chance of obtaining any is either to lie up for them, or, in Spanish fashion, to use a stalking-horse. Their numbers vary considerably in different years; and they do not seem to stay long in the same district, as some hundreds may be noticed one day and hardly any on the next. The passage continues far into the month of March, by which time they are well advanced in their rufous breeding-plumage; and this ruddy appearance shows much when they are on the wing. The earliest assumption of this dress was observed on the 24th of February. Immense quantities are brought into Seville market for sale during March; and the latest seen there was on the 6th of April. In that district their local name is *Sarseruélo*; but about Casas Viejas they are known as *Abujéta*, evidently a word of Moorish origin.

They are excellent eating and fully deserve the derivation which has been given of their English name "Godwit," *i. e.* good food (from "good," and "wihta," animal).

I have no note of their autumnal migration; but occasionally they are met with in winter, usually solitary birds, as I killed one on the 5th of December at Tapatanilla, and have seen others now and then obtained in January.

Larger than last; upper tail-coverts white; tail black, with white base;

white bar across wing; axillaries white, but sometimes barred with brown.

In summer. Breast reddish, belly white, barred with blackish brown.

In winter. Ashy brown above, below greyish white. Length 16–20 inches.

322. Numenius arquata (Linnæus). The Common Curlew.

Moorish. Bou-khalal (Father of the toothpick or pin). *Spanish.* Zarapito.

"This bird is, near Tangier, only a winter resident, which arrives in September and October and leaves during March. They frequent the mouths of rivers and the sea-shore in large numbers, but they are very wild and difficult to get a shot at." —*Favier.*

When at Larache towards the end of April I observed several Common Curlews; and a Spaniard who resided there asserted that they nested near the town. No doubt if any Curlew breeds there it would be the next small species.

The Common Curlew is very plentiful near Gibraltar during the winter months, being, perhaps, most frequent in February; but is very wary, as everywhere else in the world that I have met with it.

Bill as in next three species, very long and curved downwards.

Crown pale brown, regularly streaked with dark brown; axillaries white, barred with dark brown; rump paler than back. Length 21–26 inches.

323. Numenius tenuirostris, Vieillot. The Mediterranean Curlew.

This small Curlew is said to occur in spring and autumn about the Straits. I never met with any, but Arévalo records them from the Province of Málaga.

Capt. Savile Reid mentions ('Ibis,' 1885) that this bird was abundant during the winter of 1884–85 in the Laraish Valley, in flocks of from twenty to a hundred. He obtained specimens there, and also saw numerous flights at Meshree el Haddar; he further describes the note as resembling that of the Common Curlew, "but not so loud or musical."

Crown *uniformly* striated, no pale streak; axillaries white; flanks marked with conspicuous dark pear-shaped spots. About size of the Whimbrel.

324. **Numenius phæopus** (Linnæus). The Whimbrel.

Favier's notes on this species are the same as on the Curlew, except that he adds "this bird arrives earlier from the north, and though very common, does not remain in the neighbourhood of Tangier for the winter, but passes on further south."

On the Spanish side of the Straits, the Whimbrel, plentiful in autumn and spring up to the end of April, is occasionally seen in winter; and, as elsewhere, is far less wary and difficult to approach than the Curlew.

Crown dark brown, with pale streak along the top; in some young birds this streak is almost obsolete, and the brown on head has a glossy sheen; axillaries white, barred more or less with brown. Length 16-18 inches.

325. **Numenius hudsonicus**, Latham. The American Whimbrel.

A specimen of this Whimbrel was obtained by Lord Lilford in the Coto de Doñana on the 3rd of May, 1872 ('Ibis,' 1873, p. 98).

About size of the last. Crown pale brown, with pale streak along the centre; axillaries *rufous*.

Order **GAVIÆ**. Family **LARIDÆ**.

Subfamily STERNINÆ. Legs and feet small and weak; bill as long as or longer than head.

326. **Hydrochelidon nigra** (Linnæus). The Black Tern.

Spanish. Cencerillo, Paino.

"This Tern is abundant near Tangier when on passage, crossing the Straits in large flights during May, and returning in

September and October. They are not seen in the winter months."—*Favier.*

The Black Tern, on the Spanish side, begins to appear about the end of April. Is rather later than the Whiskered Tern, nesting also later in the same situations as that species, but not in such numbers. I have noticed quantities crossing the Straits on the 10th of May, and they are often seen on arrival, hawking about over cornfields and low ground near water.

Head, neck, breast, and belly black; vent and under tail-coverts white; under wing-coverts pale grey; rest of plumage slate-grey; bill black; legs reddish brown. Length 10 inches.

Autumn. Forehead, throat, and nape white; below barred with white.

327. Hydrochelidon leucoptera (Schinz) **The White-winged Black Tern.**

On the African side the only instance recorded of the occurrence of this bird is a single specimen shot in May, 1869, at Sharf el Akab, near Tangier. It is not included in Favier's list; and we never met with any on either side of the Straits, but three shot in the marisma are in Lord Lilford's collection; probably they rarely wander so far west. I have several times imagined that I saw some, but upon shooting the birds found them to be fine old *H. hybrida*, which, when flying in the bright sunshine and showing the blackish belly, is very apt to be mistaken for the present species.

Head, neck, underparts, and under wing-coverts black; vent, tail, and tail-coverts white; bill dark red; legs scarlet. Length 9½ inches.

328. Hydrochelidon hybrida (Pallas). **The Whiskered Tern.**

Spanish. Paino mayor (Málaga) (*Arévalo*).

"This Tern is scarce near Tangier, and seen only on passage during April, returning south in August. Immense numbers are found breeding at the lakes of Ras el Doura, where, nesting together in vast colonies, they bear the local name of *Mershik.*"—*Favier.*

WHISKERED TERNS AT HOME.

On the Spanish side the Whiskered Tern arrives about the middle of April, and is only seen near Gibraltar on migration. Hovering over every swamp and wet spot, they soon pass on to their breeding-haunts in the Laguna de la Janda and the marisma, where, among rushes and sedges, they nest about the middle of May in colonies. Like other Terns, they lay three eggs; of a pale green ground-colour, with variable markings of blackish brown.

I saw a large flock of these Terns on the sea near Cadiz on the 18th of July. Verner visited a breeding-colony of these birds at La Janda on the 7th of May, 1875, and found several hundred nests floating on the top of the water; they were simple platforms of reeds and rushes, and were kept from drifting to some extent by the young rushes growing up in the water. Only two nests contained a single egg. Five days later over thirty nests had eggs. In the interval between the visits a strong wind had arisen and blown many of the Terns' nests along the water till they were packed in a dense mass on the lee side of the laguna.

Forehead, crown, and nape black; chin and sides of neck white; belly very dark brown, almost black; rest of plumage grey or white; under wing-coverts white; bill dark red; legs vermilion. Length 11¼ inches.

329. Sterna anglica, Montagu. The Gull-billed Tern.

Spanish. Cágalo (*Arévalo*).

Strangely enough, no mention is made of this Tern in Favier's MS.; but we found them in great numbers about the lakes of Ras el Doura towards the end of April. As far as we could ascertain from the Arabs, they said that these birds remained in the neighbourhood and bred a little later on in the season. Essentially a freshwater or marsh-frequenting species, I never noticed the Gull-billed Tern on the sea-coast. Some of those we shot had been feeding on green frogs; their note, loud and frequently repeated, is (as near as I can render it) *kŭh-wŭk, kŭh-wŭk*. I never noticed the present species about Gibraltar, but it occurs in the marshes of the Guadalquivir towards San Lucar, breeding there in considerable numbers, and its eggs from thence have been supposed to belong to *Larus melanocephalus*.

Head and bill black; lower mandible slightly angulated or "Gull-billed"; tail bluish grey. Length 13–14 inches.

330. Sterna caspia, Pallas. The Caspian Tern.

Spanish for all Terns. Golondrina de mar.

This large Tern is stated by Favier to be "very rare near Tangier," he having only obtained a single specimen (in February, 1844), which occurrence I can supplement by one which occurred in the winter of 1869.

Near Gibraltar I did not meet with any, though two were obtained by Lord Lilford near the Isla Menor, below Seville, in April, 1883. They are only accidental stragglers so far west, but further east in Spain, near Mar Menor, they are reported by Guirao to be common.

The largest of the Terns.
Head black; tail white; bill coral-red, dark at tip; legs black. Length 19–21 inches.

331. Sterna maxima, Boddaert. The Royal Tern.

This Sea-Tern was once obtained by Favier in the Straits and is described in his MS. The specimen, which I purchased from his successor, was an adult bird in winter plumage, and is now in the possession of Lord Lilford. Two specimens shot near Tangier in December, 1882, are in Mr. J. J. Dalgleish's collection, to whom I am obliged for this information.

Crown black and slightly crested; bill orange-red. Length 19 inches.

332. Sterna cantiaca, J. F. Gmelin. The Sandwich Tern.

Spanish. Charrán (Málaga) (*Arévalo*).

"This Tern is seen near Tangier in abundant flocks from November to February."—*Favier.*

They were very numerous at the mouth of the river at Larache during April.

The Sandwich Tern is very common in the Straits in autumn, winter, and spring. Sometimes thirty or forty may be noticed sitting together on the small isolated rocks near Cabrita Point, and will allow a boat to approach within a few yards. They pass north about the first week in April, when I killed an old male tinted on the breast and under wing-coverts with a beautiful pink blush, just as is sometimes found in the spring on old males of the Brown-headed Gull (*Larus ridibundus*). They nest in the marisma and, according to Arévalo, near Málaga.

Head black; tail white; bill black, with yellow tip; legs black. Length 15 inches.

333. Sterna media, Horsfield. The Allied Tern.

"This species is one of the least common of the Terns near Tangier, and only occasionally met with. Further south, in the vicinity of Larache, it is more frequently seen; and I found it there during September, October, and November, in company with *S. cantiaca*, which species it resembles in habits."—*Favier*.

This Tern occurs in the Straits in spring. Two, both males, were shot near Tarifa on the 20th of April, 1873, and many have been obtained near Tangier. Probably they breed on the coast.

This bird is very much like the Sandwich Tern (*S. cantiaca*), but is a trifle larger and has the bill *yellow*. I found, on comparing male specimens shot on the same day, that it differs from that species also in having the bill stouter in proportion, and the lower mandible slightly angulated, or "Gull-billed." The feathers of the black crest are more elongated, and the upper tail-coverts and tail are grey, the same colour as the back. The primaries underneath are more broadly marked with grey next the shafts; and the tarsus is rather longer.

334. Sterna macrura, Naumann. The Arctic Tern.

I obtained this Tern in winter plumage in the Straits of Gibraltar; and there is no doubt that they occur regularly on migration; but it was very difficult to get specimens of the Terns for identification.

Crown black; below as grey as the back. First primary with the grey stripe along the shaft of the inner web no broader than the outer web; bill and legs coral-red; legs shorter than in next. Length 15 inches.

335. Sterna fluviatilis, Naumann. The Common Tern.

Favier includes this species in his notes, and states that they are found near Tangier in large flights on the coast during migration, passing south during September and October. Possibly he may mean the previous species.

The Common Tern is frequently seen in autumn and spring in the Straits, and may very possibly be found nesting near Cadiz.

Crown black, below white.
First primary with the grey stripe along the shaft of the inner web twice as broad as the outer web; bill and legs coral-red; bill blackish at tip. Length 14 inches.

336. Sterna minuta, Linnæus. The Little Tern.

Spanish. Catalinita (*Arévalo*).

"This small Tern is seen near Tangier, passing in small flights along the coast and on the rivers and lakes. They arrive during May, and return in September, some, however, remaining in the country to breed. They all retire south for the winter."— Favier.

The Little Tern occurs on the Spanish as on the Moorish side and, keeping to the sea-coast, is the latest to arrive of all the family. They are nowhere very abundant; but a few nest near the mouth of the Guadiaro about the end of May, as well as in other localities on the coast.

The earliest date on which noticed was on the 10th of May; and the latest was on the 25th of October.

Primaries white, with black tips, edged on the *inner* web with black and usually on the outer web. Length 15-16 inches.

Subfamily LARINÆ. Legs and feet large and strong; bill shorter than head.

Moorish for Gulls. Garvia or Kerzeit. *Spanish.* Gavióta.

337. Larus minutus, Pallas. **The Little Gull.**

Favier only mentions having once obtained this diminutive Gull near Tangier, in February, 1854. I have seen them in some numbers, though very irregularly, in winter. Verner says a small flock frequented the Laguna de las Jabas in February, 1892. I saw two sitting on the bowsprit of a yacht anchored at Gibraltar on the 24th of March, 1894.

Spring. Head black.
Winter. Head white, with a few dusky spots.
Young. Head brownish, marked with black and grey.
Smallest Gull, length of wing under $9\frac{1}{2}$ inches. Length 10-11 inches.

338. Larus ridibundus, Linnæus. **The Brown-headed Gull.**

According to Favier this Gull is the most common species around Tangier, arriving chiefly during November, and departing north in March.

Is found as above on the Spanish side, and was noticed as late as the 10th of April, 1894, at the Laguna de la Janda.

Head *sooty brown* from about March 1st to August 1st.
Winter. Head white, with grey patch behind eye.
Young. Marked above with brown, and, as in all *black-headed* Gulls, has a blackish bar at the end of tail.
Primaries white, with black tips, edged on the *inner* web with black and usually on the outer web. Length 15-16 inches.

339. Larus melanocephalus, Natterer. **The Adriatic Black-headed Gull.**

This Gull may occasionally occur in the Straits in winter; but I never obtained one, and Lord Lilford tells me that he never saw any westward of Málaga.

Mr. H. Saunders writes to me as follows:—" There has been a

good deal of confusion about the supposed breeding of this bird in Spain, and as I have in some degree contributed to this I will do my best to clear matters up. I saw and have specimens of this Gull from Málaga and also from the Trocadero, near Cadiz, and I *had* eggs—*said* to have been taken with the birds (which I examined) in the marisma. I also saw a colony, apparently breeding, below Huelva, but the steamer in which I had taken my passage whistled me back before I could land. The eggs above mentioned have proved to be those of the Gull-billed Tern; so were those obtained by Mr. Abel Chapman ('Ibis,' 1884, p. 86), who shot an Adriatic Gull near them*; so were those acquired by Mr. Dresser (save one, which is a Sandwich Tern's); and I do not know of an authenticated egg of *L. melanocephalus* from Spain.

"Of course I had not seen the eggs when I inserted the 'advanced notes' furnished by Mr. Dresser in my 'Manual of British Birds'; the whole account will be cancelled in the next edition.

"I think it is probable that the species will be found nesting along the coast or on the étangs of the Landes between Bayonne and Bordeaux, because the birds visit St. Jean de Luz in spring and also the mouth of the Gironde."

Bill *stouter* than last.
In summer. Head jet-black.
Adults. Primaries white, except the first, which has the *outer web* margined with black.
Young. Outer *webs* and *shafts* of first five primaries dark brown, outside of inner web of third primary white. Length 15 inches.

340. Larus canus, Linnæus. The Common Gull.

This Gull is not mentioned by Favier, but is during some winters common in the Straits of Gibraltar.

In spring. Head and neck white; mantle pale grey; bill and legs greenish yellow; former yellow at point.

---

* But this bird was not brought home for identification.

In winter. Head and neck streaked and spotted with brown; legs pale brown.

Young. Head, neck, and underparts white, mottled with light brown; tail with black band at end. Primaries black or dark brown, with white spots at the end or next the end. Length 18 inches.

341. Larus audouini, Payraudeau. Audouin's Gull.

This Mediterranean Gull is recorded by Natterer as having been once obtained near Tarifa, and has since then occurred at Málaga.

Lord Lilford, who discovered them breeding in 1874 off the south of Sardinia on a rocky island, and also found them on the island of Alborán in April, 1879, kindly gave me the following notes of the colours of the soft parts, which will serve to distinguish the adults of this species:—

"Feet and legs *very dark grey*, claws black. Bill brilliant *coral-red*, with *one broad black* band. Iris brilliant hazel, pupil black. Inside of mouth pale flesh-colour. Eyelids *coral-red*."

The following are the measurements (in inches) of a pair, taken from the dried skins:—

	♂.	♀.
Bill from gape	3·00	2·80
Wing, carpus to tip	15·75	15·75
Tarsus	2·45	2·30
Tail	6·00	6·00

Length 20 inches.

342. Larus gelastes, Lichtenstein. The Slender-billed Gull.

Favier only records a single specimen of this Gull as obtained by him near Tangier, in 1852; but he remarks that the feet of the immature birds are orange-yellow, which would lead to the supposition that he observed them more often.

They are not uncommon in spring on the coast of Southern Spain, nesting near the mouth of the Guadalquivir, where

Verner, when with the Crown Prince of Austria, found eggs about the 27th of May, 1879.

Bill slender, as long as head.

Head, nape, and neck white. Bill, eyelids, legs, and feet vermilion. Irides white. Length 16 inches.

343. Larus argentatus, J. F. Gmelin. The Herring-Gull.

The Herring-Gull is stated by Favier to be "as common near Tangier during winter as *L. ridibundus*, arriving in August, September, and October, and returning north in March, April, and May."

This bird and the Lesser Black-backed Gull feed in large numbers on the refuse from the slaughterhouses at Gibraltar; and it is not uncommon to see three or four hundred of them together there.

Perhaps some of the immature birds remain during the summer; but all the adults disappear by about the 15th of April.

Head and neck white; mantle *pale grey*; legs and feet flesh-colour; eyelids yellow.

Young. Feathers above brown, with pale edges; tail barred with brown; underparts white, streaked with brown. Length 22–24 inches.

344. Larus cachinnans, Pallas. The Southern or Yellow-legged Herring-Gull.

Favier remarks that "this Gull is not very common near Tangier, where it consorts with *L. fuscus* and *L. argentatus*."

This race of Herring-Gull is common about the Straits and southwards from Santander, where it occurred abundantly in May, 1876.

The adult birds are distinguishable by the colour of the legs, which are yellow, as in *L. fuscus*; the eyelids are scarlet, the back being much lighter in colour, but darker than in the next.

The size of the three species is about equal, and the birds in immature plumage appear identical.

345. Larus fuscus, Linnæus. **The Lesser Black-backed Gull.**

This Gull is merely included in Favier's list, but it is one of the most abundant species of Laridæ in the Straits in winter. The greater part pass northward by the end of March; but some few pairs remain to nest on the rocks of the African shore, laying about the end of April.

Head and neck white; mantle *slaty black*; legs and feet yellow; primaries nearly uniform dark brown.

Young. Like last. Length 21–23 inches.

346. Larus marinus, Linnæus. **The Great Black-backed Gull.**

This large Gull is, according to Favier, found about the Straits in small numbers from January to March, and he further states that he never saw any but immature birds; this agrees with my own observations, except that I have occasionally seen adults.

Resembles the last, but larger. Legs and feet flesh-colour; distinct wedge on third and fourth primaries.

Young. Like last. Length 26–33 inches.

347. Larus glaucus, O. Fabricius. **The Glaucous Gull.**

This Arctic Gull is not mentioned by Favier, but was once obtained by him in immature plumage near Tangier.

Adult. Entirely *white*, except grey mantle; head and neck streaked with ash-grey in winter.

Young. Dull white, mottled with pale brown; primaries greyish white; for a short time before assuming adult plumage the mantle is entirely white. Length 26–33 inches.

348. Rissa tridactyla (Linnæus). **The Kittiwake.**

"This species is nearly as common during winter in the Straits as the Herring-Gull, appearing during the month of November and leaving in March."—*Favier.*

The Kittiwake is to be seen in the Bay of Gibraltar during winter, sometimes in great abundance, at other times hardly any are to be found; their presence or absence is due to the state of the weather. They are often seen about the Laguna de la Janda, where, in February, 1892, Verner reports seeing vast numbers and caught two alive so gorged with black worms as to be unable to fly. He examined one and found a round mass of these worms, of the size of a golf-ball, in its throat.

Hind toe absent or rudimentary.
In summer. Head, neck, and tail pure white; bill greenish yellow.
In winter. Head and neck slate-grey.
Young. Bill black; brown feathers on back; tail with black band at end. Length 15 inches.

Subfamily STERCORARIINÆ. ROBBER-GULLS.

Base of upper mandible covered with a cere or skin, and hooked at the point.

349. Stercorarius catarractes (Linnæus). The Great Skua.

Favier records a single specimen obtained near Tangier, in December, 1852. It occurs regularly, but not commonly, during winter in the Straits.

General colour above dark brown; below lighter brown; axillaries dark brown; primaries blackish brown, bases white, forming a well-marked band. Tail dark brown, white at the base, but this is hidden by the coverts; two centre feathers very slightly longer than the others. Length 24-25 inches, leg $2\frac{3}{4}-3\frac{1}{4}$.

350. Stercorarius pomatorhinus (Temminck). The Twist-tailed or Pomatorhine Skua.

Stated by Favier to be very rare near Tangier; and he only mentions one specimen, obtained as far back as November, 1845. Is recorded from Málaga.

Two forms or races are found, both dark brown above. The dark form as dark below as above; the light form white below, barred on flanks and tail-coverts with dark brown, white on the throat, tinged with golden yellow, and sometimes extending round nape.

Two centre tail-feathers 4 inches longer than the others, and twisted upwards.

Young. Above dark brown; below paler, with buff margins to the feathers; tail brown, two centre feathers only very slightly longer than the others. Length 21 inches, leg 2.

351. Stercorarius crepidatus (J. F. Gmelin).   Richardson's Skua.

Spanish. Cágalo (Málaga) (*Arévalo*).

Favier only mentions one specimen of this Skua, killed near Tangier in 1844. It is, however, not uncommon in winter. Was often seen off Málaga in March, 1882.

Two forms or races are found.

Dark race. Adult uniform sooty brown, to which the name *Richardson's* is strictly applied; but the name *Arctic*, also employed, is a misnomer, as this bird breeds and also migrates further south than any of the other northern Skuas *.

Light race. Adult nearly as those of next species, but two centre tail-feathers only 3 inches longer than the others. Legs black.

Young. Sooty brown; paler below; centre tail-feathers little longer than the others.

All primaries with white shafts.

Length, including centre tail-feathers, about 20 inches.

352. Stercorarius parasiticus (Linnæus).   The Long-tailed or Buffon's Skua.

This Skua is recorded by Favier as twice obtained near Tangier—in 1846, and in October, 1858, the first being an immature specimen.

Adult. Crown black; above brownish grey; below white; sides of neck white, tinged with yellow; legs slate-grey. Two central tail-feathers about 9 inches longer than the others.

Young. Sooty brown; flanks and tail-coverts with buff margins; centre tail-feathers little longer than the others.

First two primaries with white shafts, but it is said that the nostrils of Buffon's Skua are nearer the frontal feathers than the tip of the bill—in Richardson's Skua the contrary being the case.

Length, including central tail-feathers, 22¼ inches.

---

* The writer has observed a light male and a dark female paired together at their nest on one of the Hebrides, where the dark and light forms were about equal in numbers.

Order PYGOPODES. Family ALCIDÆ.

353. Alca torda, Linnæus. **The Razor-bill.**

Moorish. Bou-drihima (*Favier*). *Spanish.* Gallaréta de mar.

Favier only says of this species that it "is found near Tangier from November to February."

The Razor-bill, in some winters, appears in the Straits in very large numbers, as in the winter of 1871-72, when, during February, they were to be seen in all directions about Gibraltar Bay, some coming into the New Mole so close to the land that we threw stones at them, and they lingered on very late, as I saw ten on the 19th, one on the 21st, and two on the 28th of March, and one on the 7th of April. In this case their appearance was, no doubt, attributable in the first instance to heavy gales and storms outside the Straits.

In 1877 I saw one at the New Mole during the last week in May. In March, 1882, there were vast numbers off Málaga.

Bill black, straight, large, much decurved towards point, with curved white line across centre on each side; upper mandible hooked, with three grooves across.

In summer. Above black, with green gloss; secondaries tipped with white, forming a band; narrow white streak from base of upper mandible to eye; below white, but chin and throat blackish.

In winter. Green gloss above nearly absent; chin, throat, and sides of head white; in young birds bill less developed. Length 17 inches.

354. Uria troile (Linnæus). **The Common Guillemot.**

This Guillemot is occasionally seen in small numbers about the Straits in winter, especially after severe weather from the westward.

Bill blackish, straight and pointed.

In summer. Head, neck, and upper surface dark brown; below white.

In winter. Throat and sides of head white. Length 18 inches.

The Ringed Guillemot is a race or variety, with a white ring round the eye and a white line running backwards therefrom.

355. **Fratercula arctica** (Linnæus). **The Puffin.**

Spanish. Frailecillo.

"This species is found near Tangier from November to March, sometimes even lingering as late in the spring as April and May. They are more abundant than the Gannet, and are frequently picked up dead on the sea-shore after stormy weather."—*Favier.*

I have seen Puffins in Gibraltar Bay as late as the 5th of March, but never in such numbers as the Razor-bill.

Bill shorter than head, higher than long; both mandibles arched (and in summer grooved across with orange).

Above black; forehead and crown greyish brown; black ring round white throat; below white; axillaries brown; legs orange.

In winter the bill is smaller and without brighter colour, the base of the bill being shed in autumn. Length 12 inches.

COLYMBIDÆ. Females smaller than males.

356. **Colymbus glacialis**, Linnæus. **The Great Northern Diver.**

Occasionally seen in winter in the Straits.

Adult: spring. Head and neck black, with purple gloss; a band of white stripes on throat, below which is another band of white stripes; bill black; iris red.

Winter. Above uniform blackish brown, more or less spotted with white; below white. Length 30–33 inches.

357. **Colymbus arcticus**, Linnæus. **The Black-throated Diver.**

Occasionally seen in winter in the Straits.

Adult: spring. Chin and *throat black*, with a purple gloss, divided by a patch of white with black lines; iris red.

Winter. Like last, but smaller. Length 25 inches.

358. **Colymbus septentrionalis**, Linnæus. **The Red-throated Diver.**

This Diver is common in the Straits in winter, and I obtained one specimen with a red throat.

Adult : spring. Throat grey, with lower part *chestnut-red.*
Winter. Above ashy grey, speckled and spotted with white, most so in the young; underparts white. Length 21-23 inches.

PODICIPEDIDÆ. Feet with lobes; no true tail.

359. Podicipes cristatus (Linnæus). The Great Crested Grebe.

Spanish. Zambullidor (applied to all Grebes and Divers).

"This large Grebe is, near Tangier, less common than *Podiceps minor.* Some remain in the country to breed; the others pass north during March. They are very abundant at the lakes of Ras el Doura."—*Favier.*

We can quite corroborate the latter statement; for when we were at those lakes at the end of April, the number of these Grebes, as well as of the next species, was perfectly marvellous. They were in pairs, but had not commenced laying. These swampy lakes, much covered at the sides with aquatic plants and sedges, must be a paradise for all Grebes and water-birds; but it is vexation of spirit and almost useless for the ornithologist to go there. The Arabs, at the egging-season, move their tents close to the lake and plunder every nest they can find, and further pester Europeans to an unbearable degree, being almost as annoying and intrusive as the mosquitoes, which were there more troublesome than in any country I have been in. Towards Casas Viejas and Gibraltar I never obtained the present species; but Lord Lilford found them breeding plentifully in May near the edge of the Coto de Doñana.

Male : summer. Crown and tufts black; tippet round face chestnut, with black edges.
Female. Rather smaller; crest and tippet not so much developed.
In winter these ornaments are scarcely present in the adult male, less so in the female, and absent in the young; all have white eye-stripe. Length 20-24 inches.

360. Podicipes griseigena (Boddaert). **The Red-necked Grebe.**

"This bird is less common near Tangier than the last, being seldom observed on passage. Some remain in the country to breed, the others migrating northwards in March, returning again during September. They are more abundant at the lakes of Ras el Doura, and are there called *Mazaa* by the Arabs."—*Favier*.

Some specimens of the Red-necked Grebe obtained in Morocco by Favier were so young that they must have been bred in the country; and we saw many at the above lakes in April, but I have no record of them on the Spanish side.

In summer. Crown, nape, back of neck black; chin and throat grey; neck in front *chestnut-red*; no tippet; bill black, base of bill yellow.
In winter. Neck in front grey; no eye-stripe. Length 16½ inches.

361. Podicipes auritus (Linnæus). **The Lesser Crested or Slavonian Grebe.**

Although Favier has not mentioned this Grebe as occurring near Tangier, I have seen one specimen obtained in the Straits in October, 1867; it probably is often to be met with in winter.

Bill straight.
In summer. With tuft of lengthened chestnut feathers on each side of head from bill to nape; crown, forehead, chin, and ruff or tippet black; neck and flanks chestnut.
In winter. As in last. Length 13 inches.

362. Podicipes nigricollis, C. L. Brehm. **The Black-necked or Eared Grebe.**

This species is the most common of the Grebes, breeding in lagoons and swamps on both sides of the Straits. In the winter they take to the salt water, and are generally plentiful in Gibraltar Bay.

Bill slightly *curved* upwards; inner four primaries *white* throughout.
In summer. Head and *neck* black, with a *stripe* from eye to nape of lengthened golden-reddish feathers.
In winter. Resembles last in plumage, except the white on primaries. Length 12 inches.

363. Podicipes fluviatilis (Tunstall). **The Little Grebe** or **Dabchick.**

Moorish. El ghotis (*Favier*).

"This small Grebe is resident near Tangier, although to a great extent migratory, passing north during April, and reappearing from October to December. They are resident and especially numerous at the lakes of Ras el Doura, where the Arabs, during the breeding-season, in a great measure subsist on the eggs of various aquatic birds, destroying a prodigious quantity."—*Favier.*

The Dabchick is resident in Andalucia, breeding abundantly in some localities; but is most common in winter; and how they reach the isolated patches of water, which are dry in summer, is marvellous, as I never saw one on the wing.

The Dabchick, in winter, is almost always to be seen on the inundation at the North Front of Gibraltar, taking no notice of the numerous passers by.

In summer. Chin black; cheeks, sides, and front of neck reddish chestnut.
In winter. Chin white, the reddish chestnut of neck replaced by brown; iris brown. Length 8–9 inches.

Order **TUBINARES**.

Family **PROCELLARIIDÆ**. Nostrils in a tube.

Oceanic birds, seldom landing except to breed.

364. Puffinus kuhli, Boie. **The Cinereous Shearwater.**

This species of Shearwater is abundant in the Straits, and is occasionally found dead on the shore. They nest about the beginning of May, under rocks and stones on islands, and a Shearwater is reported to breed at the back of the Rock.

Head, nape, and back dull brown; cheeks and chin *grey*; below *entirely white*.
Bill yellowish, tips horn-colour; legs flesh-colour (10th March). Length 18 inches.

Puffinus gravis, likely to occur in the Straits, is similar in size, but has head and nape dark brown, forming a cap; cheeks and chin *white*; centre of belly *brownish*. = *P. major*, auctorum.

365. **Puffinus anglorum** (Temminck). **The Manx Shearwater.**

Spanish. Animas (souls), Diablos (devils) *.

Favier states that this Shearwater is "found from August to November, and usually picked up dead on the sea-shore."

It is common in the Straits in autumn, occasionally coming close in to the land in the Bay of Gibraltar.

They seem to feed where porpoises swim at the surface of the water, and were thus seen in flocks of forty and fifty off Málaga in March, 1882, often sitting together on the water in company with *P. kuhli*. We shot a great many of both species, which were eaten by the yacht's crew.

Mediterranean specimens have the back lighter than northern birds, and are marked with grey on the flanks. This climatic race has been named *P. yelkouan*, Acerbi.

Head, back, wings, and tail blackish brown; breast and flanks white; rest of underparts dark smoky grey; bill and legs bluish grey. Length 13–14 inches, wing $9\frac{1}{2}$.

366. **Puffinus obscurus** (J. F. Gmelin). **The Dusky Shearwater.**

Recorded from Málaga.

Smaller than Manx Shearwater. Above blackish brown; underparts pure white; axillaries white. Length 11 inches.

367. **Procellaria pelagica**, Linnæus. **The Storm-Petrel.**

This little Petrel is frequently seen skimming about in the Straits, and, no doubt, nests on some of the small islands or patches of rock on the coast, as they are reported to do near Cabo de Palos, Mar Menor.

Above slaty black; upper tail-coverts and sides of vent white; below darker; tail slightly rounded; legs and feet black. Length $5\frac{1}{4}$ inches. Smallest web-footed bird.

---

* This Shearwater is very numerous in the Bosphorus and Dardanelles, passing continuously up and down in small flights, never being seen except on the wing; they are known as the "souls of the damned," who are allowed no rest.

368. Procellaria leucorrhoa, Vieillot. **Fork-tailed Petrel.**

This species is stated by Favier to be of rare occurrence in the Straits. Those which he obtained were all found dead on the sea shore after storms. He mentions picking up six in 1846, and one in each of the years 1852, 1854, and 1858.

Is recorded from Málaga.

Slate-black above, darker below ; upper tail-coverts white ; tail long, *deeply forked*. Length 7¼ inches.

369. Oceanites oceanicus (Kuhl). **The Long-legged** or **Wilson's Petrel.**

This wide-ranging Petrel was obtained near Málaga by Francisco de los Rios.

Sooty black, darkest below ; upper tail-coverts and sides of vent white ; tail almost *square* ; hind toe absent.

Legs 1½ inches long and slender, covered with large scales ; toes black, with the *centre* of the webs *yellow*. Length 7½ inches.

LAJA DEL CISCAR.

APPENDIX.

The following list of Lepidoptera may be of use to collectors, and is chiefly compiled from "Notes on Lepidoptera from the Region of the Straits of Gibraltar," by James J. Walker, R.N., F.L.S., published in the 'Transactions of the Entomological Society of London,' 1890, pp. 361-391.

Most of the Butterflies have been obtained by my son, L. P. Irby, 60th Rifles, and myself; possibly a few more species may be found.

The list of Moths is incomplete, and is almost entirely from Mr. Walker's paper, to whom I am much indebted for permission to make use of his notes and for his kind assistance in looking over this list.

Those species marked with an asterisk occur on the Rock of Gibraltar. All the Moorish specimens were found by Mr. Walker.

RHOPALOCERA (Butterflies).

*Papilio podalirius, L. Gibraltar (L. P. Irby).
P. machaon, L. February to October.
*Thais rumina, L. March, April.
*Pieris brassicae, L. All the year.
*P. rapae, L. All the year.
P. napi, L. Cork-wood (L. P. Irby).
*P. daplidice, L. March to November.
*Euchloë belemia, Esp. January, February (ab. glauce, Hb.).
E. belia, Esp. February.
E. tagis, Esp. March.
E. cardamines, L. Cork-wood, 18th April, 1894.

APPENDIX.

Euchloë euphenoides, Staud. March, April.
E. eupheno, L. Morocco only. March.
Leucophasia sinapis, L. March to July.
Colias edusa, F., and ab. *helice*, Hübn. All the year.
Gonopteryx rhamni, L. (Hibernates.) June.
G. cleopatra, L. (Hibernates.) May, June, July.
Thecla spini, Schiff., and ab. ♀ *lynceus*, Hübn.
T. ilicis, Esp., v. *æsculi*, O. May, June.
T. quercus, L. July.
T. roboris, Esp. June.
T. rubi, L. February and March, in numbers.
Thestor ballus, Hübn. February to April.
T. mauritanicus, Lucas. Morocco only. March, April.
Polyommatus phlœas, L. All the year round, and v. *eleus*, F., in summer.
Lycæna bœtica, L. All the year.
L. telicanus, Hübn. March to October.
L. theophrastus, F. Only near Tetuan. July.
L. baton, Berg, v. *panoptes*, Hübn. May.
L. lysimon, Hübn. August, November.
L. astrarche, Berg. All the year.
L. icarus, Rott. February to November.
L. bellargus, Rott. April and July.
L. minimus, Fuess., v. *lorquinii*, H.-S. May 16th.
L. melanops, Bdv. April, May.
L. argiolus, L. January to July.
Charaxes jasius, L. Rare at Gibraltar; one in 1872. Common at Tangier in September.
Vanessa polychloros, L. (Hibernates.) June.
V. urticæ, L. (L. P. Irby.) Also included by Rosenhauer.
V. atalanta, L. All the year.
V. cardui, L. All the year.
Melitæa aurinia, Rott., v. *desfontainii*, Godt. May 27th.
M. phœbe, Kn., v. *ætheria*, Hübn. May.
Argynnis latona, Esp. June.
A. pandora, Schiff. May to July; September, Gibraltar.
Danais plexippus, L. One, Gibraltar, Oct. 24, 1886 (J. J. Walker.
Melanargia ines, Hfsgg. (*thetis*, Hübn.). April, May.
Satyrus fidia, L. June to August.
S. statilinus, Hufn., v. *allionia*, F. July, August.
Pararge mæra, L., v. *adrasta*, Hübn. April.
P. megæra, L. January to October.
P. ægeria, L. All the year.
Epinephele janira, L., v. *hispulla*, Hübn. May to August.
E. ida, Esp. May to September.

Epinephele pasiphae, Esp. April to June.
Coenonympha arcanioides, Pierret. Morocco only. **March.**
C. dorus, Esp. July.
**C. pamphilus*, L. May, June.
**Spilothyrus alceae*, Esp. May, June.
S. althaeae, Hübn. All the year.
Syrichthus proto, Esp. May, July.
S. fritillum, Hübn. July.
S. sao, Hübn., v. *therapne*, Rbr. April, July.
Hesperia thaumas, Hufn. May, June.
H. acteon, Esp. May, June.
**H. nostradamus*, F. June to September.
H. zelleri, Lederer. Morocco only. July to November.

HETEROCERA (MOTHS), to end of GEOMETRÆ.

SPHINGES.

**Acherontia atropos*, L. Many larvæ on *Solanum sodomæum* (L. P. Irby, 1894).
**Sphinx convolvuli*, L.
**Deilephila euphorbiae*, L. Many larvæ (L. P. Irby, 1894).
**D. livornica*, L. Summer.
**Chærocampa celerio*, L. September, October.
Smerinthus populi, L. Morocco.
Pterogon proserpina, Pall. Larvæ common on *Œnothera*, June (J. J. Walker).
**Macroglossa stellatarum*, L. All the year.
**Sciapteron tabaniforme*, Rott. July.
Sesia ramburi, Staud. June.
**Paranthrene tineiformis*, Esp. June.
Zygæna sarpedon, Hübn. May, June.
Z. stœchadis, Bork. June.
Z. lavandulæ, Esp. May.
Z. bœtica, Rbr. May, August, September.

BOMBYCES.

**Nola cicatricalis*, Tr. April, October.
*Emydia cribrum, L., v. *candida*, Cyril. May, August, September.
**Deiopeia pulchella*, L. All the year.
Euchelia jacobææ, L. June.
*Euprepria pudica, L. August, September.
Arctia villica, L. March, April.
A. casta, Esp. April.
Phragmatobia fuliginosa, L. Esmir, Morocco.
**Porthesia auriflua*, L. June.

Orgyia josephinæ, Oberth. Esmir, Morocco.
O. trigotephras, Bdv. June.
Ocneria dispar, L. June. Larvæ in astonishing abundance near Algeciras, June 1888 (J. J. Walker).
O. atlantica, Rbr.
Cossus ligniperda, L.
Zeuzera pyrina, L. June.
Bombyx neustria, L. September.
B. trifolii, L. June.
Megasoma repanda, Hübn. August.
Saturnia pavonia, L. April.
S. pyri, L. March.
Cerura vinula, L. Tangier, May.
C. bifida, L. August.
Pygæra bucephala, L. March.

NOCTUÆ.

Raphia hybris, Hübn. July.
Acronycta psi, L. Morocco, April.
A. rumicis, L. Morocco, February.
Bryophila muralis, Forst., v. par, Hübn. July.
B. ereptricula, Tr. August, September.
Tapinostola musculosa, L. May.
Leucania loreyi, Dup. October.
L. l-album, L. October, November.
Caradrina exigua, Hübn. October.
C. ambigua, W. V. April, October.
Pachnobia rubricosa, W. V. May.
Orrhodia erythrocephala, W. V. October.
Triphæna pronuba, L. Summer.
Agrotis dahlii, Hübn. November.
A. saucia, Hübn. All the year.
A. leucogaster, Frr. One, Tetuan.
A. puta, Hübn. October.
A. segetum, Schiff. October, November.
A. spinifera, Hübn. February, October.
A. ypsilon, Rott., *suffusa*, Hübn. October.
A. crassa, Hübn. September.
Brithys pancratii, Cyr. February, November. Larvæ on *Pancratium mauritimum*.
Dryobata saportæ, Dup. October, November.
Mamestra serena, W. V. March.
M. dysodea, W. V., *chrysozona*, Bork. April.
M. oleracea, L. October.

Trigonophora flammea, Esp. (*empyrea*, Hübn.).
Eriopus latreillei, Dup. October.
Calocampa vetusta, Hübn. October.
  Calophasia platyptera, Esp. Tangier, September.
  Cleophana antirrhini, Hübn. May.
  C. yvanii, Dup. May.
Cucullia verbasci, L. April.
C. chamomillæ, W. V.
Eurhipia adulatrix, Bdv. September.
  Heliothis armigera, Hübn. October.
  H. incarnata, Fr. May, July.
H. peltigera, W. V. May to July.
Plusia chalcites, Esp. October.
P. gamma, L. All the year.
  Acontia luctuosa, W. V. May to September.
  A. lucida, Hübn., v. *albicollis*, F. Sierra Retin, March 28, 1894.
Catocala elocata, Esp. September.
  C. dilecta, Hübn. July.
  C. promissa, Esp. June.
  C. conversa, Esp. June.
  C. nymphagoga, Esp. June.
  Cerocala scapulosa, Bdv. April, May.
  Ophiusa bifasciata, Petagna. Tangier, September 1888.
  O. algira, L.
  Pseudophia lunaris, W. V. March.
P. tirrhæa, Cr. Larvæ on *Schinus molle*.
  Spintherops spectrum, F. June.
  Agrophila trabealis, Scop. August.
  Prothymia conicephala, Staud. July.
Thalpochares ostrina, Hübn. April to October.
T. parva, Hübn. August.
Metoptria monogramma, Hübn. April, May.
Herminia crinalis, Tr. October.
H. lividalis, Hübn. June, October.
H. obsitalis, Hübn. October.

GEOMETRÆ.

Nemoria herbaria, Hübn. October.
  Acidalia vittaria, Hübn. April, June.
  A. ochrata, Scop. June.
  A. perochraria, Rössl. June.
  A. nexata, Hübn. June, October.
A. virgularia, Hübn. October.

Acidalia elongaria, Rbr. May.
A. *circuitaria*, Hübn. Morocco only. June.
A. *ostrinaria*, Hübn. June.
A. ? *transmutaria*, Rbr. June.
A. *promutata*, Guén. (*marginepunctata*, Göze). July.
A. *luridata*, Zell. September.
A. *emutaria*, Hübn. Esmir, Morocco. November.
A. *imitaria*, Hübn. July.
A. *ornata*, Scop. May to August.
Zonosoma pupillaria, Hübn. July.
Z. *porata*, F. July.
Pellonia calabraria, Zell. April, May.
Abraxas pantaria, L. April, July.
Terpnomicta dilectaria, Hübn. Tangier, September.
Boarmia gemmaria, Brahm (*rhomboidaria*, W. V.). June.
Pachycnemia hippocastanaria, Hübn. May.
*Gnophos respersaria, Hübn. June.
*G. *mucidaria*, Hübn. October.
Anthometra plumularia, Bdv. June.
Fidonia plumistaria, Vill. Sierra Retin, 26th March, 1894.
Selidosema ericetaria, Vill. Summer and autumn.
Thamnonoma gesticularia, Hübn. May, June.
**Aspilates ochrearia*, Rossi. April.
Lozogramma obtusaria, Walker. A New-Zealand species, once taken near Gibraltar by Mr. J. J. Walker, 19th March, 1888.
Ligia opacaria, Hübn. October.
*Sterrha sacraria, L. All the year.
*S. *consecraria*, Ramb. Once in October.
**Lithostege griseata*, W. V. May.
Anaitis plagiata, L. May, June.
Chesias rufata, F., v. *obliquaria*, W. V. March.
Ortholitha peribolata, Hübn. October.
**Cidaria fluctuata*, L. Autumn.
*C. *fluviata*, Hübn. All the year.
C. *basochesiata*, Dup. October.
C. *bilineata*, L. July.
**Eupithecia centaureata*, W. V. (*oblongata*, Thnb.). Spring and autumn.
E. *satyrata*, Hübn. May, June.
*E. *pumilata*, Hübn. Spring and autumn.

INDEX TO BIRDS.

Accentor, Alpine, 49.
Accentor collaris, 49.
—— modularis, 49.
Accipiter nisus, 186.
Acredula caudata, 71.
—— irbii, 71.
—— rosea, 71.
Acrocephalus aquaticus, 58.
—— palustris, 58.
—— phragmitis, 58.
—— streperus, 57.
—— turdoides, 57.
Aedon galactodes, 56.
Ægialitis cantiana, 270.
—— curonica, 269.
—— hiaticula, 268.
Ægithalus pendulinus, 74.
Alauda arborea, 118.
—— arvensis, 117.
—— bætica, 120.
—— brachydactyla, 120.
—— calandra, 121.
—— cristata, 118.
—— macrorhyncha, 119.
—— theeklæ, 119.
Alca torda, 304.
Alcedo ispida, 130.
Anas boscas, 220.
—— strepera, 221.

Anser albifrons, 217.
—— brachyrhynchus, 218.
—— cinereus, 216.
—— erythropus, 217.
—— segetum, 218.
Anthus campestris, 116.
—— cervinus, 115.
—— obscurus, 115.
—— pratensis, 115.
—— richardi, 116.
—— spipoletta, 116.
—— trivialis, 114.
Aquila adalberti, 171.
—— chrysaëtus, 170.
—— nævia, 173.
—— rapax, 174.
Ardea alba, 202.
—— bubulcus, 203.
—— cinerea, 200.
—— garzetta, 202.
—— purpurea, 200.
—— ralloides, 204.
Ardetta minuta, 206.
Argya fulva, 70.
Asio accipitrinus, 139.
—— capensis, 140.
—— otus, 139.
Astur palumbarius, 185.
Avocet, 274.

Babbler, North-African, 70.
Bee-eater, 131.
Bernicla leucopsis, 218.
Bittern, Common, 206.
———, Little, 206.
Blackbird, 35.
Blackcap, 51.
Bluethroat, Red-spotted, 46.
———, White-spotted, 46.
Botaurus stellaris, 206.
Brambling, 104.
Bubo ignavus, 143.
Bulbul, White-vented, 67.
Bullfinch, Desert, 106.
Bunting, Cirl, 108.
———, Corn, 107.
———, House, 110.
———, Little, 110.
———, Ortolan, 109.
———, Reed, 109.
———, Rock, 110.
———, Snow, 111.
Bustard, Great, 253.
———, Little, 257.
———, North-African, 260.
———, Ruffed, 260.
Butcher-bird, 88.
Buteo desertorum, 169.
——— vulgaris, 168.
Buzzard, Common, 168.
———, Honey, 189.
———, Rufous, 169.

Caccabis petrosa, 239.
——— rufa, 237.
Calidris arenaria, 280.
Caprimulgus europæus, 125.
——— ruficollis, 126.
Carduelis elegans, 98.
——— spinus, 100.
Carine glaux, 145.
——— noctua, 144.
Certhia familiaris, 75.
Certhilauda bifasciata, 117.
——— duponti, 117.
——— lusitanica, 117.

Cettia cettii, 61.
Chaffinch, European, 102.
———, North-African, 103.
Charadrius fulvus, 267.
——— pluvialis, 266.
Chelidon urbica, 94.
Chiffchaff, 63.
Chough, Red-billed, 80.
———, Yellow-billed, 80.
Chrysomitris citrinella, 100.
Ciconia alba, 207.
——— nigra, 210.
Cinclus albicollis, 76.
——— aquaticus, 76.
Circaëtus gallicus, 182.
Circus æruginosus, 163.
——— cineraceus, 167.
——— cyaneus, 166.
——— swainsoni, 166.
Cisticola cursitans, 69.
Clangula glaucion, 229.
Coccothraustes vulgaris, 97.
Coccystes glandarius, 136.
Columba livia, 234.
——— œnas, 233.
——— palumbus, 232.
Colymbus arcticus, 305.
——— glacialis, 305.
——— septentrionalis, 305.
Coot, Common, 248.
———, Red-lobed, 249.
Coracias garrula, 130.
Cormorant, 198.
———, Green, 198.
Corn-Crake, 244.
Corvus corax, 84.
——— cornix, 86.
——— corone, 86.
——— frugilegus, 86.
——— monedula, 83.
——— tingitanus, 84.
Cotile riparia, 95.
——— rupestris, 96.
Coturnix communis, 240.
Courser, Cream-coloured, 263.
Crake, Baillon's, 245.

INDEX TO BIRDS.

Crake, Corn, 244.
———, Little, 245.
———, Spotted, 244.
Crane, Common, 249.
———, Demoiselle, 252.
Creeper, Rock, 75.
———, Tree, 75.
Crex pratensis, 244.
Crossbill, Common, 106.
———, Parrot, 107.
Crow, Carrion, 86.
———, Grey, 86.
———, Hooded, 86.
Cuckoo, Common, 135.
———, Great Spotted, 136.
Cuculus canorus, 135.
Curlew, Common, 290.
———, Mediterranean, 290.
———, Stone, 262.
Cursorius gallicus, 263.
Cyanopica cooki, 82.
Cygnus musicus, 215.
——— olor, 216.
Cypselus apus, 122.
——— melba, 124.
——— murinus, 123.

Dabchick, 308.
Dafila acuta, 222.
Daulias luscinia, 47.
Dendrocopus major, 126.
——— mauritanus, 127.
——— medius, 127.
——— numidicus, 127.
Dipper, Grey-backed, 76.
Diver, Black-throated, 305.
———, Great Northern, 305.
———, Red-throated, 305.
Dotterel, 268.
Dove, Common Turtle, 234.
———, Egyptian Turtle, 235.
———, Ring, 232.
———, Rock, 234.
———, Stock, 233.
Duck, Black, 229.
———, Brahminy, 219.

Duck, Ferruginous, 227.
———, Marbled, 223.
———, Scaup, 229.
———, Spiny-tailed, 230.
———, Tufted, 228.
———, White-faced, 230.
———, Wild, 220.
Dunlin, 281.

Eagle, Bonelli's, 174.
———, Booted, 180.
———, Golden, 170.
———, Sea, 174.
———, Short-toed, 182.
———, Snake, 182.
———, Spotted, 173.
———, Tawny, 174.
———, White-shouldered, 171.
———, White-tailed, 174.
Egret, Little, 202.
Elanus cœruleus, 190.
Emberiza cia, 110.
——— cirlus, 108.
——— citrinella, 108.
——— hortulana, 109.
——— miliaria, 107.
——— pusilla, 110.
——— saharæ, 110.
——— schœniclus, 109.
Erismatura leucocephala, 230.
Erythacus rubecula, 46.
Erythrospiza githaginea, 106.
Eudromias morinellus, 268.
Eupodotis arabs, 260.

Falco æsalon, 194.
——— babylonicus, 192.
——— barbarus, 192.
——— cenchris, 196.
——— eleonoræ, 193.
——— lanarius, 192.
——— peregrinus, 190.
——— punicus, 191.
——— subbuteo, 193.
——— tinnunculus, 195.

Falco vespertinus, 195.
Falcon, Barbary, 192.
——, Eleonora, 193.
——, Peregrine, 190.
——, Mediterranean, 190.
——, Rufous-naped, 192.
Fieldfare, 35.
Finch, Citril, 100.
——, Serin, 101.
——, Snow, 104.
Flamingo, 213.
Flycatcher, Collared, 92.
——, Pied, 92.
——, Spotted, 91.
Francolin, Double-spurred, 240.
Francolinus bicalcaratus, 240.
Fratercula arctica, 305.
Fringilla cœlebs, 102.
—— incerta, 106.
—— montifringilla, 104.
—— spodiogenys, 103.
Fulica atra, 248.
—— cristata, 249.
Fuligula cristata, 228.
—— ferina, 226.
—— marila, 229.
—— nyroca, 227.
—— rufila, 226.

Gadwall, 221.
Galerita macrorhyncha, 119.
—— theclæ, 119.
Gallinago brehmi, 279.
—— cœlestis, 278.
—— delamottii, 279.
—— gallinula, 279.
—— major, 277.
—— russata, 279.
Gallinula chloropus, 247.
Gannet, 199.
Garganey, 225.
Garrulus cervicalis, 82.
—— glandarius, 81.
Gecinus canus, 129.
—— sharpii, 128.
—— vaillanti, 128.

Gecinus viridis, 128.
Glareola pratincola, 261.
Goatsucker, 125.
Godwit, Bar-tailed, 288.
——, Black-tailed, 288.
Golden-eye, 229.
Goldfinch, 98.
Goosander, 231.
Goose, Bean, 218.
——, Bernicle, 218.
——, Grey-lag, 216.
——, Lesser White-fronted, 217.
——, Pink-footed, 218.
——, Solan, 199.
——, White-fronted, 217.
Goshawk, 185.
Grebe, Black-necked, 307.
——, Eared, 307.
——, Great Crested, 306.
——, Lesser Crested, 307.
——, Little, 308.
——, Red-necked, 307.
——, Slavonian, 307.
Greenfinch, 98.
Greenshank, 286.
——, Lesser, 286.
Grosbeak, Scarlet, 106.
Grouse, Black-bellied Sand, 237.
——, Pin-tailed Sand, 236.
Grus communis, 249.
—— virgo, 252.
Guillemot, Common, 304.
Gull, Adriatic Black-headed, 297.
——, Audouin's, 299.
——, Brown-headed, 297.
——, Common, 298.
——, Glaucous, 301.
——, Great Black-backed, 301.
——, Herring, 300.
——, Lesser Black-backed, 301.
——, Little, 297.
——, Slender-billed, 299.
——, Southern, 300.
——, Yellow-legged Herring, 300.
Gypaëtus barbatus, 156.
Gyps fulvus, 147.

INDEX TO BIRDS. 321

Hæmatopus ostralegus, 273.
Haliaëtus albicilla, 174.
Hammer, Yellow, 108.
Harrier, Hen, 166.
——, Marsh, 163.
——, Montagu's, 167.
——, Pale-chested, 166.
Hawfinch, 97.
Hawk, Black-shouldered, 190.
——, Many-banded, 168.
Hedge-Sparrow, 49.
Heron, Buff-backed, 203.
——, Cattle, 203.
——, Common, 200.
——, Great White, 202.
——, Night, 205.
——, Purple, 200.
——, Squacco, 204.
Himantopus candidus, 274.
Hirundo rufula, 94.
—— rustica, 93.
Hobby, 193.
——, Western Red-footed, **195**.
Hoopoe, 134.
Houbara undulata, 260.
Hydrochelidon hybrida, 292.
—— leucoptera, 292.
—— nigra, 291.
Hypolais icterina, 65.
—— olivetorum, 66.
—— opaca, 65.
—— polyglotta, **65**.

Ibis, Glossy, 212.
——, Red-cheeked, **211**.
Ibis comatus, 211.
Iynx torquilla, 129.

Jackdaw, 83.
Jacksnipe, 279.
Jay, Algerian Black-headed, 82.
——, West-European, 81.

Kestrel, Common, 195.
——, Lesser, 196.
Kingfisher, 130.

Kite, Black, 187.
——, Red, 187.
Kittiwake, 301.
Knot, 281.

Lämmergeyer, 156.
Landrail, 244.
Lanius algeriensis, 87.
—— collurio, 88.
—— meridionalis, 87.
—— minor, 88.
—— pomeranus, 89.
Lanner, 192.
Lapwing, 271.
——, **Black-bellied, 272.**
Lark, Andalucian Short-toed, 120.
——, **Desert Curved-billed, 117.**
——, Dupont's, 117.
——, Calandra, 121.
——, Crested, 118.
——, Horned Desert, 121.
——, Short-toed, 120.
——, Sky, 117.
——, Small Curved-billed, 117.
——, Wood, 118.
Larus argentatus, 300.
—— audouini, 299.
—— cachinnans, 300.
—— canus, 298.
—— fuscus, 301.
—— gelastes, 299.
—— glaucus, 301.
—— marinus, 301.
—— **melanocephalus, 297.**
—— minutus, **297.**
—— ridibundus, 297.
Ligurinus chloris, 98.
Limosa belgica, 288.
—— lapponica, 288.
Linnet, Common, 104.
——, Mountain, 105.
Linota cannabina, 104.
—— flavirostris, 105.
—— rufescens, 105.
Locustella luscinioides, 59.
—— nævia, 59.

Y

Loxia curvirostris, 106.
Lusciniola melanopogon, 61.

Machetes pugnax, 283.
Magpie, Common, 82.
———, North-African, 82.
———, Spanish Azure-winged, 82.
Mallard, 220.
Mareca penelope, 225.
Marmaronetta angustirostris, 223.
Martin, Crag, 96.
———, House, 94.
———, Sand, 95.
Melierax polyzonus, 168.
Merganser, Red-breasted, 231.
Mergus albellus, 232.
——— merganser, 231.
——— serrator, 231.
Merlin, 194.
Merops apiaster, 131.
Milvus ictinus, 187.
——— migrans, 187.
Monticola cyanus, 36.
——— saxatilis, 38.
Montifringilla nivalis, 104.
Moorhen, 247.
Motacilla alba, 111.
——— borealis, 114.
——— cinereocapilla, 114.
——— flava, 113.
——— lugubris, 112.
——— melanope, 112.
——— raii, 114.
Muscicapa atricapilla, 92.
——— collaris, 92.
——— grisola, 91.

Neophron percnopterus, 152.
Nightingale, 47.
Nightjar, 125.
———, Rufous-naped, 126.
Nisaëtus fasciatus, 174.
——— pennatus, 180.
Nucifraga caryocatactes, 80.
Numenius arquata, 290.
——— hudsonicus, 291.

Numenius phæopus, 291.
——— tenuirostris, 290.
Nutcracker, 80.
Nuthatch, Common, 74.
Nycticorax griseus, 205.

Oceanites oceanicus, 310.
Œdemia fusca, 230.
——— nigra, 229.
Œdicnemus scolopax, 262.
Oriole, Golden, 76.
Oriolus galbula, 76.
Ortolan, 109.
Osprey, 197.
Otis tarda, 253.
——— tetrax, 257.
Otocorys bilopha, 121.
Ouzel, Ring, 36.
———, Water, 76.
Owl, Barn, 137.
———, Brown, 141.
———, Eagle, 143.
———, Little, 144.
———, Long-eared, 139.
———, Marsh, 140.
———, Scops, 142.
———, Short-eared, 139.
———, Southern Little, 145.
———, Tawny, 141.
———, White, 137.
———, Wood, 141.
Oystercatcher, 273.

Pandion haliaëtus, 197.
Panurus biarmicus, 70.
Partridge, Barbary, 239.
———, French, 237.
———, Western Red-legged, 237.
Parus ater, 73.
——— cœruleus, 72.
——— cristatus, 73.
——— ledouci, 73.
——— major, 71.
——— palustris, 73.
——— teneriffæ, 72.
Passer domesticus, 101.

Passer hispaniolensis, 102.
—— montanus, 102.
Pastor roseus, 79.
Peewit, 271.
Pernis apivorus, 189.
Petrel, Fork-tailed, 310.
——, Long-legged, 310.
——, Storm, 309.
——, Wilson's, 310.
Petronia stulta, 102.
Phalacrocorax carbo, 198.
—— desmarestii, 198.
—— graculus, 198.
Phalarope, Grey, 275.
Phalaropus fulicarius, 275.
Phœnicopterus roseus, 213.
Phylloscopus bonellii, 63.
—— rufus, 63.
—— sibilatrix, 63.
—— trochilus, 64.
Pica mauritanica, 82.
—— rustica, 82.
Pigeon, Wood, 232.
Pintail, 222.
Pipit, Meadow, 115.
——, Red-throated, 115.
——, Richard's, 116.
——, Rock, 115.
——, Tawny, 116.
——, Tree, 114.
——, Water, 116.
Platalea leucorodia, 210.
Plectrophenax nivalis, 111.
Plegadis falcinellus, 212.
Plover, Asiatic Golden, 267.
——, Golden, 266.
——, Green, 271.
——, Grey, 267.
——, Kentish, 270.
——, Little Ringed, 269.
——, Ringed, 268.
Pochard, Common, 226.
——, Red-crested, 226.
——, White-eyed, 227.
Podicipes auritus, 307.
—— cristatus, 306.

Podicipes fluviatilis, 308.
—— griseigena, 307.
—— nigricollis, 307.
Porphyrio cæruleus, 247.
Porzana bailloni, 245.
—— maruetta, 244.
—— parva, 245.
Pratincola rubetra, 43.
—— rubicola, 43.
Pratincole, 261.
Procellaria leucorrhoa 31
—— pelagica, 309.
Pterocles arenarius, 237.
—— senegallus, 237.
Pteroclurus alchata, 236.
—— pyrenaicus, 236.
Puffin, 305.
Puffinus anglorum, 309.
—— gravis, 308.
—— kuhli, 308.
—— major, 308.
—— obscurus, 309.
—— yelkouan, 309.
Pycnonotus barbatus, 67.
Pyrrhocorax alpinus, 80.
—— graculus, 80.
Pyrrhula erythrina, 106.

Quail, Andalucian Bush, 241.
——, Button, 244.
——, Common, 240.
——, Three-toed, 241.
Querquedula circia, 225.
—— crecca, 224.

Rail, Water, 246.
Rallus aquaticus, 246.
Raven, Common, 84.
——, Tangier, 84.
Razor-bill, 304.
Recurvirostra avocetta, 274.
Redpole, Lesser, 105.
Redshank, Common, 287.
——, Dusky, 287.
Redstart, Black, 45.
——, Common, 44.

Redstart, Moussier's, 44.
Redwing, 35.
Reedling, Bearded, 70.
Reeve, 283.
Regulus cristatus, 66.
—— ignicapillus, 66.
Rissa tridactyla, 301.
Robin, 46.
Roller, 130.
Rook, 86.
Ruff, 283.
Ruticilla cyanecula, 46.
—— moussieri, 44.
—— phœnicurus, 44.
—— suecica, 46.
—— titys, 45.
—— wolfi, 46.

Sanderling, 280.
Sand-Grouse, Black-bellied, 237.
——, Pin-tailed, 236.
Sandpiper, Common, 285.
——, Curlew, 280.
——, Green, 284.
——, Marsh, 286.
——, Purple, 282.
——, Terek, 286.
——, Wood, 285.
Saxicola albicollis, 40.
—— leucura, 41.
—— œnanthe, 39.
—— stapazina, 40.
Scolopax rusticula, 276.
Scops giu, 142.
Scoter, Common, 229.
——, Velvet, 230.
Serinus hortulanus, 101.
Shag, 198.
Shearwater, Cinereous, 308.
——, Dusky, 309.
——, Manx, 309.
Sheld-duck, 219.
——, Ruddy, 219.
Shoveler, 222.
Shrike, Algerian Grey, 87.
——, Hooded, 90.

Shrike, Lesser Grey, 88.
——, Red-backed, 88.
——, Spanish Grey, 87.
——, Woodchat, 89.
Siskin, 100.
Sitta cæsia, 74.
Skua, Arctic, 303.
——, Buffon's, 303.
——, Great, 302.
——, Long-tailed, 303.
——, Pomatorhine, 302.
——, Richardson's, 303.
——, Twist-tailed, 302.
Smew, 232.
Snipe, Common, 278.
——, Great, 277.
——, Sabine's, 279.
——, Solitary, 277.
Sparrow, Hedge, 49.
——, House, 101.
——, Rock, 102.
——, Spanish, 102.
——, Tree, 102.
Sparrowhawk, 186.
Spatula clypeata, 222.
Spoonbill, White, 210.
Squatarola helvetica, 267.
Starling, Common, 77.
——, Rose-coloured, 79.
——, Spotless, 78.
Stercorarius catarractes, 302.
—— crepidatus, 303.
—— parasiticus, 303.
—— pomatorhinus, 302.
Sterna anglica, 293.
—— cantiaca, 294.
—— caspia, 294.
—— fluviatilis, 296.
—— macrura, 295.
—— maxima, 294.
—— media, 295.
—— minuta, 296.
Stilt, Black-winged, 274.
Stint, Little, 282.
——, Lobed-footed, 275.
——, Temminck's, 283.

INDEX TO BIRDS. 325

Stonechat, 43.
Stone-Curlew, 262.
Stork, Black, 210.
——, White, 207.
Strepsilas interpres, 273.
Strix flammea, 137.
Sturnus unicolor, 78.
—— vulgaris, 77.
Sula bassana, 199.
Swallow, Common, 93.
——, Red-rumped, 94.
Swan, Mute, 216.
——, Whooper, **215**.
Swift, Alpine, 124.
——, **Common, 122**.
——, Mouse-coloured, **123**.
——, White-bellied, 124.
Sylvia atricapilla, 51.
—— cinerea, 50.
—— conspicillata, 51.
—— curruca, 50.
—— hortensis, 51.
—— melanocephala, 54.
—— orphea, 52.
—— subalpina, 53.
—— undata, 55.
Syrnium aluco, 141.

Tadorna casarca, 219.
—— cornuta, 219.
Tchagra, 90.
Teal, 224.
——, Summer, 225.
Telephonus erythropterus, 90.
Tern, **Allied**, 295.
——, Arctic, 295.
——, Black, 291.
——, Caspian, 294.
——, Common, 296.
——, Gull-billed, 293.
——, Little, 296.
——, Royal, 294.
——, Sandwich, 294.
——, Whiskered, 292.
——, White-winged Black, 292.
Thrush, Blue Rock, 36.

Thrush, Mistle, **34**.
——, Song, 34.
——, White-backed Rock, 38.
Tichodroma muraria, 75.
Tit, Algerian Coal, 73.
——, Blue, 72.
——, Crested, 73.
——, European Coal, 73.
——, Great, 71.
——, Marsh, 73.
——, Penduline, 74.
——, Spanish Long-tailed, 71.
——, Ultramarine, 72.
Totanus calidris, 287.
—— **canescens, 286.**
—— **cinereus, 286.**
—— fuscus, **287**.
—— glareola, 285.
—— hypoleucus, 285.
—— ochropus, 284.
—— stagnatilis, 286.
Tringa alpina, 281.
—— canutus, 281.
—— **minuta, 282.**
—— striata, 282.
—— subarquata, 280.
—— temmincki, 283.
Troglodytes parvulus, 75.
Turdus iliacus, 35.
—— merula, 35.
—— musicus, 34.
—— pilaris, 35.
—— torquatus, 36.
—— viscivorus, **34**.
Turnix sylvatica, 241.
Turnstone, 273.
Turtle-Dove, Common, 234.
——, Egyptian, 235.
Turtur communis, 234.
—— senegalensis, 235.
Twite, 105.

Upupa epops, 134.
Uria troile, 304.

Vanellus gregarius, 272.

Vanellus vulgaris, 271.
Vultur monachus, 145.
Vulture, Bearded, 156.
——, Black, 145.
——, Cinereous, 145.
——, Egyptian, 152.
——, Griffon, 147.

Wagtail, Blue-headed Yellow, 113.
——, **Grey,** 112.
——, Grey-headed, **114.**
——, Yellow, **114.**
——, Pied, 112.
——, White, 111.
Warbler, Aquatic, 58.
——, Black-headed, 54.
——, Bonelli's Willow, 63.
——, Cetti's Bush, 61.
——, Chestnut-breasted, 53.
——, **Dartford,** 55.
——, **Fantail,** 60.
——, **Furze,** 55.
——, **Garden,** 51.
——, **Grass,** 69.
——, **Grasshopper,** 59.
——, **Great Reed,** 57.
——, **Marsh,** 58.
——, **Moustached Swamp,** 61.
——, Reed, 57.
——, Savi's, 59.
——, Sedge, 58.
——, Short-winged Yellow **Tree,** 65.

Warbler, Spectacled, 51.
——, Subalpine, 53.
——, Western Orphean, 52.
——, Western Pallid, 65.
——, Western Rufous, 56.
——, Willow, **64.**
——, Wood, **63.**
Waterhen, **247.**
——, Purple, 247.
Wheatear, **Black, 41.**
——, Black-eared, 40.
——, Common, 39.
——, Western Black-throated, 40.
Whimbrel, 291.
——, American, 291.
Whinchat, 43.
Whitethroat, **Common, 50.**
——, **Lesser, 50.**
Wigeon, 225.
Woodcock, 276.
Woodpecker, Algerian Green, 128.
——, Algerian Pied, 127.
——, Great Spotted, 126.
——, Grey-headed Green, 129.
——, Middle Spotted, 127.
——, South Spanish Green, 128.
Wood-Pigeon, 232.
Wren, 75.
——, Fire-crested, 66.
——, Gold-crested, 66.
Wryneck, 129.

www.ingramcontent.com/pod-product-compliance
Lightning Source LLC
Chambersburg PA
CBHW020320240426
43673CB00039B/867